*August 27*

*To Steve*
*With very...*

*Neil (...*

*#13 of second ever... un!*

*☺*

*If we always think*
*What we have always thought,*
*We will always be*
*What we have always been.*

*Neil Tuson*

1

# What people are saying.

"Neil? He doesn't say much. But when he does, it's worth listening to."

*Nic*

"I'd pay £50,000 to know what Neil knows."

*Gary*

"Your honesty shines through. Your story will help people. It will give them the clarity they are looking for in their lives."

*Chris*

"This is very good. Well done!"

*CD*

"A page-turner. Flows very well."

*Rob*

"A long and passionate piece of writing. I was engaged and entertained."

*Kay*

"This is a great reminder of the challenges you have faced and the determination you have applied to overcome them. It is full of brilliant anecdotes."

*David*

"Very entertaining and a source of wisdom."

*Hervé*

"Neil is like a wise older brother.
This book will help you find the right way on your own.
I cannot recommend it more highly."

*James*

"This book has transported me from a state of vulnerability and negativity to a place of trust, ambition, and positivism. My opportunities are endless."

*Carla*

"I enjoyed this book enormously."

*Christine*

"This is world-class. I am going to re-read it."

*Peter*

"Congratulations on completing this important book."

*Hannah*

*For my parents,*
*Jean and Ralph*

# Neil Tuson – Perfect Teams

## *"Nobody is perfect, but your team can be."*

N eil is a graduate of Marine Engineering and has sailed around the world as a ship's engineer. Somewhere on that voyage, he discovered a passion for personal development. Landing in California, he worked for Dale Carnegie before returning to the UK to build a business for them in South London. Being entrepreneurial, he soon set up his own coaching and consultancy business. He has had the privilege of working with more than 7000 people within 257 businesses in the US, Europe, and the Middle East.

Neil loves creating innovative approaches to helping businesses develop individuals, teams, and divisions, which resulted in the formation of Perfect Teams in 2016. Using a unique algorithm, 'Perfect Teams' has become the new standard for helping businesses understand the mix of people in their teams.

Perfect Teams have, in turn, licensed their exclusive Intellectual Property [IP] to help consultants and clients make sense of the people equation in an increasingly chaotic, office-fearing, and fragmented workplace.

People often describe Neil as— 'Enigmatic, Quiet and Driven'. When not consulting or coaching, you will find Neil running or trekking the Surrey Hills or similar terrains around the world.

He'd love to give a TED talk on 'Perfect-Teams'.

Introductory Video: https://youtu.be/0DUWaf6HdzM
Client Testimonial Video: https://youtu.be/F6sh_ZENKLU
Client Presentation Video: https://youtu.be/p-d6kHGeE-4
LinkedIn: https://www.linkedin.com/in/neiltuson/
First Showing of 37 Years: https://youtu.be/xyehO88mOXA

૭

# LISTENING, LAUGHING AND LEARNING

## Wisdom creeps up on you!

*Neil Tuson*

Published by Filament Publishing Ltd
14, Croydon Road, Beddington,
Croydon, Surrey CR0 4PA
+44(0) 208 688 2598
www.filamentpublishing.com

Listening, Laughing & Learning by Neil Tuson
Initial Cover Design – Rob Arnold
ISBN 978-1-915465-46-7
First published in Great Britain in 2024
Copyright © Neil Tuson 2024

# CONTENTS

**PART FOUR**
Mastery

## PART FIVE
### Teacher

## PART SIX
### Leader

## APPENDICES

# PREFACE

One of the advantages of being at the older end of the spectrum called life is that you have done so much listening and learning. Over the past 37 years, I've collected and curated 1931 quotes, which is just about one per week. Amidst all this, I've learned some profound lessons. Here are 53 of mine. Please do with them what you will. Hopefully, they will help you or someone close to you.

I've had an extraordinary life. Not great like Churchill, but exceptional, nonetheless. This statement prompted the following conversation with my publisher:

"People don't know anything about you. Who are you? You are a bloody genius, but you need to be visible. The problem is not enough people know about you. You need to get yourself known in the world."

"People buy people, and no one knows anything about you. What right do you have to give anyone any advice? You're an enigma. You have so many qualities and great ideas that would help people, but they need to know about you first. What is your story? How did you come to learn what you've learnt and develop the philosophy that has helped so many people?"

"Frankly Neil, you're still missing … you haven't turned up for your own party."

With these words ringing in my ears, I turned around, walked away, and thought, "Why would anyone be remotely interested in me and my story?"

I turned the corner and heard my father's words, "Nail your flag to the mast, son," I decided there, and then, if that is what the publisher required, I'd write my story. I'd defiantly refuse to surrender. I'd fight to get my book published.

Here's my story, warts and all.

*Neil*

Neil Tuson - December 27th, 2023

# Author's statement

By the end of August, I had completed the first draft and sent it to a few people for feedback. I naïvely thought when I'd finished, "OK. That's that. It'll be an instant storming success!" Guess what? It wasn't. The work had only just begun. Some of the initial feedback:

> *"Being blunter than a very blunt tool, there is a thread of repeated life mistakes within the book, and it prompts the reader to ask whether the author has learned anything from his 37 years."*

> *"I came away thinking why had this chap had so many jobs and partners ... perhaps he's not actually acted on the listening prowess that he advocates."*

The comments were totally valid on one level. I sulked. I went for a walk. I quickly realised that this book needed some context and provisos for it to make sense to anyone who doesn't know me.

The thing is, a life lived is continually unfolding. It will consequently come with its share of bumps, upsets, and pitfalls. It's never going to be the perfect finished article. These lessons are merely signs of my continuing success in overcoming the multitude of obstacles that inevitably accompany a life well-lived. This book doesn't presume to be an idealised, utopian blueprint on how to live the perfect life.

It's merely an aide that will hopefully help some of you to navigate your own storms, struggles, and stumbles, the shadow side of life.

And if I keep making mistakes, as I no doubt will, then that's perfectly OK. It simply means that I'm still alive. And if I'm still alive, I'm still ready to learn some more and experience yet another lesson. I hope I live long enough to have another fifty-three.

It may appear trite when you come across it, but the expression 'Shake it off – Step up' is simply a metaphor for picking yourself up, dusting yourself down, and returning to the game. To be honest, if you're looking for the perfect solution to salvation, you'll find plenty of charlatans ready and prepared to help you in any town of your choosing. Likewise, if you're looking to read this and get some tips on how to be rich, put it down now. You'll be better off writing a book yourself on how to rob a bank.

If, however, you've reached a level of insight to realise that your own salvation comes from within, then perhaps one or two of these fifty-three lessons will help.

At no point have I given up. A good friend once told me, "Neil, you're a survivor. You always bounce back." That's not because I'm physically made of rubber, but because I've developed the mental ability to consistently flip the coin, to turn a negative into a positive, and proverbially, to turn lemons into lemonade.

## Bonus Tip: Never give up

# Reader's Guidance

1. If you are easily offended, then please choose not to read this book. Learn to live with the offence.

2. I am not going to pander to the recent fashion of intolerance and self-censorship on the grounds that someone may choose to get offended.

3. I am a fan of George Orwell. His statue and the following quote are outside the BBC centre in London:

   "If liberty means anything at all, it means the right to tell people what they do not want to hear."

4. I am what I am. Love it or loathe it.

5. Ultimately, your attitude is your own choice.

6. I am all for 'Diversity and Inclusion', but not at the cost of freedom of speech and the scourge of cancel culture.

7. If you connect with the ideas here – great – use them! If you don't, then simply screw them up into a mental ball, and toss them aside. I won't be offended.

## Part One - Childhood

# CHAPTER 1
## Competition is part of life
### Coming second is OK

I began at a quarter past midnight on the 6th of November 1954. The family joke was that if I'd been fifteen minutes earlier, I'd have been called Guy, not Neil. I doubt it would have made much difference to the life that was about to unfold. I was born to Ralph and Jean Tuson in a small village called Portchester just outside Portsmouth, which was the powerful home of the Royal Navy and in which my father served. With the sea at the bottom of the road, I was probably already in the hands of destiny.

But if you think this is going to be a story about fate and a life pre-determined by destiny, then think again.

My first conscious memories are around three and a half: my brother Mark was born, and my oldest friend Steve came back from kindergarten with newfound knowledge of what a 'Copper' was besides being the penny we all coveted as pocket money. I have a recollection of being slightly jealous of Steve's advanced learning.

I didn't have to wait too long, though, before we were both enrolled at Manor House Infants School, and my lifelong passion (with a few detours) for learning began. I do know that I was a very talkative little boy because Mrs. Ricketts, our form teacher, would sit Steve and I together so she could hit us with a green garden stick whenever we started talking. It didn't work, but what did was Steve being put in another school at the west end of the village. The interesting thing about this is that at four or five, I was an extremely talkative and extroverted child. Years later, I was in the front room of the old family home with my five-year-old son James. He was being boisterous, talkative, and noisy, and my mother shouts out, "Neil. Control your son. We wouldn't let you act like that!"

I looked at my mother and asked, "Do you mean I used to be just like that?" And she replied, "Oh yes." I simply looked at James and said, "Carry on son." The adage of the day was 'Children should be seen but not heard'. Years later, I heard a great story about George Bernard Shaw. He was a famous author and playwright a hundred years ago. He was at a dinner when Beatrice Webb, one of the early patrons of the Fabian Society, a forerunner of the Labour party, said to him, "Mr. Shaw, why do you write in the Manchester Guardian under the nom de plume of 'Cornetto Bassoon'?" He replied, "A man can write alone and not be known unless he blows his own trumpet! Cornetto Bassoon is Italian for loud trumpet." George Bernard Shaw, to use modern parlance, was bigging himself up.

When I was growing up, the national mood was the exact opposite. Everyone was to know their place, be quiet, be modest. It was, in a way, the national depression of losing an empire, of no longer being the preeminent power in the world, a collective loss of self-esteem, and a growing antipathy to the new kids on the block— The Americans with their loud, overly confident swagger, and an incessant air of self-promotion, much like George Bernard Shaw in his day.

Another one of the truisms of the time in which I was raised was, 'Spare the rod and spoil the child'. Unfortunately, the rod was not spared in my case, and perhaps the child was spoiled because that natural exuberance and extroversion were well  and truly beaten out of me either at home or school. I can still see the ruler with blue and white inch squares coming down firmly on the palms of my hands just because I thought the long white corridor to the play area could do with some brightening up with coloured crayons as we crowded forward during morning recess. Some eagle-eyed teacher was looking out for the culprit as we returned.

It struck me years later that it was never ever the punishment that deterred the behaviour. If you were caught, you just accepted the punishment and wore the badge with pride. I did hear years later that our local doctor, Dr. Coventry (who treated my asthma) called my father 'A martinet' (someone who demands exact conformity to rules and forms, a strict disciplinarian). About as far removed from my evolving character as one could possibly be.

These early school days were a blur of activity and hazy memories of 'show-and-tells' with Yvonne in the hedges around the playground. Before I knew it, I was moving on to Castle Street Junior and my first experiences of being graded and ranked. I was ranked second in my first year and missed out on a scholarship to Portsmouth Grammar School. Top in my second, but no cigar. Somewhere in this was the 1963 winter of snow, which was quite magical for a child, with garages buried in snow drifts and endless ice slides in the schoolyard. It didn't matter that the garages became buried as no one had cars anyway, and walking and buses were enough to get you anywhere you needed at a penny a trip. The village had by this time grown into a small town, and there were now three junior schools to cope with the burgeoning explosion of children, which would later be called 'The Baby Boom'. Mine in the east, with the remaining 'Creek-Boys', Steve's in the west, and a new mysterious one in the north where several of my former friends from Manor House had disappeared, never to be seen again until the next big event in my life; the infamous eleven-plus held in a vast hall at the secondary school. I can't say I gave it any thought at the time as it was just a puzzle to be solved, but it did leave me with an awareness of comparisons being made and unfairness, particularly (as I found out later) towards the girls. Many girls who should have passed didn't purely because there were not enough places allocated. A sword had come down and divided us all in two. There were those who went on to grammar school and those who went to the local secondary school. It did leave some friction and a lingering animosity.

## Tip #1: Coming 2nd is OK, but 1st feels so much better

# CHAPTER 2
## A sunny disposition
### Independence is forged in struggle

In 1966, there were two significant events. One was England winning the World Cup. The other was me going to Prices Grammar School in Fareham. The World Cup, of course, lives on. My arrival at Prices does not.

It was quite grand in its way. Founded in 1721 with a big old rickety schoolhouse, quadrangles, a library, fields, a swimming pool, a tuck shop, a smoking lounge for the teachers, and six hundred boys. Amidst the intake of the new year were some I hadn't seen in three years, and strangely, three of them remain friends to this day: Rob, Bob, and Paul. Three new friends to make were Ade, Charlie P, and Tim. Steve, for some obscure reason, had gone to yet another different school.

My abiding memories of this new school were of routine, discipline, and homework, which was quite an alien concept.

The routine was my first introduction to time management. However, no one ever called it that in those days; it was simply our weekly class timetable arranged to keep us perpetually on our toes and engaged in all the new and fascinating topics that were hurled our way: Physics, Chemistry, Biology, Latin, French, History, Geography, Woodwork, Technical Drawing, English Literature and English Language, and last but not least Mathematics my absolute favourite. On top of all this, there were sports, combined cadet forces, debating societies, chess clubs, rifle shooting and probably others long since forgotten. It was a pretty packed agenda for a twelve-year-old, but you simply got into the swing of it and off your education went.

It went well for the first three years. I occasionally aced things and came top or second in a particular subject, usually maths or geography. I certainly never came top of the class. Fifth or sixth was my usual position. That grading and ranking system was well and truly entrenched in my teenage psyche, which was about to morph into adolescent rebellion and a three-year battle of wills with my parents. There is an inherent truth in the saying that numbers don't lie. There's clearly something amiss when you go from fifth or sixth to seventeenth to twenty-seventh in little over a year. What was amiss was my abiding interest and passion for learning. I really couldn't be bothered to use a now topical phrase. What I was bothered with was girls, music, and drinking. I was too young looking myself to get into pubs (yet). However, Andy and I could still convince the cashier in the local supermarket to sell us cans of IPA quickly supped before descending on the various local youth clubs for dancing and carousing. Looking back, it was a disastrous recipe. My father was away on a deployment to the Far East for two years, and my poor mother certainly couldn't control me, although she did try once by picking up the bamboo cane so often used before. I just looked at her, grabbed it and broke it in two, throwing it at her as she shouted, "Just you wait 'til your father gets home," which was, of course, an idle comment as that was two years away or so I thought.

What was it all about? In reality, it was the age-old transition from childhood to young adulthood. When I was at school, you could leave at fourteen and go to work. I was myself already working to a degree with a paper round in the morning and work in a supermarket at weekends and evenings. The beers snuck with Andy weren't free, and we didn't steal unless you count the lead stripped from Cams Hall, which we sold for a pretty penny. We seem to lack acknowledging this important transition in modern life (unless you're Jewish and have your Bar-Mitzvah at 13). Instead, it's all about troubled teenagers. No, it's about the transition to adulthood and a deep-seated instinct to be independent. Cocooning and forcibly extending childhood is the real recipe for disaster here. Fortunately, I didn't land myself in too much trouble and managed to pull myself back from the brink just in time for my O-Levels. I didn't cover myself in glory, but I passed six, which was enough to get me back in the lower sixth for A-Levels.

Just as my rebellious phase started, there was a watershed moment that has resonated throughout my whole life. I was in the kitchen with my mother. Not sure what we were talking about, but she suddenly said to me, "Oh Neil, stop dreaming you've got your head in the clouds again!" I can distinctly remember replying, "No, Mum. My head's not in the clouds at all. It's above them." "What are you talking about?" she spluttered. "Well. It's always sunny up there." My optimistic, sunny, and positive view of life has a long pedigree.

The sixth form did acknowledge a transition of sorts. I wore a suit, not a uniform, and there were acres of space in the timetable supposedly for the extra study required to ace the exams and get to university. Didn't quite work out that way for me. Although I'd made it to the sixth form there was still an underlying stand-off going on at home with my parents. My father had by this time returned and was about to leave the Navy after twenty-five years and enter civvy street. Perhaps it was a bribe, or he was feeling particularly generous, but I was allowed to go on the annual school cruise on the SS Uganda. I had gone on her two years previously, but that piece of the story fits in better later. There was a small group of us this time, Ian, Charlie, and Peter, who would become head boy and eventually the Bishop of Bath and Wells. I have no idea where we went, but it was a blast. Another boy in our year who would go on to become John Major's favourite author was a young Robert Goddard.

If it was a bribe to get me to settle down and attend to my studies, I'm afraid it just didn't work. With scores of 34%, 19% and 13% in Maths, Further Maths, and Physics, university was looking (at this point) decidedly unlikely. I wasn't taking responsibility once again, and my passion for learning had deserted me. It was at a Wishbone Ash concert in Portsmouth Guildhall that my friend Paul convinced me to leave and get myself an apprenticeship. He had already left the year before and was working at a local shipyard and loving it.

This was a boy who'd turned down a scholarship for Winchester he was so bright. Perhaps things moved quicker back then, but I do know that I had guaranteed myself an Engineering Cadetship with the Royal Fleet Auxiliary within a month of that conversation, quit school and had a full-time job in a Schweppes bottling factory on the princely sum of twenty-five pounds per week. Happy Days!

## Tip #2: Develop your own sunny disposition

## Part Two - Young Adulthood

# CHAPTER 3
## Delay the gratification
### Stay active

I t's funny, but the real lessons in life come when you leave school. School is all about lessons, but they're not of life. Perhaps a great educator will come along one day and rectify this logical conundrum. I had seven months before I had to get my hair cut, don my new uniform, move to Southampton, and take a pay cut to ten pounds per week. And that was perhaps the first lesson. Sometimes in life, you must make a sacrifice, delaying the gratification. There were people in the factory who told me I was mad to leave, that I'd make much more money staying. Would anyone today leave a seventy-five grand a year job for one only paying thirty? Well, I did, and years later, I summed it all up in a lesson called 'Invest in Yourself'. It's not just about the money. It's about the opportunities that open up when you go away. It's the people you meet and the friendships made. It's the broader horizons.

Last year, we had a fifty-year reunion of our cadet class— seventeen of the fifty-six plus partners. My wife said it was like being with a group of sixty-eight-year-old teenagers!

The truth is, we all still have an incredible zest for life, and every one of us has a story to tell that is full of lessons and learning, but let's get back to the timeline.

Fifteen pounds a week down but quids up in future opportunities, I commenced my cadetship in September 1972. Unlike school, I took to the lessons because they were about tangible things that worked and helped. After all, we were being trained to be ship's engineers and ultimately in charge of keeping Britain's (then immense) fleet working ploughing the seven seas and contributing to the nation's wealth. Not many people were aware of the massive structural changes coming our way. The cadetship was divided into three phases: two years at college, a year at sea, and a final year back at college. After this, we would return to sea as Junior Engineering Officers when the real work would begin. Abiding memories of this time are Triumph Spitfire road trips to Anglesey, racing Royal Enfield continentals, Matchless sidecar combinations veering off the approach road into the avenue of trees, cadets falling out of windows, and a general feeling of all being well with the world.

And it was the world that we all saw in our year at sea. Well eventually. I spent my year at sea with another cadet, Andy from Gosport. We were instructed to join RFA Pearleaf, a fleet tanker, in Invergordon north of Inverness. The thing is, we could both quite clearly see it sitting alongside in Portsmouth dockyard. We called to say so but were told to proceed to Invergordon, where she was nowhere to be seen. A weekend was spent in a Scottish castle waiting for her, and when we joined, we promptly sailed back to Portsmouth via Swansea. This was my first introduction to Kafkaesque bureaucracy and inefficiency. The world was now open to us. South Africa, the Persian Gulf, Singapore, Gibraltar, the Mediterranean, North America, South America, Puerto Rico, and the Caribbean where I ran my first road race. When people ask me how I started running, I can honestly tell them I started running in the middle of the Atlantic. The fleet was heading to Puerto Rico. Andy and I are in the Wardroom having a drink and a smoke when the Second Engineer walks in and points at Andy and I, saying, "You two on the deck in two minutes in plimsols and shorts. You're now in training." The two Junior Engineers sitting next to us started laughing, at which point the Second said, "And you two can wash those smirks off of your faces and join them. You are now this ship's fleet relay team."

The thing is I took to it and thus began my lifetime love of running and endurance walking. Perhaps the funniest recollection from my year at sea is being taken ashore in Rio de Janeiro by the senior officers for a meal. When the appetisers turned up, they all looked to me and Andy, the other cadet to start. We'd never seen anything like it, and we promptly tucked in and quickly spat things out. We'd both chomped into the Oyster shells to hysterical laughter from the officers. Being working-class boys from Portsmouth, we'd never seen an Oyster in our lives! I don't know if it's a saying, but if it's not, it should be, "Go to sea a boy, and come back a man."

It certainly felt a lot different for all of us when we returned to do the third phase. Many of us were turning twenty-one, and we were already on forty quid a week, which would be eighty when we finished so good things were coming to those that wait. And good things certainly felt abundant. We were living. We were laughing. We were learning. And boy, were we loving. There was a very famous author at this time, Leslie Thomas. He wrote a book called the 'Virgin Soldiers', which was all about his time in National Service, and it would be turned into a great movie starring Lynn Redgrave, Hywell Bennett, and a young David Bowie. In 1972, he also wrote a book called 'Arthur McCann and All His Women'. Many of us are convinced it's about our year to this day and are waiting patiently for the call to be in the film.

With the third phase rapidly coming to an end, there was one event that would sow a seed for my future. My oldest friend Steve of 'Copper' fame had by this time been at university for two years studying psychology. We would meet up occasionally and compare notes on how things were going. I can acknowledge that my competitive nature was aroused, and I thought to myself, 'If Steve can get to university, then so can I'. The hare had started running, and I was going to chase it.

## *Tip #3: Learn to delay gratification*

# CHAPTER 4
## First impressions can be wrong
### Life turns in an instant

I must admit I loved going to sea until I didn't. Acres of time to just be. To be yourself. To read. To study. To write. We would write letters constantly to our family, friends, and girlfriends in those days. My girlfriend at this time was Rosie. She was studying fashion at Portsmouth Art College and was soon to work in London, where I would join her during the long leaves I had between ships or on weekend trips back from Chatham Naval Dockyard in Kent. I was by now a Junior Engineer on RFA Bacchus, a very appropriately named ship indeed. We had frequent trips around the Mediterranean, visiting Gibraltar, Crete, Cyprus, and Iskenderun in Turkey. The Third Engineer I kept watch with was a young man called Paul Henry, who would win a posthumous George Cross in the Falklands War six years later for giving his air-breathing apparatus to a young cadet on RFA Galahad after two Argentinian 500lb bombs hit the ship and caused fires, one in the engine room, whilst they were moored in Bluff Cove. Andy Morris and Chris Hailwood, who I studied with, would also perish. Andy was an amazing stunt car driver.

The Bacchus was a small ship but had a captain with a big chip on his shoulder. We used to enjoy watching movies at sea on an old reel-to-reel projector. One of my duties as a junior officer was to set them up in the bar. One day, for some reason, the captain missed a showing of Private Benjamin with Goldie Hawn and demanded that it be shown the following night. Well, he failed to show again at the appointed time, so I put on The Green Berets with John Wayne, which had been scheduled, whereupon he burst in, switched on the lights and raged that his film wasn't being shown. I looked at him squarely and said, "Do you really want to see it?" "Yes. I do." To which I replied, "Well show it your fucking self," and walked out. There was a knock on my cabin door shortly afterwards, and the Fourth Engineer told me the captain had stormed off. I returned to the bar, and we watched The Green Berets. I'll never know how I got away with it, especially as every time the captain walked into the bar afterwards, the other officers would whistle the tune to the Green Berets. My parents heard about this two years later when visiting some friends, Harry and Gloria, in Canada. Harry worked for a Canadian shipbuilder, and one of his engineers was an ex-Royal Fleet Auxiliary chap.

In 1977, I joined RFA Resurgent at Wallsend Slipway, where she had just completed a refit. Little did I realise that the whole trajectory of my life was about to change. Two days later, a young navigating officer joined. I thought he was an absolute twat. Once we sailed, we were both on our respective watches (four hours on and eight hours off). I'm on the 8 to 12 and wander up to the bridge shortly after midnight, where I find the twat on his watch. I decide to get to know him better and ask, "Where are you from, Vaughan?" "Winchester," he replies. "Oh. I only ever knew one girl from Winchester. I met her on a school cruise when I was fifteen." "What was her name?" asked Vaughan. "Jane Snelgrove." "Really. I live next door to her!" Long story short, we become the best of friends. On a run ashore in Edinburgh, we meet these three American girls, all called Debbie, one of whom I end up marrying, but I'm getting way ahead of myself here, and apologies to Rosie.

The Resurgent was my favourite ship. She'd started life as a cargo/passenger liner for the China Navigation Company before the Communists under Mao Tse Tung took over. As such, she was solid, ornate, and luxurious with a big old, opposed piston Doxford engine thumping away at her heart. I can't remember much about where we went. We were in Rosyth a lot, and I paid off in Lisbon. I do know that I'd started applying to university and had to get a letter from my old headmaster at Prices. It was pretty funny seeing him again after six years. I turn up on my motorbike dressed in my leathers. He ushers me into his office, and as I'm sitting down, I can still see in my mind's eye the last time I'd been there and him giving me six of the best for setting off fireworks in the Chemistry lesson. The cane was still in the corner behind his desk. He peers at me with his big, bushy eyebrows and says, "Well, Tuson. The only thing I remember about you was your inordinate desire to leave us!" I laughed and agreed with him, and we nattered for a good fifteen minutes or so, and he wrote me a stunning letter, which must have helped because I was offered a place at Newcastle.

When you finish your cadetship, you need eighteen months sea time as a Junior Engineer to be able to study for your Second Engineer's Certificate of Competency. With Baachus and Resurgent behind me, I still needed another eight months, and so early in 1978, I flew out to Gibraltar to join RFA Cherryleaf. She was a small fleet tanker, and we set sail to the Persian Gulf via the Suez Canal. After loading in Bahrain, we stopped off in Mombasa, waiting for the fleet to arrive and do any replenishments required. There was a lot of waiting around in those days. During one spell in early April, we simply drifted in the Red Sea and did some main engine maintenance. I did not know it but my life was about to turn in an instant.

When you do main engine maintenance on a marine diesel engine, you need to use an auxiliary piece of equipment called the turning gear. This involves a worm wheel to engage with the massive flywheel so you can electrically turn the engine. For some reason, the Second Engineer insisted that we manually turn it with a wrench attached to the end of the drive shaft. It worked well putting it in, but after the work had been done, the engine's momentum kept binding the worm and flywheel. Being the junior, it was my job to turn the wrench, thus turning the worm wheel. The Third Engineer became fed up with this and did the usual thing of quickly starting and stopping the electric motor, forgetting that I was on the wrench. As a result, the wrench caught me by my arms and legs, twisting me like a Catherine wheel, missing my head by millimetres, and throwing me twenty-five feet across the engine room. I tried to get to my feet but immediately collapsed, screaming. I now had extra joints in my forearms with bones sticking out and blood all over the place. It was all quite dramatic, to say the least, but quite amusing once they gave me some morphine, which really is magical stuff.

Fortunately, the fleet had arrived by this time, and I was airlifted by helicopter to HMS Tiger, where they patched me up, reduced the fractures the best they could and sent me back to work. No. I'm fibbing now. I remained on Tiger until we arrived at Malta three weeks later, and I was transferred to the Naval hospital. I had to wait for a few days before being flown back to the UK, which gave me and another patient time to escape in our wheelchairs to some of the local bars, but sadly not 'Strait Street', which was a step, or chair, too far. Back in the UK, I was taken to Royal Naval Hospital Haslar, which was not too far from home, and my parents were able to see their sorry son before he underwent surgery to repair his arms with steel plates and screws. The resulting scars are a talking point and a marvel to this day. Needless to say, I was out of action for six months, which delayed me getting my required sea time to do my second's ticket.

There were several bonuses, though, one of which was being able to take a 'Grand Tour' around Europe with my old schoolmate Paul, who had by now left the local shipyard and gone to sea himself with P&O. We set off in his Mark III Cortina and took in Paris, Cannes, Monaco, Pisa, Florence, and Venice where Paul lost the car keys on the camp-site, but we found them in a puddle. The luck! Our luck followed us. Crossing the Italian Alps into Austria, we ran out of petrol at the top of the pass and cruised to the next petrol station down the mountain. From there, it was Salzburg, Vienna, Munich, The Black Forest, and home.

Following this jolly, I ventured up to London on my motorbike with Winchester Vaughan to arrange my next trip to sea. We went out for a night in the bright lights of Finsbury Park, where I took a tumble and broke my wrist, much to the chagrin of HQ. Three months later, I was finally able to join Sir Bedivere (a sister ship of Sir Galahad) to get that vital sea time. What's the first job the Second Engineer gives me? Putting in the turning gear. I froze to the spot, as if welded to the engine room plates, but immediately saw the gallows humour. Sir Bedivere was an interesting ship used to transport troops and tanks either to Belfast, where the troubles were still ongoing, or Norway for Arctic training. Just as I'd first started running in the middle of the Atlantic, I learnt clay pigeon shooting off the flight deck in the middle of the North Sea. Frustratingly, I was still three weeks short of the magic eighteen months of sea time.

## Tip #4: Life turns in an instant

# CHAPTER 5
## Continue to learn
### *Competency brings responsibility*

I joined RFA Grey Rover, a small fleet tanker, as the Fourth Engineer. Unfortunately, we didn't stray much further than Gibraltar, but it gave me an opportunity to participate in the famous (in Navy terms) top-of-the-rock race. It's gruelling. It's hot. It seems never-ending, and the only real supporters are the rock's famous Barbary Apes clapping as you navigate yet another precipitous hair bend. Very satisfying, though, to finish, and there's a terrific party afterwards down below on Main Street. Other duties on Grey Rover were being a training target for a troop of SAS, SBS, and an assortment of international special forces bods to practice their covert, night-time ship-boarding skills whilst steaming up and down the coast off Portland Bill. True to form, they kept themselves to themselves, bunking down in one of the holds, cooking and catering with complete self-sufficiency. I've never seen a more motley and scary gang. The similarity to a pirate crew was very easy to make.

It's funny how certain things stand out when you cast your mind's eye back over life. After our run-in with the pirates, we headed for Chatham Naval Dockyard on the Medway to the East of London.

The novel thing about the Rover class of ships is that they had what was called 'Bridge Control'. The main engine orders of Full-Ahead, Half-Ahead, Slow, Dead Slow, Stop, Half-Astern, etc., were done directly from the bridge rather than being communicated by a ship's telegraph, and us engineers altering the engine speed accordingly.

So, there we are in the engine control room when there's this almighty thump and a shudder through the whole ship. This is immediately followed by a plaintiff call down from the bridge with the captain saying, "We are going full-astern, aren't we?" "No, Sir! Still half-ahead!" We had just gayly gone and hit the aircraft carrier HMS Triumph broadside. Good job she was in reserve and not on active duty.

Finally, I had the sea time in the bag, back to college. My enthusiasm for learning has increased as I get older. It's probably due to the ability to self-select what I wish to learn and seeing the utility in what I'm learning.

This time round, it's about convincing the examiners that you are competent enough to take on the responsibility of being a Second Engineering Officer, effectively the Chief Operating Officer of the engineering department of an ocean-going ship. I'm fortunate that my friend Paul is also on the course, so we travel to Southampton every day from Portchester. I wouldn't say I aced the course (Paul certainly did), but I did enough to convince them of my competency. The three months flew by aided and abetted by the two one-gallon flagons of navy pusser's rum I'd smuggled back from Gibraltar on Grey Rover. Because of my accident, Newcastle had kindly deferred my entrance for a year, which had given me time to finish my ticket. It also helped me put some money aside for university. Three years on a student's grant was not going to be enough for this global explorer with a rapacious appetite for life. The immediate consequence of passing was a promotion to Third Engineer and a posting to RFA Gold Rover. But first I had some leave to use up.

## Tip #5: Continue to learn

# CHAPTER 6
## Developing a 'Can-Do' attitude
### Making friends

This time, I headed west instead of south. My American adventures were about to start. I'd been to the States twice on ships. Mayport Naval Station near Jacksonville, Florida, and Norfolk, in Virginia, where the Ark Royal was berthed alongside the Nimitz and looked like a tiny lifeboat in comparison. My abiding memories are of Disneyworld (a day I never stopped smiling) and Williamsburg, which, with Jamestown and Yorktown, is the triangular heart of the American Revolution and the origins of the colony itself. This time, though, I was heading far away from the coast into the heartland of the continent itself and guaranteed to strike fear into all seafarers. First things first though. I had to get there. Freddie Laker (bless him) had introduced tickets to the US for £59 one way, which was an incredible bargain when comparable fares at the time were £200 plus. I went one better, though and got there for £9. Because I was in the Royal Fleet Auxiliary, I qualified for an indulgence flight from RAF Brize Norton to Washington DC. Besides getting the best deal on the planet, you learn a curious fact. RAF passenger plane seats all face backwards towards the tail of the plane. This way, if you do crash, there's none of this 'Brace-Brace-Brace' nonsense, which would just smash your face in any way; the crash would be comfortably cushioned by the full armchair effect of the chair you're sitting in. Only image and PR nonsense stops commercial airlines from doing what is best for safety.

My plan once in Washington was to buy a motorcycle and do the whole Route 66 thing to Denver, my destination. That didn't work out as planned. I did the next best thing and took a train via Chicago. What a journey. Two whole days and a carriage load of characters, including myself! We arrived at Denver Union Station in the heart of old downtown Denver around seven in the morning, after a night of partying on the train, and there to greet me on the platform was the sole reason for this trip. Debbie. Do you remember the three Debbies met with Winchester Vaughan back in Edinburgh? Well, here she was in the flesh, A blue-eyed Scandinavian beauty with an uncanny resemblance to Sharon Stone. She was now head curator at the Denver Art Museum, one of the largest art museums in the country and known for its collection of American Indian art. I arrived with one bag, a bottle of Glenmorangie whiskey and the intention of staying for three weeks.

I left three months later, having fallen in love with Denver, America, and, of course, Debbie. I do remember one evening overhearing Barb, Debbie's roommate, whispering, "When's he going to leave?" There is an old saying about guests, 'They're like fish they go off after three days'. Well, this one was salted, marinated, pickled, cured, and canned. As with any period of elapsed time, there will be some highlights, and the ones that have stuck with me are Mexican food, Skiing in the Rockies, and Charlie. Debbie, like most Americans, was very religious. Charlie was one of her friends from Church. He, too, was from Minnesota, known as the state with 10,000 lakes, and therefore another pure-bred Viking. Charlie was studying for his Masters in Hospital Administration just around the corner from Debbie's apartment. We met for lunch one day at the College Inn after his classes, played some pool, and sealed the beginnings of a great friendship by necking that bottle of Glenmorangie I'd brought with me. As he left the Cherry Street apartment on his bike, he did look a tad wobbly and, as I found out later, fell into Cherry Creek, next to the Bull and Bush, on his way back to Glendale.

Shortly after this memorable introduction, Charlie introduced me to the delights of skiing. Denver is known as the 'Mile-High City', being 5,280 feet above sea level. It is also the gateway to the Rocky Mountains, a magnificent range of peaks running three thousand miles from Canada to New Mexico. That gateway is speared by highway I-70, and off of it are many fine ski resorts, Loveland, Winter Park, Breckenridge, Aspen, and Vail. It's a great place to learn how to ski.

One of the things I love about Americans is their 'Can-do' attitude. They are vested in improving themselves and, therefore, invest in themselves. They will, thus, often be working while attending college, and it seems one of the rites of passage is tending tables in bars or restaurants. One of Debbie's friends, Linda, was an example of this and my introduction to Mexican Food at Las Delicias in Glendale. I'll forever love tacos, enchiladas, and burritos.

Have you noticed that you always remember the first time but rarely the second or third? Anyway, Debbie and I would make Mexican food our signature dish, but more on that later.

My brother Mark happened to pass through Denver around this time, too. He wasn't on a gap year but was taking some time to consider his options, one of which was to go to sea himself. He caused quite a stir and I do know Linda took quite a shine to him. Another stir was us playing pool one night in the College Inn. Because we both played snooker, pool seemed simple in comparison, and it riled the Americans no end that they couldn't get us off the table all night.

I can't close out this chapter without mentioning one more highlight. Debbie's family had property on one of those ten thousand lakes, and we took a road trip there and back. It was both a delight and an agony. Driving at fifty-five miles an hour on those wonderful, great open highways is unmitigated torture for Europeans. The delights were meeting up with Winchester Vaughan, who had also flown over to see one of the Debbie's in Grand Forks, North Dakota, and meeting Debbie's parents, Jay and Florence. The day after we arrived, it was straight off to Round Lake, near Lake Bimidji, on the road to Duluth. Minnesota is known for its 10,000 lakes. It's lesser known for its state bird 'The Mosquito'. We were there for two glorious weeks, and it gave Vaughan and I time to renovate an old wooden canoe, which promptly sank when we launched it. Our seafaring skills obviously didn't work this far from the ocean. It's indicative, though, of another trait I've seen in Americans – their openness and ability to welcome people into their homes. I'd first seen it in Norfolk when I was a cadet, and personally, I find it very heart-warming—a window into the true human spirit.

On the long drive back to Denver, we took a more northerly route across the South Dakota Great Plains and Wyoming rather than the Nebraskan. We got to take in places like Sioux Falls, The Badlands, Rapid City, Mount Rushmore, Casper, and Cheyanne, but missing Laramie, the heart of the lawless Wild West with its famous 'Bucket of Blood' saloon. Sheer delight for a boy brought up on a diet of wild west cowboy and Indian films. The other delight was Barb's. My three months were at an end, and it was time to return to duty with a helping hand from Freddie Laker. I left with one bag, a T-shirt emblazoned with 'I'd rather be in Denver', and a skateboard.

## *Tip #6: You make friends by sharing new experiences*

# CHAPTER 7
## Travelling opens your eyes
### Relish being shocked

Third engineer. Two gold stripes and qualified for three. I felt like I'd arrived, but I was already planning on leaving. I joined RFA Gold Rover in Portland on July 1st, 1980, and would leave on August 27th. My eight years with the Royal Fleet Auxiliary were rapidly drawing to a close. Had the boy become a man? Well, not yet. He was a bit of a lad if the truth be known, and Paul would sum it up beautifully years later in a song he'd write for my sixtieth birthday. It hadn't gone to my head, but years earlier, people often mistook me for David Cassidy, who was incredibly popular at that time. I found it amusing, flattering, and occasionally embarrassing. However, when this striking Austrian girl came up to me in The Cormorant in Portchester and asked for my autograph, what was a lad supposed to do? I loved the way she spoke, "You will come to London." To her, it was a question; to me, it was an order, and so to London with Christina, I went! Paul and I visited her in Salzburg when we were on our 'Grand Tour' and stayed with her and her parents at their holiday home on Lake Attersee, a glorious lake to the east, much favoured by the Viennese painter Gustav Klimt and an angler's delight. We headed to Vienna after our sojourn at Attersee and took in the magnificence of the Hapsburg legacy. Having both been imbued, throughout our schooldays, with the glories of the British Empire, we were both shocked by the grandeur of the Austro-Hungarian one. The eagle atop the orangery in the Schönbrunn Palace Gardens has stuck with me ever since. The one regret we have both had since those days is that we didn't strike north from Vienna and cross over the 'Iron Curtain'. Instead, we headed west to Munich, the Black Forest, France, and home.

My remaining two months of service with the Royal Fleet Auxiliary are a blur, to be honest. Navy Days in Portland and Portsmouth come to mind, but not much else. Navy Days was an opportunity for the public to explore the historic docklands and the assortment of ships that were not overseas or on active duty alongside vessels from Canada, the US, Australia, and other NATO fleets. It was the annual 'Show Time' for the Navy and a huge boost for recruitment. For the 'lads', it was an endless beauty parade.

I finally paid off Gold Rover at anchor off Portland. I disembarked by liberty boat, and I have to admit I had a tear in my eye as I looked back and the boat ashore powered forward.

## Tip #7: Allow your perceptions to be shocked

# CHAPTER 8
## Learning to teach myself
### Planning to fail in order to succeed

I absolutely loved university. Debbie was over for a couple of weeks and helped me move my stuff up to the shared Richardson Road flat before flying back to Denver. When I returned on my motorcycle, I started to meet my five flatmates. There was Bob, who had also been in the merchant navy; Martin, an ex-Trappist monk studying philosophy; David, who founded the university's first gay society; married Dave doing a post-grad in hydrology; and Peter, a lost New Zealander. I thought Bob was drunk when we first met, but it was just his stammer getting in the way and strangely enough, I'd never met anyone with one before. We immediately clicked and went doon the toon for a broon or two. I have to say the Newcastle dialect was a mystery to me, but Debbie, who spoke fluent Norwegian, understood them completely.

What did I love about university? The freedom, the space, the opportunity to learn. I've told numerous people ever since, "University teaches you how to teach yourself." You're not spoon-fed. You're introduced to subjects, and slowly, you find the way to mastering them yourself. Being a mature student and not having A-Levels, I had to work twice as hard to catch up, and this was particularly true with Mathematics. The other mature students on the course, Peter and John, also knuckled down and collectively, we all ended up doing very well. The students who had come directly from school with straight A's seemed to flounder. They were all a little out of their depth and lost, it seemed to me.

He wasn't on our course, but one of the freshers straight from school was William Gladstone, the fourth. Gladstone, the great Victorian Liberal prime minister, had been his great-great-grandfather. He was a flamboyant, colourful character with a booming, plummy, and authoritative voice. Seeking a position in the student politics of the time, he was sorely disappointed. That patriarchal and conservative style didn't cut it with Tariq Ali in the ascendancy and the NUS (National Union of Students) pretty much sewn up by Trotskyists, International Marxists, and The Socialist Workers Party. I liked him though.

The first term flew by, and I was straight on a plane to Denver. Didn't bother with Freddie. The RAF were now unavailable. It cost a small fortune. I spent five hours a day (including Christmas and the New Year) digesting Stroud's Engineering Mathematics and doing past exam papers for the three weeks I was there. Why? Because it was imperative that I pass the catch-up exam upon my return to maintain my place. I achieved my first 'First'.

By now, we were beginning to settle into the life of being students. Bob was also studying Marine Engineering and had been at sea for nine years. All the flats in Richardson Road had the same floor plan. Enter the front door into a common shared area with comfy chairs, a shelf above head height on the wall opposite, a kitchen to the left or right, two bedrooms off the common area and a hallway down to the other rooms, toilet, and bathroom. Quite quickly, that top shelf in every flat became full of empty wine bottles except in ours. Ours was full of bourbon, whiskey, and rum bottles. On Sundays the kitchen to the left was a theatre to the delights of 'Spag-Bog'. Our 'Spag-Bog' became legendary, and we would often have a queue of people waiting at the front door.

Like the first term, the second flew by, and I was on a plane again. This time, it was all about prepping for the finals. I made a strategic decision and mentally dropped two subjects, machine dynamics and materials. Naturally, when it came to the finals, I failed them, but I now had the whole summer to prep for the resits I was allowed before commencing my second year. My tutor remarked that he had never seen anyone fail so spectacularly and return with such magnificence.

Before flying west for the fourth time in a year, I had a few things to attend to. One was finding some accommodation for next year, and another was preparing for the first Great North Run. The accommodation was sorted with four of us going in on a house, 194 Sandiford Road between Heaton and Jesmond. I had kept my running going through the years and would regularly run around the Town Moor and through Jesmond Dene. The Great North Run was brought together by Brendan Foster, an Olympic 10,000m medalist and a local lad. On June 28th, 1981, an estimated half a million people (several of them outside the North Terrace) turned out to watch over 12,000 runners leave the town moor and run half a marathon to South Shields, making it Britain's biggest road race at the time. Kevin Keegan, who was an immensely popular footballer, ran it in a respectful one hour and fifteen minutes. I was fifteen minutes behind him. You won't find my name in the results because I borrowed another student's number who couldn't do it. I made sure I enrolled for the next two, and my times improved. Kevin Keegan must have loved it because he joined Newcastle United the following year.

With the first year drawing to a close and me about to jet off, what had we all learnt? Bob was still finding himself. David was making a name for himself. Peter found his way back home. Martin, with his vows of celibacy, gave in to a muse named Sophie. Dave, with his vows of fidelity, gave into the charms of a young Swedish post-grad. I, who hadn't taken any vows as yet, just gave into everything. What would the summer of '81 bring?

## Tip #8: Learn to teach yourself

# CHAPTER 9
## Second again
### *I'm officially an 'Alien'*

1 981 was famous for several things. President Reagan and the Pope were both shot, and the first case of HIV/AIDS in the USA was announced. On my Easter trip to Denver, when I was frantically swotting for my finals, Debbie and Barb had had a party. I'd gotten into a conversation with a chap who worked for the CDC (Centres for Disease Control and Prevention) in Atlanta. He casually mentioned that they were very concerned about a new virus that was very much like the Green Monkey Disease. This was the very beginnings of the AIDS epidemic, which would have such tragic consequences.

The positives of the year were Indiana Jones had his very first adventure, Charles and Diana had the fairy tale wedding of all weddings, and Debbie and I married. It happened very quickly, and no shotguns were involved. We were up at Round Lake in Minnesota. Debbie had expressed an interest in moving to the UK, and I had told her that I wasn't going to be able to afford to fly over again. What's the solution? I simply said, "Why don't we get married?" So, we did ten days later in Denver on August 27th, exactly a year after I left RFA Gold Rover. Amazingly, my parents and brother were all able to make it, and following a very short honeymoon in Winter Park,

I flew back to prepare for my resits and clear the decks for Debbie's arrival. I'm well aware that that statement leaves some questions, but let's leave them behind.

As my tutor remarked, my resits were magnificent, so I was able to continue with my second year. It was a good year academically. Because I had now caught up, all that extra energy was transferred into concentrating on the moment, and I found myself 'in the flow'. I particularly remember one thermodynamics exam. I sat. I looked at the paper. And then, as if in a trance, I completed the paper without consciousness of time passing. I walked out thinking that was very strange indeed and when I got the result 'First-Class' it was still stranger.

1981 morphed into 1982, and in April, something that had never happened in my lifetime occurred: The Falklands War. In the scheme of things, it was only a little war, but it certainly had enormous consequences for those who died, and of course, I knew people down there who did. If I hadn't left to go to university, I would have been down there too. It was, therefore, quite personal to me. Winchester Vaughan was there on RFA Sir Geraint, and I recently found a letter he wrote [I've abridged it]:

*May 29th, 1982*
> *Dear Neil & Debbie,*
> *Just a quick line again from the front line.*
> *Today, we heard about our capture of Goose Green. The general feeling is that it won't be long before Stanley and we can get back home …*
> *As for the guys aboard? The 2nd mate, Third Engineer,*

*and Chief Lecky (Electrician) are all scared shitless and*
*on Valium.*
*The rest of us are all in good spirits ...*
*Toodle pip, take care and regards to all at 194*

Bearing in mind that this was just a week before Sir Galahad was bombed and two weeks before the Argentinians finally surrendered, I find this pretty stoic stuff. One thing I do know is that just like Steve had inspired me to go to university, I also inspired Vaughan, who was to follow me to Newcastle after I graduated.

Then it was finals again. Every day and night was spent feverishly studying, cramming, and absorbing up until about 10:10 pm and then dashing down to The Punchbowl on Jesmond Road for last orders and getting three or four pints down before repeating it all again the next day. The camaraderie of studying like this was missed in my final year.

The second year came to an end, and I found a small, terraced house around the corner on Goldspink Lane for Debbie and I. On reflection, I spent too much time doing it up and not enough studying. But it was only £5 per week which was cheap even for Newcastle. Bob decided to go live in a construction site back on Claremont Road next to the North Terrace. It would be the scene of many raucous parties in my final year with a fabulous soundtrack of Bowie's Let's Dance, The Eurythmics' Sweet Dreams, The Police's Every Breath You Take through to Talking Head's Burning Down the House and Cyndi

Lauper's Girls Just Want To Have Fun towards the end. Classic times.

Debbie was well settled in Newcastle by now, and one day, exploring Fenwicks, she found the holy grail, 'Taco Shells'. Our housewarming party was una fiesta Mexicana with Tacos, Enchiladas, and Burritos. Not quite as good as my first meal in Las Delicias, but pretty damn close.

I took my eye off the ball in my final year. And I found out later that I'd missed a first by 2%. Two per cent! At the time, I was pretty philosophical about it, but truthfully, I was gutted.

It was a bit like coming second to Ian Johnson at Castle Primary and not getting the scholarship to Portsmouth Grammar. My tutor, Graeme Armstrong, asked if I'd stay to do a PhD, but Debbie was set on us moving to the States. I remain to this day a frustrated academic in one sense but a liberated generalist in another.

The whole emigration process was exhaustive and tedious with several trips to the American embassy on Grosvenor Square. Whilst this was ongoing, we took the opportunity to travel. First up through Scotland – Loch Lomond, Loch Fyne, Glencoe, Fort William, Invergarry, The Kyle of Lochalsh, beautiful Skye itself, and then the highland train from Mallaig to Inverness. Back in Newcastle, we jumped on a ship to Bergen and did something similar in Norway. The train journey from Bergen to Oslo has to be one of the greatest in the world.

I'm not much of a fan of unions, but all this largesse was due to the efforts of the Merchant Navy & Airline Officer's Association (MNAOA), who had quietly but diligently been fighting on my behalf for compensation from my engine room accident five years ago. It wasn't a fortune, probably about one year's salary, but it was like winning the lottery for a student at the end of three years of studying. It paid for the extended holiday, and when the embassy signed off on my eligibility to be a 'Resident Alien', it paid for us to move to the States and ship some of my stuff. I don't know when it happened, but it wasn't just me, a bag, a bottle of whiskey or a skateboard anymore.

# Tip #9: Be 'stoic' in the face of adversity

*Part Three – Maturity*

# CHAPTER 10
## Doing things, I don't like to do
### Willpower

The real lessons begin. Before emigrating, there were some people to see. My oldest friend Steve, of 'Copper' fame, was living in Wandsworth with his girlfriend Karen. He'd graduated years before and now worked in marketing for an international pharmaceutical company. I liked Karen. She was very intuitive and perceptive. She said something that night that stuck. "Neil. You've lost the sparkle in your eyes. What's going on?" Karen had known me before I'd even gone to university. I simply shrugged it off as I usually do, but what was going on?

We flew to the USA on October 30th, 1983. The final agony before leaving was giving Paul my beloved 750cc Motorcycle to sell on my behalf.

Winter in North Dakota-Minnesota is a body shock; it's so cold. The lakes and rivers freeze over, and the locals drive and fish on them by cutting holes through the ice. You get used to it though. Your body adapts and adjusts to this 'new normal'. The weekend after arriving, Jay, my father-in-law, took me hunting with a group of his buddies up near Round Lake. There's something exciting, scary, and primaeval about six blokes trekking around the wilds of Minnesota with thousand-yard Winchester 308s, equipped with telescopic sights, swigging cherry brandy, or peach schnapps tracking a stag. The highlight of the trip for me was seeing the Northern lights for the first time. These great shimmering sheets of luminous green light pulsing and dancing to an eternal tune. It was awesome.

After an initial emotional hiccup with me walking back to the airport at three in the morning in minus fifteen Fahrenheit with flurries of snow, I began to settle into my new life and seriously started looking for meaningful work. I say meaningful because the day after we arrived, I had already received my social security number and taken casual work moving furniture and building a grain silo on the outskirts of Grand Forks. There was a recession at the time, and the chances of an English marine engineer finding work in his profession in the potato capital of the world was negligible. I quickly noticed something. Every time I looked through the job ads, I saw hundreds of jobs in sales. Now, sales to a professional in England at this time (and still today in some circles) is a very dirty word. I swallowed my pride and followed up on an ad that said: sports-minded people wanted for an opportunity in sales. Own car required. Flexible hours. Before you can say, "Bob's your uncle," I found myself selling Kirby vacuum cleaners, door-to-door, in the winter, in North Dakota. I was rather good at it.

One day, I knocked on a door in Grafton, sweet-talked my way in for a 'Demo' and left with a leaflet. The guy had given me a copy of Albert Gray's essay, 'The Common Denominator of Success'. I was pretty miffed at the time and tossed it on the front seat of the big old Oldsmobile 80 that Jay had loaned me.

A couple of weeks later, I'm sitting in said car on the outskirts of Red Lake Falls, Minnesota, having been kicked out of town by the local sheriff for unsolicited selling; I'd knocked on his door without a permit! Feeling pretty sorry for myself, I saw the leaflet I'd tossed aside a few weeks back and started reading it. And there, bang between the eyes, was the lesson, 'Successful people do the things that failures don't like to do'. It hit home. I started the car, drove to the next town, Thief River Falls, and sold three vacuums. What I had begun to discover was the power of exercising my own individual will: The power of doing things that initially feel uncomfortable.

I find it strange that something so important is never taught. But why would it be? Most people will probably dismiss it anyway. Did anyone listen to the teacher or parent shouting, "Come on, pull your socks up," or Norman Tebbit admonishing everyone, "To get on their bikes."

No. I've discovered that it's easier to subtly put it out there that willpower is the gatekeeper to change. When one learns to exercise it by consciously doing things that initially feel awkward, hard, or uncomfortable, that's when mindsets start to change.

My mindset started to change. Wayne, who ran the Kirby franchise, was big on personal development and encouraged me to buy Zig Ziglar's 'See You at the Top'. Did you notice the subtle difference there between an English way and an American way? He persuaded me to buy it. He didn't give it to me, which would have been the English expectation. The great thing about learning is that it opens up new pathways, and my neurons were firing down different avenues. I was, for a while, the top salesman for Kirby, and I won an off-road three-wheeler, which was perfect for Round Lake. I also won an all-expenses paid trip to Las Vegas for me and Debbie. Staying in the MGM Grand and wandering down through the strip was an experience but not something I'd rush back to. Forty years later, I still haven't.

On the plane back from Vegas, I decided that I would seek proper work that had a wee bit more intellectual satisfaction than flogging vacuums door-to-door. The conversation with myself went thus: "I like this new world of selling. I have this terrific background in engineering. Why don't I combine the two?" I wrote down a long list of all the equipment I'd worked on in the Navy: turbines, diesels, turbo-generators, pumps, filtration systems, boilers, purifiers, electrical switchgear, controls, hydraulics, winches, air compressors, refrigeration, and air-conditioning. The next day, I talked my way into UND's (University of North Dakota) library and started researching American manufacturers of said equipment. Then, along with a smartly produced resume, I started sending out cover letters to all the appropriate manufacturers, saying that I was looking for a position in technical sales. It's often said that once you make a decision providence moves too and helps you. Sitting in the university library one afternoon, I came across a marketing magazine. Thumbing through it, I stumbled upon an article about the National Sales Director of York International, a man named Josh Costell. I had just sent a speculative letter to them a week before but decided to send another immediately.

> *Dear Mr. Costell,*
>
> *Congratulations on the article in Marketing Monthly. I liked what you said about attitude being all important in the arena of sales.*
> *You will no doubt have seen my recent enquiry about a sales position with York. Any advice you can give me on securing a position will be gratefully received.*
> *I'm enclosing my resume again in case it has slipped to the bottom of the pile.*
> *Very best wishes – Neil*

He was on the phone by the end of the week, asking me to come for an interview.

# Tip #10: Willpower is the gatekeeper to real change

"Success is achieved by the minority: so, it is unnatural and not achieved by following our natural likes and dislikes."

**Albert Gray**

# CHAPTER 11
## Remember people's names
### *Relish encouragement*

I flew to Chicago to meet with the Regional Sales Director, Al Dering, and the local sales manager, Steve Graham. That went well because I then flew to St. Louis, where they had an opening, to meet with Jack Betzold, the sales manager, David, a senior sales engineer, and Stewart, the service manager. At the end of the day, Jack said, "Well, Neil, there's just one more person to meet. If she likes you, the job's yours." He introduced me to Theresa, the office manager, and fortunately, we clicked; the job was mine, and Jack took me out to dinner. Al told me a couple of years later that they gave me the job because no one had ever asked them so many questions. For a blog, I was asked recently what the secret to finding and keeping good people was, and I reflected on this particular time in my life. It's a two-way process. Bees are attracted to honey, so as an employer, you must create a compelling narrative that attracts good candidates. You then must have an interviewing process that introduces multiple touchpoints. Most employers try to do it too quickly. If you only have one or two interviews, it's a 50/50 chance it will work out at best. Three touchpoints increases that to 70/30, four 80/20, five 90/10.

You'll make your fortune if you know how to get to 100/0! As a potential employee seeking employment, look for personal connections, things that can spark a conversation, and ask a ton of questions. They're selling you just as much as you're selling yourself.

Debbie and I were on the move: Nine hundred miles south and east to St. Louis, where the Missouri River meets the mighty Mississippi. It's easy to forget just how vast North America is. I was now a sales engineer for York International, a major air-conditioning and refrigeration equipment manufacturer. To begin with, I was put under Stewart's wing and tasked with selling service contracts to clients who had already purchased our equipment. I was quickly moved into product sales, which suited me as a product is more tangible than service. It's a funny thing, but I noticed it when I was studying. Mechanical systems made more sense to me than electrical. A big diesel that goes thump and you can bash with a hammer is real to me, whereas that spooky at a distance electromagnetic stuff that can invisibly zap you wasn't. Air conditioning had come a long way since Willis Carrier had introduced it to the world by installing the first plant in the Metropolitan Theatre in Los Angeles in 1921. The biggest plant was York's, though. They had four 12,500-ton machines sitting in the basement of the Twin Towers of the World Trade Centre in New York City. I saw them. They were as big as any ocean-going ship's steam turbine. To put that in perspective, an average home would require two tons of a/c, so the plant in the Twin Towers was sufficient to cool 25,000 homes. A ton is simply the unit used to describe the cooling capacity of the machine. And it was my duty to sell this stuff – fabulous and way better than vacuum cleaners.

One of my early lessons in sales followed an important sales call with Josh, who'd flown down to St. Louis to see how I was doing. As we drove up to the facility, he said, "Always look to get on first name terms with your client." This was in the 80s when things were much more formal than nowadays. We're ushered into a grand oak-panelled boardroom and introduced to the President of the company and the rest of the board. Josh starts the conversation by saying, "So Frank, you don't mind me calling you Frank, do you?" Whereupon the President of the company retorts, "You can call me what you want, Sonny, but my name's Fred!" Not the best start to a meeting I'm sure you'll agree. The principle, though, is sound. About a year after this, I found myself reading Dale Carnegie's seminal work 'How to Win Friends and Influence People'. The sixth principle in the book states, 'Remember that a person's name is to that person the sweetest and most important sound in any language'. I had to chuckle as I recalled Fred's sour and sardonic reply to being called Frank.

People's names are important. Remember them. But get them right. I once heard that Bill Clinton was the master of remembering names. He'd work a room and remember the names of people he'd met years ago. Remembering names is the first step to building a relationship. If you do get it wrong, though? Simply apologise or ask them to repeat it.

Just like all those early pioneers who saw St. Louis as the gateway to the west (immortalised by Eero Saarinen's stunning archway) it was a pivotal transit point in my life, and I did indeed eventually head west.

Three significant things happened in my first year in St. Louis. The first was Debbie introducing me to our new neighbour in Creve Coeur, Kirk Simpson. Kirk was a wiry little Afro-American pharmaceutical salesman. He was hugely disciplined, getting up at five every morning to go running before hitting the road for the day job and then hitting the track two evenings a week for interval workouts and racing most weekends. In St. Louis running circles, he was a legend and effectively became my running mentor, introducing me to the St. Louis Track Club and Gateway Athletics. I started racing and getting up early too, not at five, more five-fortyish. Within three months, my times for a 10K had dropped from over forty minutes to under thirty-five. Kirk also had impeccable taste. Besides having the most sublime Hi-Fi I'd ever seen; he had an Eames armchair and ottoman right in the centre of the room. On the walls were Agam prints. Agam was a modern artist I'd fallen in love with back in Newcastle, and we had a couple of his prints ourselves downstairs. Most importantly, Kirk introduced me to the St. Louis running community, and I formed some terrific friendships.

The second thing was some encouragement from my secretary Diane. When I was at school, there were two subjects I loved, with two teachers who couldn't be more unalike. One of them, Jock, the Math's teacher, was always full of encouragement, jiving the class on to do better, to be better. "And it doesn't matter if you make mistakes, just learn from them," he would say. The English class was just so different. It didn't matter how much I loved reading; it mattered not that I wrote poems and loved reading them; the English teacher, Gus, was constantly deriding, criticising, shouting, "Do not do that. Do not sing when you read. Now, stand on your chair and read it. Do not ever sing it." The embarrassment! I just wanted to crawl away and hide in a corner. And that is, in a sense, precisely what I did when it came to English.

Although it was my favourite subject, I left school with no English qualifications whatsoever. English language and literature were dead to me. Dead through a lack of encouragement. What happened in St. Louis was Dianne saying to me one day, "Do you know, you really are a very good writer; the way you word your letters is like nothing I've seen before. There is almost a lyrical quality to them." "Do you think so?" "Yes, I do." "Thanks, Dianne," I said, pleased as punch and smiling like I hadn't smiled in a long time. 'I'm a good writer', I thought to myself, 'I always knew it. Much more than that old so-and-so knew'. With her encouragement, I started to write again.

The third thing? Sadly, and unfortunately, I got divorced. Looking back on it now, I was a real cad and certainly not made for marriage.

## Tip #11: Remember people's names

# CHAPTER 12
## Having a daily discipline helps

### *What is age anyway?*

I'm an Englishman in St. Louis. I was thirty, gainfully employed, and fit. I started training more seriously now, still not as disciplined as Kirk, but moving closer. I'd meet the lovely Lynn DeNinno every morning at 5:45 at the corner of Olive and Tempo, and we'd run to Lake on the edge of the Missouri River and back. Lynn was an amazing runner, slightly quicker than me, but that was OK. She was about to go off to an Olympic training camp. Lynn's boyfriend at the time was a champion triathlete, and he was tragically killed on a training bike ride on that same road to Lake. My girlfriend at the time was my vivacious, vibrant, but volatile hairdresser, Sandy. Her best friend from high school, Patti, was married to Jimmy Connors, an East St. Louis boy famous for his intense rivalries with Björn Borg and John McEnroe. We spent a magical weekend in Chicago, the windy city on the shores of Lake Michigan, famed for its deep-dish pizza, created at Uno Pizzeria in 1943. All those years at sea and the only time I've been seasick in my life was on a boat on Lake Michigan six hundred miles from the ocean. Sandy would tragically shoot herself some years later.

I ran my first marathon in St. Louis, my second in Minneapolis-St. Paul, and my third in New York, which began a love affair with that city. The city that never sleeps. It always has something going on with a constant backdrop of yellow cabs honking their horns whether you're on the way to Guido's Supreme Macaroni (used as the backdrop restaurant for that superb movie Leon with Jean Reno and Natalie Portman), McSorley's the oldest Irish saloon in the city, or Veronica's Italian restaurant in the garment district where you would carbo load for the race to come the following day. New York was my second experience (after the Great North Run) of massive crowds willing on all the competitors. As you cross the bridge from Brooklyn into Manhattan and turn the corner up 1st Street, the sheer energy is breathtaking and never forgotten, unlike my times, which shall remain buried and never talked about. Running marathons is an art unto itself, and it took me a couple of years to master it.

Back in St. Louis, I moved to Ralph Terrace in Richmond Heights and began a Master's in International Affairs at Washington University in St. Louis. I was now only a mile away from Forest Park, a real jewel in the heart of St. Louis. It was also home to the famous 6:20 running club started by 'The Colonel' Gary K, who happened to own the Colonel Day's chain at the time and lived in a colonial-style mansion in Clayton. The 6:20 was famed for meeting at 6:20 every morning on the corner of Skinner and Forsyth and running the 6.2-mile perimeter of Forest Park at 6 minutes 20 seconds a mile pace. In the winter, when it was minus 25 Fahrenheit, you had to wear insulated underpants to preserve your crown jewels. It was not for the faint-hearted, and it attracted the best runners in the city. One of them was an academic at Washington University. One day, as we ran around the park, he explained his research into the emerging field of tectonic plates. I was fascinated by the notion that the earth's continents were just the uppermost parts of huge crustal plates that were constantly moving, diving, crashing, and emerging in an eternal dance on the earth's surface. Many of the group were veteran marathon runners. Some, Gary included, did ultra-marathons like the Western States 100, the world's oldest 100-mile trail run with 18,000 feet of climbing, all in under 24 hours. Over the years, the 6:20 also attracted media interest with numerous articles and TV features being made. On weekends, the runs were extended to venture down to the Mississippi and back, taking in the famed gateway arch, Busch Stadium (the home of the St. Louis Cardinals baseball team) and Union Station undergoing a terrific refurbishment.

In 1904, Forest Park hosted the World's Fair and its legacy lives on in the local naming of an area to the south of the park, which you will not find on any maps. One of the so-called 'exhibits' at the fair was an indigenous tribe from the Amazon with their camp along the park's south side. Over the course of a few weeks, news articles started appearing in the St. Louis Post Dispatch (founded by Joseph Pulitzer himself) about the mysterious disappearances of local pet dogs. It was discovered that the tribe went out hunting for them at night, and the area will forever be known as 'Dog Town'.

With the daily discipline of running with the 6:20, track workouts with Kirk and his crew and racing most weekends, I started to win some 30–35-year-old awards. Within three years, I had a shelf full of cups and medals.

One weekend, I ventured out to St. Joseph, to the west of St. Louis, for a 10k road race in aid of the local hospital. Looking around the other runners on the start line, I didn't recognise any of the usual suspects. The starting gun fires, and we're off. Strangely, I found myself out in front. Forbidding myself to look back and see who was behind me, it stayed that way to the finish line. I'd won my first ever race.

The overriding goal for any marathon runner at this time was to qualify for Boston. You had to run a qualifying marathon in under three hours to do that. I was inching ever closer. Three hours and five minutes in New York in 1986 and finally two hours and fifty-eight a year later. My friend Charlie joined me on these trips to New York. He'd become quite an accomplished runner himself, and I couldn't believe that he beat me across the line in '86 until I remembered his girlfriend Katy whispering something in his ear just before we boarded the bus to the Staten Island start. He had looked at me with a gleam in his eye. She'd made him a promise. All he had to do was beat me. Charlie was motivated that day, for sure.

1987 was the year that things began to click. I was invited to run in the Peoria Steamboat Classic. Peoria is a town halfway to Chicago on the Illinois River, which joins the mighty Mississippi just north of St. Louis. The Steamboat Classic was quite a well-known race on the road-running circuit, attracting several of the top runners of the time, Grete Waitz, the New York champion, being one of them. I found myself in the bar the night before the race, drinking it away with Henry Rono, who would break the 10,000m world record the following year. He said, "It's not the night before that matters Neil. Just make sure you don't do it two nights before!" True to form, Henry came second, and I got a personal best of 51:30 for fifteen kilometres.

I entered the Philadelphia Distance Run in September as a warmup for the New York marathon. This very fast half-marathon was legendary for giving runners some of their personal bests, and this year was no exception. Getting to Philly a couple of days ahead gave me time to scout the route. Much of it was flat along the Schuylkill River. Naturally, I had to find the 72 steps Rocky had run up at the Philadelphia Museum of Art entrance and strike a similar pose. The race itself was brilliant. The aftermath even more so from a learning perspective. I'd run a personal best of 1hour and 18minutes.

I stuck around for the awards ceremony. They started with the usual countdown from the higher ages. The bit that took my breath away was, "And in the 60-65 age category, with a time of one hour and eight minutes, and he's 64 today, folks, Norm Green." I just walked away amazed. I had just run my absolute best, and this man who was exactly twice my age had run a half-marathon ten minutes faster. This is when the life lesson that age doesn't matter was conceived.

I was warmed up for New York, though. This year, instead of going to Supreme Macaroni or Veronicas for our pre-race carbo load, Charlie and I went somewhere posher downtown, probably because his parents were in town. I can remember amazing Charlie's parents by consuming two meals. They were also awestruck because sitting directly behind me was Sting noshing away with Trudie Styler—an Englishman in New York.

## Tip #12: Age doesn't matter

# CHAPTER 13
## Beware the Bear
### Storms ahead

All the work finally paid off. Two hours and fifty-eight was enough to get me into Boston. Life wasn't all about running, though. I had a job. I was studying. I had girlfriends. I had friends and family. I was travelling.

Iain, one of my old friends from university, was working for BP in Alaska. One summer, I flew up to Anchorage to see him. He took me to the Hilton hotel in the centre, and there in the foyer was this gigantic polar bear. It was standing on two feet, and with its front paws raised, it reached the ceiling. Incredible. Next to the hotel was a small gift shop. Quietly browsing, I picked up this book entitled 'Bear Tales'. To this day, I've never come across a better opening line in my life. "And as the bear's teeth crunched through my skull, I passed out." I still kick myself for not buying it. Down on the waterfront, there were three-hundred-pound halibut hanging from wooden gantries. You just got the impression that everything was big in Alaska. Funnily enough, it also proved to be small.

Iain and I went fishing for King Salmon down on the Kenai peninsula. Blasting back up the Seward Highway in his

Chevy Corvette, we stopped at the famous Bird House Bar. This quirky bar was all set at an angle due to the 1964 earthquake. The bartender would slide your drinks down to you. The walls were covered in cards, messages, and women's panties. I was 4,000 miles from home in St. Louis but sat there in the corner was someone I knew from Clancy's, my local bar, and she wasn't with her husband. She was mortified. I smiled, waved, and left her to it. I never found out if she left her panties, but I did write her a small ditty, "Bumped into Bonnie in the Birdhouse bar bonking with her boyfriend." I would sing it to her back in Clancy's (egged on by my friend Phil Johnson) whenever Greg, her husband, went to the restroom. She would blush every time. The Bird House Bar unfortunately burnt down in 1996. The beautiful thing about Alaska in the summer is the perpetual daylight. You don't need to sleep. You have endless energy. I was only there for five days, and I maybe dozed for five hours. One of those hours was in a tent at the foot of Mount Denali with brown grizzly bears sniffing around outside. It was the middle of the summer, and the peaks still had snow. One memorable day, we hiked to the top and slid back down on our bums using our elbows as brakes—the best two-thousand-foot slide of my life.

My brother Mark had by this time married Vanessa, given up on the idea of going to sea, and taken a position in Brunei looking after the Sultan's small fleet of fast patrol boats. I requested a three-week holiday to go out and visit them (Americans rarely take more than two weeks of vacation). It was granted, and off I set. Getting off the plane in Banda

Seri Begawan was like walking into a sauna. I loved it. Once we'd dropped the bags, my brother immediately took me off into the jungle as it was the weekly 'Hash'. The 'Hash House Harriers' is essentially a drinking club with a running problem. There are 'Hashs' all over the world, and they are a core ingredient of any British ex-pat community. The idea is that a couple of 'Hares' set off, leaving a trail of flour, chalk marks, and toilet paper. Twenty minutes later, the 'Harriers' give chase, attempting to catch the hares before the finish line. My brother was doing a recce for an upcoming hash once when he came face to face with a King cobra.

Scary stuff, and here was me, I'm petrified of snakes, running through the jungle sixty minutes after getting off the plane. After forty minutes of running, we get to the end and the real business of drinking starts. One of the highlights of this trip was meeting Jane, an English teacher who had taken a couple of years out to teach English as a foreign language (TEFL). We immediately clicked and spent many a night skinny dipping in the surf of the South China Sea, supping Verve Clique champagne. One night, we went sailing in her small yacht, anchored off the coast, and swam in the phosphorescence. It was a fantastic experience. Back on board, she asked me, "Neil, do you have a girlfriend back home?" I replied, "Of course I do." Cheeky for sure, but totally honest.

This was Sandy. We'd had a pretty tumultuous time over the two years we'd been seeing each other. I got up and left her apartment one night due to some instinct I had. She told me, some years later, that she would have shot me if I hadn't left. This was no idle threat as she did indeed shoot herself. On reflection, Sandy was probably bipolar using today's terminology because she could undoubtedly swing from euphoria to the deepest of depressions. My parents loved her, though, and one night, when they were over, we went to the newly opened Grand Union Station, which was now full of fine dining establishments and shops. I know it was October 19th, 1987, because that was 'Black Monday', the day the world's financial markets went into meltdown and mortgage interest rates went through the roof. It was also only a few days after Michael Fish famously said, "We'd never have a hurricane In England." My parents returned to a devastated land. With a storm in England, little did I know one of my own was about to start.

## Tip #13: Expect storms

# CHAPTER 14
## Steps and breaths
### *What is the greatest motivator?*

My Master's in International Affairs course covered a curious range of subjects. One of the delights of studying is you meet interesting and clever people. She was also beautiful, mysterious, and full of life, and she was called Lisa. She had gone to university when she was sixteen, was finishing an MBA, and was in a rush to get on with life, and that rush caught me up in her slipstream for the next year. We fell for each other just before I flew off to do that year's New York marathon, where I would qualify for Boston. Upon my return, I had some decisions to make. I had invited Jane over from Brunei for Christmas that year and had to cancel. It didn't go down too well. I also had to make a final break with Sandy, which, to my amazement, she accepted. I think she knew that our relationship had run its course. There was never any bitterness when we met up a couple of years later. There was a third piece to this puzzle, but that's a story for later. With the decks cleared once again, I walked into the slipstream with my eyes wide open, but perhaps a tad blinded and infatuated.

My eyes were wide open when I found myself next April in a New England village at six in the morning, on a freezing, wet, grey spring morning, with next to nothing on. I am there with a dozen friends and six thousand semi-naked strangers. A gun goes off. Shuffling forward like an army of zombies, we break into a trot after a couple of hundred yards. Full stride came after a quarter of a mile. Before I knew it, I had run six miles. I'm getting warm, the sun's coming out, and I'm settling down to a good rhythm and pace. An hour goes by. "Can you hear that?" Gary asks. I hear this growing noise. We look at each other, shrug our shoulders, wonder what it is, and run on. As we run, the noise just gets louder and louder. We turn a corner. There is a relentless roar, a massive wall of sound: roars, screams and whoops of delight. In the wall, there are all these smiling, enticing, and encouraging faces. All the sorority girls of Wellesley College are lining the streets, cheering us all on.

For a mile or so, I am utterly oblivious to anything except the surge of energy their cheers and encouragement have given me—the whole middle mile floats by. Six miles further on, there is a hill. It is not named 'Heartbreak Hill' for nothing. It comes at precisely the wrong point. It rears up at the exact moment when people want to lie down as they start to feel the effects of the distance they have run. I fly up 'Heartbreak Hill', passing over fifty runners on the way. At the top, it is all downhill—a six-mile coast to the finish in the city centre. I've always told people that a marathon is simply a twenty-mile warm-up with a 10k race at the end.

As I cross the finish line of my first Boston Marathon, I feel motivated, exhilarated and very alive. What strikes me, though, is that here I am, that skinny little asthmatic, finishing the greatest marathon in the world. How did I do it? What has changed for me in all those years? What miracles have transpired to allow such a transformation? Well, one thing I can say, without a shadow of a doubt, is that not one of the steps on the way could have been missed. Not one of the breaths either, and there were only four thousand one hundred and ninety-two of those. Each and every step and breath was as important as the next. It was Lao Tzu who said: "A thousand-mile journey begins with a single step." The miracle was realising the value of good, consistent training and coaching and pushing the boundaries every week, digging down inside and finding the will to get up at five-thirty on cold winter mornings and go for a training run, and then doing it all again the next day. It certainly helped that the lovely Lynn DeNinno would be waiting for me up on the corner of Olive and Tempo, but we are talking about motivation here, and it comes in many different guises! Gaining and getting the support of fellow runners is incredibly valuable. The most crucial factor of all, though, is that I wanted to run the race. I had thought about being there. I'd seen myself crossing that finish line. I knew in my core that 'The greatest motivator of all is love. Love what you do and love who you are'. I simply love running and love what it does for me. I realised that the moment I do anything that does not have an element of love within it, then I am kidding myself about the potential outcome.

Back from the triumph of Boston, Easter term is upon us. Lisa is going to graduate and has started looking for potential work. I still have at least three classes and my thesis— 'Peace-making in Northern Ireland' to finish. Then it's summer. We had already planned a trip to the UK, Lisa's first, and I hadn't been back for a few years. We stopped at a country pub for some lunch, driving down to Portchester. Pulling out of the car park, I momentarily forgot where I was and started driving down the road on the right. There was an extremely hairy moment before I pulled us back to the left. Habits, eh? Useful when they help. Dangerous when they don't. The ten days we were over was a blur of activity. My Grandmother and Great- aunt were totally mesmerised by my new exotic girlfriend. She, in turn, was fascinated by the rich history all around us and loved the view from the top of Portchester Castle with its panorama of Portsmouth harbour, the Isle of Wight, and Portsdown Hill behind us guarding it all, just as Palmerston intended.

We were only back in St. Louis for a week before flying out to Los Angeles. Lisa had accepted a position with Proctor & Gamble on their graduate management programme. I was meeting with Steve Graham, who was now the local area manager, to see if I could get a transfer. I must admit I loved California so much that for the first and only time in my life, I missed my plane. Fortunately for me, being a day late back in the office didn't count against me, and I was given the transfer.

## *Tip #14: The greatest motivator of all is 'Love'*

# CHAPTER 15
## Visions and failure
### The day my 'English' charm disappeared

If St. Louis was my gateway to the West. Seal Beach was my portal to the Pacific. Our apartment was a stone's throw from the beach. Throw it the other way, and you could break a window in Walt's Wharf on Main Street, a laid-back fresh seafood restaurant with an amazing pleasure of Californian wines. Clos du Bois from Sonoma County became a particular favourite. One autumn evening in this Main Street haven Lisa asked me to marry her. A month later, she decided she'd had enough of P&G and moved back to St. Louis. That slipstream had turned into a whirlwind, and I found myself battered and bruised on the shores of the Pacific. Some research has been done on genetic compatibility. If someone smells awesome to you, it probably means that your chromosomes will also love each other. That you're a good match genetically. If it smells 'off', then it's a warning sign that you perhaps shouldn't hook up. Lisa was half-Mexican, and she sure smelt right to me. Our paths never crossed again, but her aroma lingered for quite some time.

The cleared deck was again cleared and now I was an Englishman in LA.

Running north along the San Gabriel River one evening, I saw some familiar signs, chalk markings, splodges of flour, and round check marks (a circle with an X through it). 'Aha! There's a 'Hash' around here somewhere'. With a little detective work and asking around the ex-pat community, I obtained the number for the Long Beach Hash House Harriers. It was on one of their regular Friday night runs that I met Richard, aka 'Churchill'. He was a Major in the Royal Marines seconded to the US Marine Corps at Camp Pendleton, down the coast. We became fast friends and often sailed his 'Hobie Cat' in the San Pedro channel between Long Beach and Santa Catalina Island. Over time, I found out that Richard had been in the SAS when the Falklands War blew up and was in one of the first special forces units air-dropped in at night to do preliminary reconnaissance before the main forces arrived weeks later. I always felt safe when Richard was around. He certainly had some hair-raising stories. He was courting Nancy, whom he would marry on the Queen Mary, which was now a hotel and moored at the mouth of the Los Angeles River at the Port of Long Beach. Right next to it was the 'Spruce Goose' Howard Hughes monster of a flying boat, which in 1947 was the largest plane ever built. It was five stories high, had a wingspan longer than a football pitch and eight propellers. Richard left the Royal Marines and thinking he needed a job, used his SAS skills to create one. He had once been undercover as a lift-engineer, or elevator-engineer as the Americans prefer to say, in Egypt. He blagged his way into getting a union card and a job with OTIS elevators as a supervisor. With a combination of his wits, sheer chutzpah, and ingenuity, he ended up running some of the biggest commercial contracts OTIS ever had in California.

What was I doing? I was still working for York, but truthfully, the wind was no longer filling my sails, and I was a little lost. Sitting on the grey sofa in my new apartment on Temple Avenue, Long Beach (I'd moved after Lisa left for St. Louis), I was contemplating, mulling, and musing on this vague 'lost' feeling when I had what can only be described as an epiphany. A sudden moment of understanding. A vision. It was weird, to say the least. I clearly saw a young boy sitting under a lush tree with the word 'FREEDOM' emblazoned in the canopy of branches and leaves. I grabbed a piece of paper and, with some crayons, drew it as a seven-year-old child would. Standing back and looking at it, I started to wonder what it meant when a series of words came to me: Face fear, responsibility, encouragement, enthusiasm, determination, opportunity, and mistakes. My lost feelings would dissolve when I faced my own fears and took responsibility. I didn't know it then, but I had stumbled over the first cycle of a book I would write a decade later.

People often ask me, "How did you get into what you do?" My answer is always the same, "I failed." I had a project running at work for Huntington Hospital Pasadena. I had a great relationship with the hospital administrator, the facilities manager, and the hospital engineers. I had also managed to get the specifying design engineer to build the specification around our equipment, which always makes it more difficult for our competitors. It was a big project. All I had to do was present our proposals, and it would be in the bag. On the fated day, I walked into the room to begin. It wasn't who I'd expected to be there.

There was a horseshoe of seventeen unknown faces. I just wanted the ground to open up and swallow me. My knees were trembling. My palms were sweating. My English charm deserted me, and I stumbled my way through it. It was an unmitigated disaster. We didn't get the contract, and it cost me thirty thousand in lost commission. On the rather tense drive back to our Cerritos office, I asked Steve what he thought I should do. "You, Neil, need to learn how to speak in public." I went away, did my research, and came back with two options. I put them on Steve's desk the following week and, pushing one forward, said, "I want to do that one." He looked at it and said, "Go on then." "But Steve. It's twelve hundred dollars." He just looked at me and mouthed, "And?" I still had an 'Access' card for an account back home, so I paid for myself to do the Dale Carnegie Course.

Remember the lesson about Americans paying their own way and investing in themselves? This was it writ large for me. The course was one evening a week for fourteen weeks. Our instructor was a very charismatic guy called Skip, who sold commercial real estate. I loved it and won the top award on the final night. A couple of months pass by. One day in the office, my phone goes and picking it up, I hear the secretary of our trade association say, "Neil. Senator Brown can't make next month's meeting; we'd like you to give the keynote." I agree, put the phone down, put my head in my hands, and momentarily panic. Catching myself, I give myself a pep-talk and say, "You can do this. This is your chance to use what you've just paid to learn." I pull the manual down, take a piece of paper and start preparing. I can still see the hotel off Pacific Coast Highway in Seal Beach, where I was to present. I walk in; there's a raised platform looking out over a room full of round tables, with three hundred and fifty people seated.

I'm ushered to the central chair on the platform. The next thing I know, I'm being introduced, and as I stand, I can see all seven hundred eyes looking at me. I start. I'm not using any notes because I have used the mnemonic techniques I learned to guide me through my presentation. Within ninety seconds, I'm conscious that I have the audience in the palm of my hand. I relax and start to enjoy it. Twenty minutes later, I get a standing ovation. Steve comes running up to me and says with some vigour, pointing his finger, "Why didn't you do that at Huntington Hospital?" I replied, "It wasn't that I couldn't. I'd never been shown how to!" As the words came out of my mouth, I immediately realised they summed up a profound lesson for me. "It wasn't that I couldn't. I'd just never been shown how to."

One of the things I'd been shown on the Dale Carnegie class was the power of a story. That a great story or narrative can convince and persuade people to do things that pure logic never will. A picture is worth a thousand words has been an advertising mantra for a hundred years, ever since Fred Barnard coined it in 1921 by saying, "One look is worth a thousand words."

Stories paint mental pictures for people, and the one that crystallised it for me was told by Cynthia Micinski. She was a graduate assistant on my class. That is someone who had already done their own class but comes back to help the instructor by giving the new class examples of what was expected from them when they came back the following week. We were to think of something that had happened in our lives that had taught us a lesson. Cynthia told us a story about when she went to a farm as a small child and how some cows taught her, in later life, to face fear.

I was so awe-struck, so taken with it, that I asked her afterwards if I could use it in a book I was going to write. I had my 'F' story. Face Fear. You can find Cynthia's story in Appendix 2. "It wasn't that I couldn't. I'd just never been shown how to." These words just kept going round my head. Being lost, I had been throwing myself into studying, grad classes at UCLA, and doing introductory classes in psychology at Cal State Long Beach. My goal at that moment was to get into a PhD program in San Diego on Cognitive Psychology (There's that frustrated academic poking out its nose again!). I was also running over a hundred miles a week and cycling two hundred. I may have been lost, but I had bags of energy, and threads of ideas were whispering.

## Tip #15: Learn to speak in public

# CHAPTER 16
## Following the muse
### Confronting prejudice

I also had a new girlfriend. Beth. She was studying law at the University of Southern California (USC) and was about to graduate. The fabulous thing about California is you can be skiing in the mountains in the morning and sunning yourself on one of the forty-five beaches, stretching from Malibu to Newport in the afternoon. Beth's family had a cabin in Arrowbear between Lake Arrowhead and Big Bear, in the San Bernardino Mountains, Northeast of LA. Many pleasant days were spent hiking the local trails. We took our last trip up there shortly before she left for Australia for the whole summer. When we returned to Long Beach the following day, I went for a run along Belmont Shore towards the breakwater at Seal Beach. I was feeling good about life but a little sad that Beth was leaving for Australia that night. As I was running, a line suddenly popped into my head. I have no idea where it came from, but it just wouldn't go away. 'There's a link between you and I' and then came another and another. Before I reached the breakwater, I had a poem rattling around in my head and couldn't wait to get back to the flat to write it down. Rushing in through the front door, I grabbed some paper and furiously wrote it straight down.

*There's a link between you and I,*
*I struggle to define it but accept it,*
*It's there between yesterday and tomorrow,*
*like the line between figure and ground,*
*between then and there.*
*It's the past that I struggle with the most,*
*for the future will take care of itself.*
*I thank you for the connection,*
*aware of the struggles you have to fathom, too.*
*Today, I'm full and aware and focussed,*
*but know that the struggle can cease or continue.*
*Take care as you follow your thread,*
*between your dreams and reality,*
*and sometime today, when you come back,*
*we'll explore the link some more*
*and struggle a whole lot less.*

I gave Beth a copy at the airport that night before she flew off. "It's beautiful," she said with tears in her eyes, "just beautiful. You should enter it into a poetry contest." I didn't but writing it was my way of letting go because Beth was off to Australia to see another admirer. I lost out once again with respect to tangible romance but gained so much more, having now been smitten by the creative muse. There is something extraordinary about 'Encouragement'. It goes back to that second thing happening in St. Louis when Dianne told me I was a good writer. It's that standing ovation at the end of my talk in Seal Beach. It's the cheering of the crowds along the route of the Boston Marathon. Compared to its evil twin 'Criticism', you can energetically feel the difference. This is a theme the muse will lead me to explore later in my life, and I also now had a story for 'E' – Encouragement.

That summer, my parents flew out to stay and surf the waves. I'm joking, but we did take a road trip up PCH (Pacific Coast Highway) to Santa Barbara. Another of my St. Louis classmates, Ruth, had moved West to do her PhD at the University of California Santa Barbara. This university is not very well known in the UK, but it is one of the top research universities in America, akin to being in the 'Russell Group'. Santa Barbara itself is a lovely city, with the Santa Ynez Mountains acting as a dramatic backdrop. Downtown is full of Mediterranean-style white stucco buildings with red-tile roofs reflecting the city's Spanish lineage. When we pull up outside Ruth's apartment, I usher my father and mother to go ahead and knock on the door whilst delaying my own arrival because I had a plan in play. Ruth opened the door with a huge smile, and the shock on my father's face was palpable. My plan had been to confront my father's racism. Ruth is from Eritrea, in East Africa. By the end of the afternoon, it was pure joy to see them walking down Stearn's Wharf, arm in arm, joking with each other towards Moby Dick's restaurant, whilst my mother and I did the same following them.

One of the things my new muse led me to do was write my first article, 'Motivation: The Power That Drives You Forward'. After reading it recently, I can see several elements that weave their way through my later creations. My father's feedback at the time? "Bit heavy and philosophical, but well thought out and put together."

Shortly after my parents left, I got a phone call from my sister-in-law, Vanessa. "Neil. Spike's going to be in LA soon and would like to meet up." Spike is Vanessa's brother. He was three years ahead of me at Prices. He's a very accomplished musician indeed, having worked with The Boomtown Rats, Dexy's Midnight Runners, Buck's Fizz, Haircut One Hundred, Peter Green and the Rolling Stones. At the time he was touring with Duran Duran, then at the height of their fame, and he invited me to their LA concert at the Universal Amphitheatre, backstage, and the after party. Star-struck? A little, but then I am an introverted character. Spike would go on to collaborate with Queen, becoming their de facto fifth member. Look him up on Wikipedia. The boy's done good.

Another reason Vanessa had called is because I was about to fly to Brunei for the second time. Chasing the sun across the Pacific, I started wondering about Jane. I'd been there a whole week before I got her attention by knocking on her window one evening. She freely admitted that she'd been avoiding me but invited me in any way. The estrangement had been healed. We went sailing again but couldn't do the Verve Clique thing in the South China Sea because the Brunei authorities had, by this time, started clamping down on the Western propensity for enjoying alcohol. I'll bite my tongue, for now, on what I think about Fundamentalist regimes. One of the funniest memories of this trip is taking a river trip into the jungle with a researcher who was absolutely obsessed with fungi. To him, it was the most fascinating thing in all of evolution. I wish I could remember exactly what it was he said, but Jane and I were in fits of hysterical laughter for a full thirty minutes. I left Brunei for the second time with a promise that she'd come to California and I wouldn't let her down.

"It wasn't that I couldn't. I'd just never been shown how to." This spoken truth was still worming its way through my mind. I started to think, 'What if I joined Dale Carnegie? I loved what it did for me. It's all about personal development, psychology, philosophy. Maybe it's not 'High-Brow' and 'Academic', but it's all about personal growth, helping people be more, and showing them exactly how to do it'. The worm kept going for a whole year.

# Tip #16: Hold up a mirror to prejudice

# CHAPTER 17
# Butterflies and chaos
## Simple visualisations

The eighties gave way to the nineties. I was thirty-five halfway to my three score and ten. I was the fittest I'd been in my life. My regular training partner now was a Scot called John. He was doing cutting-edge genetic research at UC Irvine into what would develop into the human genome project. He was a terrific runner and taught me a technique known as the 'Golden Thread'. When it starts to get tough, imagine a golden thread ahead and behind you. As you run and breathe in, the thread pulls you forward. As you breathe out, it gently pushes you. It's a simple visualisation technique, but it certainly helps when you're doing tough interval workouts, which we often did on UC Irvine's world-class track. Being from England, I was always so gob-smacked at the quality of the sporting infrastructure in the US, especially the college and university facilities, which at the time put anything in England to shame. English first division football teams could only dream of playing in stadiums as good as those of American colleges.

The run that sticks in my mind from this year is the Carlsbad 5000, the world's fastest 5k, held each spring. It's legendary because it's so flat and so fast, and so it proved for us. John ran it in 15 minutes 40, and I was six seconds a kilometre slower in 16 minutes 10, which was my all-time best.

Paul, my inspiration-to-leave-school friend, was finally getting married, and I flew back. The significance of this was his speech at the reception in the village hall. It was highly unusual as he started talking about 'The Theory of Chaos' and 'The Butterfly Hypothesis'. He said that if a butterfly in China flaps its wings, it can affect your life right here in Hampshire, or California, or wherever you may live. You see, if one single butterfly flaps its wings, it moves some air, and if a field of butterflies flap their wings, they move a lot of air. Now, a lot of air moving in China will alter the weather patterns locally. The patterns changing in China will cause changes in the patterns and winds in Hampshire. He finished by thanking the butterfly that had initially moved and brought Clare into his life to be his wife.

On the flight back to LA, I reflected on Paul's butterfly story. I mused, 'Aren't we all sometimes a little like a butterfly? We flap away. Sometimes, nothing happens. Sometimes, good happens. Sometimes, bad things come our way. Friends appear and sometimes disappear. As a rule, though, if we flap out the good stuff, if we put out the good thoughts, the good deeds, somewhere down the road, maybe tomorrow, perhaps next week, but sometime, the good will be returned, just like the wind'. 'Be like the butterfly', I began to think. Put out excited, enthusiastic, positive thoughts that have the potential to be returned one hundredfold.

I wrote it all down during the flight back, and another piece of the 'Freedom' puzzle fell into place.

Spring gave way to summer and promises made were kept. Jane came over. Being an engineer, I had an engineer's car. It was a SAAB 9000-Turbo. It was technically perfect and the only new car I've ever had in my life. I picked Jane up at LAX, and on the drive back to Long Beach, she started squirming in her seat. She was pretty British about it until she saw me smirking and cried out, "What have you done?" The beauty of SAABs at the time was they had heated seats for all that winter driving in Sweden but just used for mischief-making in Sunny California. We went sailing to Santa Catalina, an idyllic island twenty-nine miles off the coast from Long Beach. It was developed as a tourist destination by the Wrigley's of chewing gum fame, in the 1920s. The main town of Avalon is dominated by an art deco Catalina casino. It's just a great wilderness to explore once you get out of Avalon.

We also visited Charlie, who was running his own business in Palm Springs, a hundred miles east of LA. Palm Springs is a desert resort famed for its connections to legions of film stars and celebrities, with streets named after the likes of Frank Sinatra, Dinah Shore, Gene Autry, and Gerald Ford. Bob Hope had a superb house built into the hillside looking over it all. Like LA, you can head to the mountains, although here it is done with a cable car taking you up to trails leading to San Jacinto Peak, a full 10,000 feet above sea level and always covered in snow. We borrowed Charlie's beloved Porsche and drove up to Idyllwild, the other side of San Jacinto. On the switchback mountain roads, you can pretend you're in the Italian Alps. Jane loved California and me, but I couldn't quite reciprocate to the same degree, so we became the best of friends. It would be nearly three years until we saw each other again, and our circumstances would be unimaginably different. It's good not to know the future.

## *Tip #17: Simple visualisations work*

# CHAPTER 18
## Pots of Gold
*Happy ever after?*

The worm turned its penultimate corner. I arranged an appointment with John Nethery, who had the license to promote Dale Carnegie Training within the southern half of greater Los Angeles. John had been the protégé of Harry O. Hamm, who had helped Dale Carnegie expand his business throughout the West and had, in turn, introduced him to his future wife, Dorothy. John's office was on Atlantic Avenue in the California Heights area of Long Beach, close to Signal Hill, which has been one of the most productive oil fields ever in California. Signal Hill is actually a tiny city entirely surrounded by Long Beach. In 1921 when oil was found, there were over one hundred producing oil derricks, and it was nicknamed 'Porcupine Hill'.

John invited me to join him for lunch at his favourite diner, 'Bake-n-Broil', two blocks up from the office. Here, I was introduced to my favourite dessert 'Pecan Pie' with vanilla ice cream. Over lunch I asked John about opportunities with Dale Carnegie. "There's always opportunities, Son, but first you're gonna have to resign from your job." "OK, Mr. Nethery. But what's the package?" "It's an opportunity, Neil. 100% straight commission. No salary. No Benefits. You sell, and we'll show you how to; you'll eat, but you gotta really want to do it."

I drove away, parked under the apartment, and took a walk down to and along Bluff Park. With the breeze off the Pacific and the sun in my eyes, I cogitated. 'I'm making $60,000 per year plus commission. I have health care. I have a pension plan. But I love this field. I reckon I could make an impact if I can absorb and learn everything Dale Carnegie offers. If I don't do it now, I never will'. The worm "It wasn't that I couldn't. I'd just never been shown how to," took its final turn, and in July 1990, I tendered my resignation to York and started working for Dale Carnegie as an Associate. Now, in a fairy tale, the ending would be, "And they lived happily ever after." This is no fairy tale. I went broke and declared bankruptcy.

But first there were some profound lessons. To sell, you have to have someone to pitch to. Customers for products like training, insurance, and encyclopaedias don't usually walk in off the street unless you were someone like me who had a very specific need when I messed up at Huntington Hospital. To find prospects in the 1990s, unless you have a slick marketing or advertising machine, it meant one of three things: Yellow Pages and cold calling; wearing out your shoe leather collecting business cards or compliment slips from business premises; sending out invitations to a promotional event. You were ultimately looking for Presidents of companies (Managing Directors back in the UK) and Vice-Presidents of sales.

Long Beach is a big aerospace centre with the likes of Rockwell and MacDonnell Douglas headquartered there. I can remember Nate (One of John's area managers) coming back from a site visit to Rockwell and saying, "I've just met HAL." For those that don't know the movie, 'HAL' was the AI computer in Stanley Kubrick's epic 1968 science fiction movie 2001: A Space Odyssey. To have seen something as advanced as that in 1990 is mind-boggling indeed. There's quite a funny story about Nate. John Nethery is being pitched to by one of Anthony Robbin's salesmen in the office one day. Robbins had written 'Unlimited Power' in 1986 and was in the process of building his vast empire. John and the Robbins guy were standing in the centre of the room. John could see the corridor behind, along which Nate was tiptoeing gingerly and theatrically as if walking on hot coals (which is Robbin's Shtick) with his big white teeth grinning at John behind the guy's back. Well, John lost it and had to show the guy out. The lesson? Never play to an audience with people behind you. One of our colleagues, Joanna, had been at high school with Robbins and said he was "Huge, Loud and a bit of an Oddball."

What of the sales process itself? Over the years, I've seen many (and later, I will give you my own unvarnished version), but Carnegie's was quite slick: 1. Establish some rapport; 2. Find out their understanding and connection with respect to the product/course; 3. Position your product favourably so they have a thorough understanding of what it is and isn't; 4. Question to find out what their specific needs and requirements are; 5. Find out why it's important to them to solve any issues; 6. Paint a picture of them now succeeding in overcoming the issues; 7. Make it easy for them to buy and gain their commitment. Naturally, this very slick process can only work if you've got potential clients to talk to. If you're a salesperson and you have an empty diary, you are effectively unemployed.

John was an inspirational man. He would have a sales meeting every Monday morning with Nate, Tom Kibling, the other area manager (who would marry Cynthia, of cow fame and eventually take over from John) and the eight associates, including me and Joanna. The recurring context was always about potential, and three examples stick out.

The first was 'General Sherman'. Not the Union Civil War general but the giant sequoia reaching 275 feet into the air in Sequoia National Park. It is currently the largest living tree on earth and is estimated to be over 2,500 years old. The seed for this tree weighed 1/16 of an ounce. To encircle its circumference would require seventeen people fingertips to fingertips. If they were to chop it down, there would be enough wood to build forty-five two-story family homes. Do you honestly believe that that sequoia seed has more potential than you and your brain?

The second example? John would say, "People are always chasing and seeking the pot of Gold at the end of the rainbow. No. It's never there. It's here now (and pointing). It's right there. You're sitting on it!"

The third? John simply looked at all the associates one morning and said, "Get a message to Garcia." He, Nate, and Tom then just got up, leaving us all looking at each other completely mystified. It took me three days to figure it out (there was no internet, remember), and John was delighted when I walked into his office and gave him Garcia's reply. For those who can't figure it out, I'll put the solution in Appendix Four later.

Was I still chasing the pot of Gold? That Christmas and New Year, I ventured back to the UK. I shouldn't have, as I was rapidly running out of money. Attempting to keep a $60,000-a-year lifestyle going with next to nothing coming in requires some sort of magic I had yet to discover. Mark and Vanessa were over from Brunei, and there was a big party thrown at Fareham Squash Club where I was to meet a pivotal person whom I hadn't seen for many years. Returning to Long Beach in 1991, I had an important decision to make. My car had just been repossessed, and I couldn't pay my rent. I did, however, have one very good friend and on the phone with him, he asked, out of the blue, "Do you need some breathing space right now?" "I sure do," I responded. "OK, start packing right now. I'll be there tomorrow with a van. You can come stay here for a while and re-group." I did the best thing that I could ever have done for myself. I cast aside my ego, threw away my stubborn pride, ditched my independent arrogance, fully accepted Charlie's offer of help, and moved to that film star's playground— Palm Springs. Thanks, Charlie.

In the following months, I was gradually able to rebuild my life. I started working in a tele-sales office and was managing it within a month. Keep the room cold and the coffee hot seems to have been the abiding lesson. In twelve weeks, I was able to save enough money for a flight back to England via St. Louis so I could say my goodbyes to Sandy and Phil.

# Tip #18: You are the pot of 'Gold'

# CHAPTER 19
## The Maltese Breaststroke
### Sales and Marketing

" **B**ut what will I tell my friends?" she said when I told her I would seek a sales position with Dale Carnegie in London. Sales to a professional in England was still a very dirty word. I firmly believed that a good salesperson will keep, on average, thirty people employed and, consequently, make three times the average earnings.

I had arrived back in London on April the 25th, 1991 and started my new life living with Liz in Blackheath. She is an exceptional architect, and her work can be seen in the gorgeous shopfronts of the Royal Opera House in Covent Garden, opposite the Apple store. If you venture up there, savour the echoes of Charles Rennie MacIntosh from her time at Glasgow School of Art. Despite her protestations, the London licensee for Dale Carnegie invited me into the fold with open arms and tasked me with building a business for them in South London, Croydon being the focal point. Two weeks after joining them, Sherman invited everyone in his organisation to attend a team-building event at Chiswick Town Hall. Here, I would meet for the first time some key individuals who are still friends today. Ian, Walter, and Paul Walsh.

A facilitator was running the team-building exercise. They divided us into two groups. The group I was in had to solve the problem. The other group had to observe. The remit, put simply, was to contain a nuclear core melt-down (some bricks) with a disparate set of objects without crossing over a circular containment line. The thing is, I immediately saw the solution. The problem was no one was listening to me. So, I commandeered one of the team members, and while they were still talking about it, we solved it. I got slaughtered in the feedback session for not being a team-player until I explained that when you are in a crisis situation, like a fire in a ship's engine-room, you are trained to take instant action. A nuclear melt-down is precisely the same, irrespective of this being a training exercise, and so I unilaterally decided to take action. I got a few cheers and claps but most of them looked at me askance. I shrugged my shoulders and thought to myself, "Civies!"

My project in South London took a while to get going. On an internal training course in Chiswick, Walter was tasked with firing me one day. He was pretty mystified when I continued to show up. No one was going to stop me from realising my dream. As in Long Beach, the primary method for generating leads was to promote an event and invite as many prospective businesspeople as you could find. Walter created the event itself, and it was brilliant in its ingenuity. Two hours of 'Wow' wrapped around something as mundane as 'Time Management'. If you were to ask me today to do it this afternoon, I could repeat it verbatim. All you had to do was find the potential candidates, and that was a painstaking process of canvassing, trawling through business directories, and talking to past and existing clients. Once you had the names, positions, and addresses, you would begin writing the envelopes, add a name to the pre-printed invitation, insert, seal, and lick the stamp. Sixty an hour was about the maximum, so 2,000 invites would take a couple of hours a day for two weeks. Two thousand invites would get you forty people in the room. Then the magic would start, and the selling could begin. The truth is everything up to now is marketing, and it's why, to this day, I hate it—such a ridiculous waste of time for a salesperson.

The outcome of all this effort is the event, and once you've wowed the audience, you have the right to call them to make an appointment. "Great to see you this morning. How does your diary look?" The simple statistics were that you'd get thirty-six appointments and twelve contracts/ clients if forty showed up. The process worked exceptionally well. I began to create a network in South London.

The biggest difference between selling in the UK versus the USA is no one is prepared to invest in themselves. The expectation always is that someone else needs to pay. I know it was this difference between the mindsets of an employee and an employer that drew me towards the world of entrepreneurship and business building. To me, this was the world in which people invested in themselves. This was the world of creating things and giving back vs the world of just taking and expecting things to be given. This world was best summed up by my father when he referred to Dom Mintoff (The Prime Minister of Malta in 1974) doing the

'Maltese-Breaststroke - Give it to me - Give it to me' with an exaggerated action of hands coming in towards his chest. I've loved his analogy ever since. I've seen this UK attitude slowly change over the years. It will always lag behind, but I do see more people firmly believing in themselves and recognising that no investment will equate to no growth.

The three individuals that I met in these early days prepared to invest in themselves were:

1. Jonathan Butterworth is the first person I ever convinced to enrol on the Dale Carnegie class in the UK. He went on to run a very successful Specsavers franchise.

2. Nic Rixon (who often says he was the first) was the second. A bit like Winchester Vaughan in part two. Nic will keep popping up in this story. The thing I remember about Nic was his first night on the class, and him saying get me up there. He immediately wanted to be an instructor. The boy loves a stage.

3. Peter Baker approached me following a talk I gave at the Old Whitgiftians Sports Club. He wanted to learn how to speak in public. Although Peter worked for BT at the time, he paid for himself. It wasn't long before his entrepreneurial streak kicked in, and he started building his own business.

By Christmas that year, I had a good core of clients. Most were young entrepreneurs. Over the holidays, I had the brainwave of bringing them all together once a month so they could all learn from each other. One client that deserves a special mention is Bryden Johnson. Gordon Bull, one of their partners, had been on a Dale Carnegie course before I got off the boat. I'd been to see him as soon as I'd been tasked to build the business, and subsequently, I'd signed up some of their people, including Neil Johnson, Paul Gould, and Jackie Marshall. Jackie's uncle was Jim Marshall, who designed the incredible speakers and amplifiers for Pete Townsend of The Who, and subsequently built a considerable business off the back of their success. Bryden Johnson agreed to sponsor my idea, and so the Croydon Movers and Shakers was conceived. On reflection, it was akin to a blend of Vistage and BNI (Business Network International), but I failed to monetise it. We kept it going for twelve years. One of our earliest members was Peter Dobner. Peter and his wife Christina had been Austrian and World Champion ballroom dancers. Along with Anne Laxholm (a Danish champion), they created a company called ChrisAnne, which designed and produced stunning outfits for ballroom dancers. Their showroom in Mitcham was a kaleidoscope of bright colours, feather boas, and glittering fabrics. Their big break would come in 2004 when Strictly Come Dancing hit our screens, and everyone was wearing their costumes.

## Tip #19: Invest in yourself

# CHAPTER 20

## Counting your blessings

### Self-sabotage and 'Suck-back'

Returning to the UK was a culture shock. I had absolutely forgotten about the class system and how one's accent can instantly define and, therefore, position you. Although this time, I didn't start walking back to the airport at three in the morning in minus fifteen Fahrenheit flurries of snow, I came perilously close. Jay, who owned the tele-sales operation in Palm Springs, offered me a way back. He'd pay for the flight and give me a $5,000 signing back-on fee! I was so tempted, I must admit. But stay I did until the Christmas. I spent it with my parents on my own and decided, despite the glimmerings of success, that I would return to the US.

I travel back to Blackheath in the new year, walk into Liz's apartment and say,

"We've got to talk."

"Yes. We do," she says.

"OK. You go first."

"I'm pregnant. What do you need to talk about?"

"It doesn't matter."

I stayed in the UK.

There's something primaeval about direct sales. It's back to John Nethery's line, "You sell, you'll eat, but you gotta really want to do it." When you are constantly prospecting, putting on events and meeting people, you find life is full of beautiful surprises, opportunities, and learnings. A key learning for me was at an early morning seminar at the Inns of Court on Chancery Lane. At the end of the workshop, it is usual to ask people what they gained from the day. This young woman stood up, thanked us for the insights, and shared the following, delivered from memory, with no notes at all:

> *"The moment one definitely commits oneself, then providence moves too. All sorts of things occur to help one that would never otherwise have occurred. A whole stream of events issues from the decision, raising in one's favour all manner of unforeseen incidents and meetings and material assistance which no one could have dreamed would have come their way. Whatever you can do or dream, you can, begin it. Boldness has genius, power, and magic in it. Begin it now."*

I can still feel the hairs on the back of my neck bristling as she recited it, and every word resonated. I pledged to myself there and then that I, too, would learn this piece verbatim. I asked my father to write it out for me in a Gothic script (he was quite the calligrapher) so I could hand it out to clients. For those who don't know, it's from Johann Wolfgang von Goethe, Germany's Shakespeare.

Opportunities? When you are in direct sales, you will eventually cross paths with others selling insurance, pots and pans, financial planning, Amway, and encyclopaedias. Anne Summers hadn't yet got going. Sales managers will recognise your skills and attempt to lure you into their orbit.

One such chap was Joe Adams. He was the UK Managing Director for Encyclopaedia Britannica. Joe had come along to one of my seminars at the Croydon Chamber of Commerce, and I made an appointment to see him at their headquarters in Wallington. Being a born salesman, he naturally tried to sell me on working for him, but I resisted his charms and sold him instead on putting someone on one of my courses. It was Chris Day who headed up their audio-visual department and is today my publisher. Joe is originally from Indiana, and in his office, he had a fabulous collection of arrowheads, which he had picked up as a boy from the land around the family homestead. Chris's background is in the theatre, and he has a collection of the loudest ties you'll ever be blessed to see.

I learnt something else from Joe that would be the seed for a future lesson. Joe had hired and developed hundreds of people to sell Encyclopaedia Britannica. The thing that always amazed him was the unerring way in which a person's background would suck them back from their newfound success. Joe was ahead of his time in granting everyone equal opportunities no matter their personal circumstances. He would train them to succeed if they were willing to make the commitment. His disappointment was when they would self-sabotage their success because they couldn't break their emotional dependencies with family and friends, who hated them for changing and improving. There had been a popular movie in 1983 called 'Educating Rita' with Michael Caine and Julie Walters. The crux of the film was exactly the same thing. Rita needed to cast off the people close to her who were impeding her development. It's the never-ending cycle of breaking free from dependence and becoming truly independent. The behaviour in my world is called 'Suck-Back'.

An aside: Everyone knows the expression, 'Is the glass half-full or half-empty?' It becomes an indicative metaphor for being optimistic or pessimistic. And then it becomes, 'Are you a half-full or half-empty sort of person?' Joe always said, "It depends on whether you're pouring or drinking!" What I love about this added dimension is the inference on whether you're taking or giving, and I'd use and expand on this concept later in life.

Surprises? You bump into people in unexpected places. A bit like Bonnie in the Birdhouse Bar! But bumping into Winchester Vaughan at Kings Cross was one delight. Another was an old university girlfriend in the Epsom post office. They say that if you stand at Piccadilly Circus for an hour, you will see someone you know. It's some statistical quirk that travel guides like to trot out. The real surprises of 1992, though? The end of the 'Cold War', Sharon Stone, who looked uncannily like Debbie, in 'Basic Instinct' and my son James being born. He began at 09:30 on August the 10th. The family joke is that he had to wait for his father to blow-dry his hair before his mother could be taken to hospital.

When I'm coaching or consulting with people, one of the exercises I do is 'Look at the wall'. Look at the wall now. Pick a blank wall in your office or home and really look at it. What do you see? If we were together, you'd probably tell me about the shadows, the smudges, the chips, the blemishes. You'd describe the edges, etc. No one has ever told me that they see the wall, the wall that supports the ceiling, that divides one room from another. You see, we're geared from an evolutionary standpoint to pick up on discrepancies in our environment, the so-called negatives. It's a sound survival technique because reacting instantly to a discrepancy could well save our life on the savannah.

The wall is a metaphor for the positives in your life. The positives that simply fade away into the background because we're wired to look at the negatives.

Ready to do some writing? Get yourself a nice hardback notebook and start tallying your victories in life. These will be moments of peak experience, bliss, happiness, and well-being. These will be smiles, jobs well done, recognition, and acknowledgements. It's been sage advice forever, hasn't it, 'Count your blessings'. But have you ever done it? Have you ever physically sat down with a sheet of paper and written them down? Probably not. Let's see if we can get you to do so. Write down fifteen today. Make it thirty tomorrow, fifty by the week's end.

I still have the piece of paper from when I first did this exercise myself. It's inside the back of my very own 'Victory Book'. It starts with my son being born on August the 10th, 1992.

# Tip #20: Look at the 'Wall' and tally your victories

# CHAPTER 21
## Walking becomes a theme
### Neil with the 'Shiny Shoes'

You've probably picked up that I wasn't getting on too well with Liz. She asked me to leave two months later. I looked at a map of South London. Studying the main transport routes between Croydon and Charing Cross (we had an office on the Strand at Queensland House), I figured Balham would be the ideal place to live. Not finding anywhere there, I ventured one stop down the Northern line to Tooting Bec and found a room for the princely sum of thirty pounds per week. I ended up living in Tooting Bec for twenty-five years, the longest I've lived anywhere.

If you walk out of the tube station at Tooting Bec, you will immediately be struck by this gorgeous Victorian pub, 'The Wheatsheaf' or the 'Wheaty' as the locals call it. Back then, the locals were predominantly Irish and had a close affiliation to the Roman Catholic Church, St. Anselm's diametrically opposite. Talk about an assault on the senses when I first walked in. Nine people in 'Black and White' tending bar and customers five to six deep, all vying for their attention. I can remember taking my small red notebook out and doing simple word sketches of what I saw. 'Stocky with a strong jaw and the demeanour of a convict about to be shipped to Australia'. 'The most foul-mouthed, voluptuous, harridan of a woman I'd ever seen and heard in my life', are two that still spring to mind thirty years later. I grew quite fond of the 'Wheaty', its customers, staff, and its evolution, near demise, and renaissance.

Jane was now back in the UK, living in Cliftonwood, Bristol, and I took the liberty to go visit. "Neil. You're so pale," were the first words out of her mouth. Those California days were long gone, as were any fringe benefits as Jane was now married to Clive, a great gregarious, rogue of a husband casting around for a new opportunity having been made redundant from a senior banking position. Their house had a lovely small backyard sitting up high over the river Avon with views of Clifton Suspension Bridge to the right and Brunel's SS Great Britain to the left. The local pub was 'The Lion', and it was undoubtedly the heart and beating soul of the community. In it, I met my first ever 4x4. John had had four kids with four different women. I'd never heard the term before, but Clive took great delight in introducing me to it. We obviously clicked. I was invited back.

Sometimes, you just click with your clients, too. I had a class running in the Great Western Hotel at Paddington. Nick D, who was an ace salesman for Konica, suggested we go for a drink afterwards. Sitting in the bar and looking very furtive was Robin Cook, who was in John Smith's Shadow Cabinet shortly before he died, and history changed with the Blair-Brown Granita Pact. Both Nick and I agreed that she wasn't his wife. As I left, Nick asked if I'd like to attend a Boat Race party that weekend.

It was being hosted by his girlfriend in a super apartment right on the river's edge, just down from the White Hart, with the Thames Path running below. At one point, I'm leaning on the balcony and looking down, and I see this absolutely gorgeous woman waving at me from the path. I smile as she takes a photo. A little later, I saw her approach me through the sitting room, and we started chatting. She hadn't been waving at me. She was waving at the chap on the balcony directly below, Jack Nicholson! She thought, though, that I looked interesting enough for her to leave Jack's company and come talk. Her name was Cherry. It was a great party, and I walked away with a grin, a bit of a swagger, and two phone numbers. I must admit it felt good to sense that my confidence was returning. I'd love to find that photo, 'Me and Jack!'

Walking became a theme for me this year. I was still running but nowhere like the levels I had achieved in California. I started going on long hikes. I dusted off my map reading skills, learned in the Boy Scouts, and ventured into the wilds. One of my favourite places was around Snowden in North Wales. I'd fallen for this area when Iolo and I had driven through it in his Triumph Spitfire on the way to Holyhead, Anglesey when we were cadets. I used to stay at Plas Y Brenin, the mountain training centre near Betws-Y-Coed, and I went on long hikes around the Snowden horseshoe. With its sheer two-thousand-foot drop, Crib Goch was scary the first time, and I practically crawled along the top. I was dancing by the third traverse. Hiking through mists using dead reckoning with the compass and coming out exactly where you wanted to be was exhilarating. Coming down the wrong side of a mountain and realising you were ten miles off-course less so. Having the right kit is paramount when you go walking in nature. It's also essential when you're in town canvassing and wearing out the shoe leather. I ensured I bought the best shoes I could afford from Jones, the bootmaker. I remember the day my shoe repairs cost me more than I used to spend on a cheap pair, but I didn't begrudge the bill because good-quality shoes worked their magic from the feet up. It became my signature, and one of my best corporate clients nicknamed me 'Neil, with the shiny shoes'.

Another of my clients also had well-polished shoes, but that was because he was in the public eye as a Member of the European Parliament (MEP). I asked him what his goal was. He puffed his chest up and boomed straight back, "To effect legislative change!" I spat my tea out, laughing so much. I challenged him and said, "You do realise how pompous that sounds don't you? It's so detached and highfaluting that no one, including yourself, will connect with it. Now, be real. What's your real goal, something you can get your teeth into?" Do you know what he came back with? To be re-elected.

## *Tip #21: Get the right kit*

# CHAPTER 22
## Living, Laughing, Loving, & Learning

### Insecurity and living on the edge

Ultimately, I wasn't rich enough for Cherry, but we had a lot of fun before we parted. I still have a memento she bought for me in Blaenau Ffestiniog. It's a phenomenal photo of a mountaineer standing on this precipitous rock outcrop, and I think it's an apt metaphor for my life. Perhaps that's why she bought it for me, knowing I wasn't looking for a life of stability and security. In fact, my favourite book at the time was Alan Watt's 'The Wisdom of Insecurity'. Someone said once, "Live on the edge. That's where the excitement is." This is a theme I will return to. I was poor, but I had potential.

Credit to Jane though. On my next trip west to Bristol, she threw a party and introduced me to Teresa. May you live in interesting times is an English expression often claimed to be a translation of an ancient Chinese curse. It's not. With typical English irony, what is delivered is a blessing enveloping the notion that chaos, trouble, and catastrophe won't be far behind. It took me a few years after returning from the States to rewire my brain and again appreciate the British admiration for biting, sardonic, sarcastic, and cutting humour. Teresa brought forth some interesting times.

One of the great things about having been in this world of personal and corporate change for so long is seeing the sudden emergence of ideas that everyone starts raving about, but they are just repackaged old ideas. Being in the zone becomes flow. The Fraud syndrome becomes the Imposter syndrome. Modelling and anchoring became Neuro-linguistic programming (NLP). Paradigm shifts become disruptors. Type A/Type B became labelling. As the philosopher Martin Cohen so aptly said, "Today's facts are never really more than opinions whose popularity is transitory and far from conclusive." Personally, I now prefer to say, "There's not a shred of evidence that life is serious." I mention this because the bandwagon that everyone was jumping on at the time was NLP. I have to say I avoided it like the plague.

Back when I was perhaps a little more serious, I can remember going on a sales call. Nic had introduced me to Petra who ran, at the time, a thriving costume jewellery business called Cabouchon. Nic did the packaging for them. I can still see the appointment running through to this day. We start with the usual preliminary pleasantries, and just before I'm about to begin my sales spiel, she cuts right in and says, "What you got?" I continue with my patter, and she again says, "OK. Just tell me what you've got." But I have a 'Winning formula' and continue, at which point she says, "Get out!" Walking back down the damp, dusky Battersea streets towards the train station, the penny finally drops. Meet direct, blunt behaviour with direct, quick answers. Never prevaricate. Instinctive people only respect equal directness initially. They will eventually warm, and their softer nature will emerge, but you usually only ever get one chance.

A chance that I did take at this time was to do some freelance work. One of the more colourful characters I'd met in Croydon was Geoffrey Cotton, an ex-PGA chairman. He owned Addington Court Golf Club and would go on to buy West Chiltington GC in Sussex with fine views of the South Downs. He asked me to do a motivational management seminar for him and his team but wanted me to use my own material. In May of 1994, I facilitated the first ever 'Freedom Seminar' and got paid the princely sum of one thousand pounds. It was a real buzz to receive a cheque made out to me for something I had created. My true entrepreneurial journey had begun, and I kept a photocopy of the cheque.

We had a European conference at the Hilton in York. What a beautiful city with such a chequered history. Right opposite the Hilton was Clifford's Tower, the site of an abominable atrocity in 1190 when the city's Jews were massacred. Things were more peaceful inside.

Three significant things happened due to this conference.

The first: We had a talk by Terry Ostrowiak, who had recently given up the South African license and returned to The Netherlands. Terry had created a product for Dale

Carnegie called 'The Executive Image Programme'. He related a story I would eventually use in 'The Freedom Tree'.

> *One day, Terry came into his conservatory and found his young daughter Orit intensely studying something on the floor. Getting down on his hands and knees, he joined her and discovered that she was observing a butterfly chrysalis. "What are you doing?" asked Terry.*
>
> *"Well, Dad, this poor butterfly inside this cocoon seems to be struggling so much, and I was wondering how on earth I could help it," replied Orit. Terry, down on the floor next to Orit, explained that she should leave it alone to allow it to find its own way out because that is the way of the world. Getting himself up and picking Orit up, they left the conservatory and went into the kitchen for some lunch. After lunch, Terry told Orit he was just popping out to pick up some bits and pieces. He would be back within the hour. When he returned, he walked into the conservatory and again found Orit looking at the chrysalis, or rather what remained of it. She was sobbing, and she snuffled that the butterfly had died. Sure enough, it was, lying a few inches away from the now-empty cocoon.*
>
> *"What happened?" asked Terry. "Well, Dad, it was struggling so much that I just had to help it. I couldn't help myself. So gently, with some small nail scissors, I released the butterfly from its cocoon, and it just fell over and died." "Well," said Terry, "That's the way of the world with butterflies. You see, the struggle of escaping from their cocoons is all part*

*of their development. The struggle itself helps them to develop the strength to use their wings. It's like accelerated weight training, and when you deny them that struggle, they don't have the strength to fly off on their own and do what butterflies do." The lesson was that opportunities are often born out of struggle. Relish your struggles and get stronger.*

The second: During a coffee break on the second day, I wandered past a group of our Swiss associates and overheard part of their conversation— "The secret is you must be Living, Laughing and Learning." That was it; that was all, just a snippet of a conversation. About what, I have no idea, but as I walked past, it captured a piece of my mind and stayed there working and growing. Now I'm a magpie for ideas. I always carry a small red notebook with me to jot down thoughts, impressions, quotes and ideas, and this little snippet went straight inside. It did more than that, though. It continued to work at me, and I found myself playing with the concept. Living, Laughing and Learning. Powerful, positive, empowering words. Words of life. When I returned from the conference, I wrote the three words up on the dry-wipe board I have in my office and let the idea stay in limbo for a while. Like any true idea, it didn't just stay still. This one started to grow slowly at first, with the addition of just one word – Loving. I felt this was a stronger message that this is what life is all about – Living–Laughing–Loving–Learning – and I adopted it as my motto. Over the next two months, three other letters appeared on my office board, attracting for a number of reasons their own words, which were:

*Fun—Free—Friends—Fame*
*Happy—Healthy—Horny—Holy*
*Energetic—Exciting—Enthusiastic—Extraordinary*

I started trying them out. People would ask, "How are you?" and I'd say right back, "Well. I'm Happy, Healthy, Horny, and Holy." Some people would look at me as if I was totally crazy, but the majority would smile. If I'd used the Es, they would say, "You certainly are extraordinary!" The point is that I was having fun with it, and I noticed other people's attitudes and mine shifted as a consequence. It sure beat that old litany of "Oh, I'm all right, how are you?" or that old faithful, "Oh, not too bad today. My neck's playing up a bit. Pity it's so cold. How about you? Still got that trouble with your back?"

As with anything that works, you start to explore it a little more. I started another notebook, indexed A-Z no less, and started jotting down all the good words I came across: Terrific, Exotic, Radiant, Enthralling, Sensational, Artistic, Alluring, Noble, Natural, Erotic, Tender, Unique, Real, Now, Enterprising, Remarkable, Inspiring, Spectacular, Beautiful and many more. As the notebook slowly and gradually began to fill up, I noticed a dramatic shift in my attitude toward situations and people. Another benefit, which proved helpful later on, was that by simply reading or speaking aloud the positive words, I could quickly change my state of mind and my attitude. Then I ran out of words. Sitting in the Wheaty with a Guinness and my old school dictionary, I began a project that would eventually result in my first book, 'The A-Z of Positive Thinking'. All because I jotted down an idea in my little red notebook.

The third: After York, I was on the train to London with Ralph Nichols. Ralph had the Dale Carnegie (DC) license for Detroit. Most licenses averaged about 1,000 candidates a year. Ralph's did 15,000. He was in with all the US car manufacturers at the time: General Motors, Chrysler, and Ford. He personally knew Kathleen Ford. I asked him what he would do if he'd been given the London license for DC. I've never forgotten his reply. "I'd take a house in Kensington. I'd then find myself the best restaurant in town, get to know the Maître D', have a regular table booked, and have the Maître D' introduce me to all the significant people in town." To this day, I still want to follow this advice. Ralph was coming down to London to attend a follow-up meeting with Sherman, the London licensee. I mentioned that I was giving a presentation at Fairfield Halls in Croydon, and Ralph said he'd like to attend. It was my first major presentation since Seal Beach. Again, there were 350 people in the theatre, and again, I felt the power of holding an audience in the palm of my hand. Ralph said, "You'll eat out on that for a month."

## *Tip #22: Always carry a notebook*

# CHAPTER 23
# The A-Z of Thought Antidotes

## *How we really communicate*

You don't, though, do you? Food is somehow more tangible than thoughts and feelings. I've had a funny relationship with money in my life. It waxes and wanes like the moon but in longer cycles. Once in Bristol, I was playing cards with a friend's daughter, who was about ten. She wanted to play for money. After the game, I asked her, "Why do you like money so much, Katie?" "Because it helps," she simply replied, and I thought, 'That is the most excellent answer I have ever heard'. Somerset Maughan famously said, "Money is like a sixth sense. Without it, you can't enjoy the other five." I think it's true to say that I've never attached myself to the need for a secure income. I've never been what I would call a slave to the salary and ended up on the hedonistic hamster wheel of keeping up with the 'Joneses'. I'm open to being called 'Irresponsible' and having a 'Peter Pan' attitude, but there it is.

I can remember Teresa moving in with me in Tooting Bec. I was still living in one room, albeit a much larger one, and when she started to complain, I simply said, "Well, it's much bigger than a cabin on a ship." I'm often asked what I would do if I won the lottery, and I always say the same thing, "I'd do precisely what I'm doing now but with much more style, panache, and reach." I suspect my DNA is missing the material/secure piece of code, and money always seems to turn up anyway. Well mostly. There's been a few tense, scarce, and scary times, but that's life on the edge, right? If you're looking to read this and get some tips on how to be rich, put it down now. You'll be better off writing a book yourself on how to rob a bank. If you're looking for some tips and insights on how to improve your own and other's lives, read on.

My Living-Laughing-Loving-Learning project finally came together with me self-publishing it in a samizdat way. I cobbled together an A4 master copy with two A5 layouts back-to-back. I asked the wonderful Patel brothers, Ilesh and Dushyant, to print multiple copies on the photocopier in their shop on Trinity Road. They would then guillotine the copies, add a rough cover, staple, and fold and voila, 'The A-Z of Thought Antidotes' (as it was originally called) was published for £3 a copy at a cost of 28p.

I published it under my pen name of, N. James. Why? Because I had a year before coined a quote, 'If we always think what we have always thought, we will always be what we have always been'. I put it on the back of my business cards and thought it would be a bit naff to put my own name to it, and there's my inherent shyness coming through. The funny thing is people would start asking me, "Who's this N. James?" When the book came out, I could say, "Oh. They wrote this fabulous little book," and people would buy it off me, but they wouldn't if I promoted myself. Technically, it's called third-person referral and works particularly well in the UK. Other people can sell you, but you can't sell yourself. That's the way it was in Britain. Of course, nowadays, everyone is promoting the heck out of themselves, and that British sense of reserve has dissipated. Book sales took off, and testimonials from readers and clients poured in. My favourite? My mother's, and I put it on the original cover with her maiden name: "Very clever and well written." Jean McCulloch.

I was still working, selling Dale Carnegie courses (Sales, Leadership, Public Speaking) to business owners throughout South London. The Movers and Shakers breakfast meetings, hosted and sponsored by Bryden Johnson, were gaining momentum. My results were rising, and I was pretty pleased when I saw myself in the top 50 table for salespeople worldwide. There were three thousand of us at the time. My friend Ian was 5th, and I was 19th. The top four were this group of phenomenal women from Sweden.

Interesting Segway here about language and the way we communicate. Everyone thinks it's all about the words, but it's not. I've always referred to it as the Birdwhistell Formula, but the formulation was originated by Albert Mehrabian, PhD, Professor Emeritus of Psychology at the University of California, in the 1950s. Mehrabian concluded that the total impact of a message is about 7 per cent verbal (words and sentences), 28 per cent vocal (tone of voice), and 65 per cent nonverbal (facial expressions, posture and other gestures). Raymond Birdwhistell, who was doing pioneering research on the interpretation of body language, facial expressions, and gestures, came up with very similar numbers. I had started my training to be a Dale Carnegie course instructor (more on this later). Our instructor (the instructor of instructors) was Mike Smith. He was asked to go to Sweden to assess a new group of instructors. Mike didn't speak a word of Swedish but was able to assess their competency using the above formula. He could see if they were performing and could see when they failed.

As a consequence of this success, I was invited to the annual conference in San Diego. It was a delightful conference for several different reasons. I received a bonus cheque—a big tick. I danced with Dale Carnegie's widow, Dorothy—bigger tick. I took Terry's daughter, Orit, to the black-tie ball—the biggest tick of all. I love San Diego (if you remember, I wanted to start a PhD there). Orit was living in Del Mar to the north, and one evening, I said I wanted to go for a run. She drove me to Torrey Pines State Beach, pointed and said, "That's a good run," and off I went. Down to La Jolla and back was a good 15k. When I returned, she had a great big grin on her face, "Good run?" My run had taken me along 'Black's Beach', which is now known as one of the best gay nudist beaches on the planet. I laughed. "Good one, Orit," and gave her a high five.

Being there also allowed me to catch up with my old university friend Bob. He was now working at NASSCO shipyard next to San Diego Naval Base. A degree in Marine

Engineering really is a passport to travel. Bob had recently admitted that he was gay and roared with laughter when I told him of Orit's jape. We went for drinks downtown in the Gaslamp distinct, and one of Bob's friends, he told me later, thought I was an arrogant tosser, which I took as an excellent compliment. I had learnt some years earlier that when people throw things your way, they're mainly talking about themselves. It's called 'mirroring', and what displeases you about someone else is often the seeds of something you see in yourself or want for yourself. As a consequence, I find myself smiling and laughing whenever someone attempts to insult me. Being called arrogant simply means I'm doing something right. I recently said to a friend, "I can't wait for the next time I'm called an arrogant c\*\*t because it means I'm back." Bring it on.

# Tip #23: Criticism? It's just a mirror

# CHAPTER 24
## Right or wrong?
## Good or bad?

*Civilisation is in the gap.*

Teresa was the harbinger of 'Interesting times'. Publishing the A-Z had been, on one level, an attempt to woo her back. It worked, but a good friend quietly told me, "Be careful what you wish for!" Looking at it now I can clearly see that duality, the black and white, the good and bad, the right and wrong. I cannot remember who told me the story, or when, but it must have been around this time. It has always stuck with me. It bubbles up when people start complaining or moaning about things that have happened and immediately label it as bad, wrong, or unfortunate.

> *There's this Chinese family. They have a young boy who is a bit of a handful and a terrible risk-taker. One day, on one of his escapades, he falls out of a tree and breaks his leg. The neighbours all congregate and start saying how unfortunate it is. The Chinese father simply responds, "Who knows? Good or bad, right or wrong, fortunate or unfortunate, it is what it is."*

> *The next day, the local warlord turns up with his troops to conscript the young men from the village.*

*They can't take the young man because he has a broken leg. The neighbours now say how fortunate the family is. The Chinese father simply responds, "Who knows? Good or bad, right or wrong, fortunate or unfortunate, it is what it is."*

As humans, we have a deep need to make sense of things and ascribe meaning to events, especially when they seem to be beyond our control. There's a compulsion to label things as good or bad, right or wrong, fortunate or unfortunate. When the lion kills the antelope on the savannah, there's immense pity for the antelope. In reality, it's good for the lion.

Right or wrong? It's just two sides of the same coin, just information that helps.

And this is where Teresa helped. She introduced me to three things. The first was Psychosynthesis and the writings of Roberto Assagioli and Piero Ferrucci. Through them, I learnt that 'Will' is the gatekeeper to personal change. If I exercise my will and choose to make different choices, then my world and the world around me changes. But nothing changes unless I exercise my will. As a consequence of this, I developed my first ever model called 'Mind-The-Gap'.

As humans, we have the ability to control our actions and behaviours consciously. Our cognition is both a blessing and a curse. It is a blessing that civilisation has thrived—a curse in that our primaeval drives and desires are sometimes thwarted. There had been a court case I'd read about where the Judge had asked the teenage defendant why he had stabbed someone.

# The Act of Will
## Mind the Gap

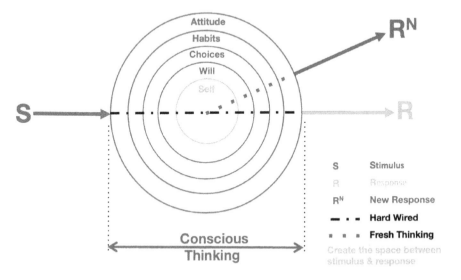

The teenager had replied, "Because he looked at me funny." It struck me that, in this very instance, we have the story of humanity neatly wrapped up. In this primaeval instinctive response, there is literally no gap between the initiating stimulus and the consequential response. The stimulus and response are hard-wired. Is that good or bad? If the reaction is one of survival in the face of imminent danger, we want a hard-wired response. Civilisation is differentiating and, evaluating and assessing the kind of response necessary. The old adage of counting to ten before responding simply introduces that civilising gap between an initiating stimulus and response. If someone is happy with a habitual response, keep the pathway going. If the habitual response is debilitating, unhelpful, or hindering, then a new pathway is required, and that is when the hard work begins.

To lay down new habits you have to activate your very own will. You then consciously choose a different outcome and act upon it. Consistently acting differently creates a new habit. New habits create new attitudes, which presents a new you to the world. Going the other way, when a stimulus hits your attitude, you now have to decide whether to accept or reject it. You can immediately see with this model why most people find change so hard. There's a lot going on.

To help, though, Assagioli talks about training your will on a daily basis by doing small daily things differently. At this time, I consciously choose to change three things. I started tying my tie the opposite way (one was expected to wear one). Instead of right over left, I turned it around and started left over right. I started finishing my morning shower by turning off the hot water and standing with the cold water washing over me for two minutes. Lastly, I started writing everything with my left hand. These conscious acts of will laid down new neural pathways and developed new habits. They reinforce on a daily basis that we can be conscious agents of change if we exercise our individual will. I am ambidextrous to this day. To my mind, a lack of will and the proliferation of excuses is society's single biggest issue. When it comes to will, I'll leave the last word to John Dewey, the American philosopher and educator: "The people I respect most in the world are the ones who say they will do something ... and do it."

The second? Teresa was taking some classes at City Lit in Holborn, central London. It is an outstanding adult education college with a wide range of part-time courses covering the humanities, science, language, arts, and life skills. Its claim to fame is that it never closed its doors during the war, even at the height of the Blitz, when they would wheel a piano underground for recitals. Teresa returned one evening raving about a lecture she'd just had from a young academic anthropologist, Robin Dunbar. She explained that there's a ratio between group sizes in primates due to brain size and language. Primates like chimpanzees will have groups that will grow to around fifty in size; above that, they will split into two groups.

What happens with chimpanzees is they form social bonds by mutually grooming each other. You scratch my back, and I'll scratch yours. Up until fifty or so, it's easy to track who's building social equity with whom. Above fifty, you begin to get freeloaders in the system, those who just take and don't give. At precisely this point, the freeloaders are exposed with the group splintering. With humans, according to Dunbar, we do our social grooming with conversations and gossip. Because we can converse, we can captivate and hold the attention of three people at once in a small group. Watch the dynamics play out next time you are at a cocktail party or small gathering. You'll be in a group holding court with three people hanging off every word. One other person will join the group, and before you know it, the group will split into three and two.

Dunbar posited that the magic number of people you will have in your circle of social relationships, the most you can maintain, will be 150, three times that of chimpanzees. Everybody I coach finds out that when it comes to building relationships, they will have a list of around 150 people that they are actively engaged with. Fascinating.

Lastly, Teresa was in correspondence with Peter Senge. According to Harvard Business School, he had written one of the seminal management books of the 20th century, 'The Fifth Discipline'. The book's core idea is that organisations need to be 'Learning Organisations', not obsessed with an endless search for a heroic leader who can inspire people to change. Businesses are dynamic systems in a state of continuous adaptation and improvement and, therefore, need people who can flex and shift with them. Senge saw that the prevailing cultural habits and systems hinder most efforts to change. To change, there must be a compelling case, time, skilled help, and constant vigilance so that new emerging problems don't derail the process. Having people who are open to learning and wish to expand their creative capacity is critical. For someone who was intimately involved in helping people be the best they could be, who was following the dance of, 'It wasn't that I couldn't. I'd never been shown how to', this was an academic acknowledgement that I was following the right path.

That path was also affirmed when I picked up a letter at my PO Box. "You must carry on your work, Neil. There is no doubt your book is food for thought for the hungry— fulfilling a great need." A letter out of the blue like that fills the sails for sure.

> *"A child becomes an adult when they realise that they have a right not only to be right but also to be wrong."*
> *Thomas Szasz*

# Tip #24: Mind the gap

# CHAPTER 25
# *Ringing the bell*
## *Factor X*

Wat doesn't fill the sails is a topsy-turvy relationship. One of my clients had recently said to me, "What I respect most in my personal relationships is emotional stability." I thought to myself, 'That would be nice!' That 'Interesting' weather front was circling.

Becoming a Dale Carnegie course instructor is quite a formidable process, and rightly so. You do the fourteen-week course. You then volunteer to help on three more as a graduate-assistant (like Cynthia, who told us the cow-story). You then do two years of pre-instructor training with someone like Mike Smith, the instructor of instructors and submit your application. The next stage is you will participate in a pilot class of volunteer candidates over a long weekend, where the instructor's examiner assesses your ability to take a class through the process. Both Nic and I had reached this stage. If we pass this part, we will then need to ride shotgun on two to three classes with a qualified instructor before going solo. If you remember, Nic was the chap who said on his first night, "Get me up there." I'd put together the pilot class for this examination, which was being held at the Croydon Park Hotel near East Croydon railway station.

We would be instructed during the day, and the class would come in at six-thirty in the evening for us to show our capabilities. On the first morning, I overheard the head examiner Alan saying as he looked through my application, "Who the fuck does he think he is?" I smiled and thought, 'Don't ask the question if you don't like the answer'. One of the questions had been, 'What are your strengths?'

With the class slowly filtering in for the evening session, your responsibilities are to create the exact same atmosphere that paying clients would experience, with the six examinees rotating through set pieces of setting the scene, giving examples, coaching, facilitating, creating crown comments for each delegate at the end of their presentations, taking the votes, presenting prizes, and ensuring all the timings are strictly adhered to. For the timing, you would sit at a back table with a stopwatch and give people verbal time checks, such as 'twenty seconds' to go. At precisely two minutes, you'd ring a bell, and that would be the timed guillotine. I'm not sure how it happened. I'm at the back table with Nic's wife, Linda, who is also a great friend. Nic is in full flow, and I ring the bell. There's absolute silence, with Nic just staring at us, mouth wide open in astonishment, and Linda says to me, "If I'd known it was that easy, I'd have done it years ago," at which point we dissolve into hysterical laughter which we can't stop. We have to leave the room with tears streaming down our cheeks. Fortunately, the head examiner did have a sense of humour, and both Nic and I passed. I gave Linda a bell as a memento.

'It's as easy to sell big as it is to sell small'. I don't know if I've just made that up or heard it somewhere, but there is a truth in it. When you sell something daily, the time taken to sell an individual contract could well have been the same amount of time spent on a contract for one hundred people. The manna from heaven for salespeople is the volume play, either in ongoing repeat business or more significant contracts. My first big contract came from the man who nicknamed me 'Neil with the shiny shoes'. It was an in-house sales training programme for all the area sales managers of a very large security company. When I looked back at my call records, I noticed a curious thing: the return on investment of my time was an order of magnitude better than any of my other sales calls. That is, it was ten times more profitable. I then made another discovery, and I have to admit it is one that still bugs me: the salesperson's dilemma, providing they have been adequately trained, is down to one thing alone: getting in front of the right people. And that comes back to the dark arts of marketing, PR, and advertising.

The training industry in the UK received a bit of a boost in the 90s. The government set up nineteen Training and Enterprise Councils (TECs) to administer publicly funded training programmes. The one covering South London was called SOLOTEC, and it had very nice offices in Bromley. Personally, I tended to avoid any connection to public sector bodies because you would become bogged down in bureaucratic red tape, qualifications, assessments, and processes. They also seemed to be run by people of a certain ilk with an air of detachment and disdain for private sector people who were creating wealth rather than consuming it. They were handing out funds to companies that qualified so you could tell potential clients that the TEC would pay half the course fees, making selling things a tad easier. The best thing about SOLOTEC was Lorna and Susan, two incredibly creative, sassy, and competent women who didn't fit the stereotype painted above. They were a joy to work with, and I know they felt the same about me because they told me one day. I was in Susan's office with Lorna. They had an inspection coming up and were discussing how they could justify the quality of the work we'd done to the inspector. Lorna suddenly said, "The problem with Neil is he's like factor X; you can't describe what he is, but you know he's great. Let's just put him in the cupboard there, and when the question is asked, we open it up, and he steps out like the man from the Woolwich Ad." I immediately blushed but realised what a massive compliment I'd been paid. It went in my Victory book that very day.

One of the last things I did working for Carnegie was coach a senior director in The Crown Agents. The Crown Agents were historically the procurement department for the British Empire. I remember being in their archives in their headquarters in Sutton. There on two shelves were the yearbooks going back to 1833. You could visibly see the rise and fall of the British Empire, illustrated by the thickness of the book's spine. The Crown Agents wanted to reposition themselves as an independent, international development company and not be a statutory body reporting to the Minister for Overseas Development. I helped the director craft his presentation to the Ministry. His presentation received a positive tick, and it was one giant step towards that independence.

I made a reference earlier to my call records. When I first started in sales many years ago, my first sales manager said to me, "Neil, the secret to sales is the following."

## The Secret to Sales

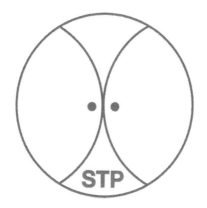

I looked at him as if he was mad and spluttered, "What?" "Yep," he said, "That's the secret to sales. See three people a day. Eyeball to eyeball, Belly to Belly, and you'll succeed!" Years later, I just translated it into 'See-The-People'.

When it comes down to it, sales, outside of technique and processes, is all about activity. If your diary has no appointments in it to see clients, you are effectively redundant. I kept a record of my calls for the five years I worked for Carnegie in the UK. I made nearly 18,000 phone calls, and every one of them took me closer to making something happen. Lao Tzu says every journey begins with the first step. In sales, every success starts with that first phone call.

| | Total | Per week |
|---|---|---|
| Phone Calls | 17,834 | 68.6 |
| Contacts | 5,801 | 22.3 |
| Appointments Set | 2,107 | 8.1 |
| Face-to-Face Meetings | 2,084 | 8.0 |
| Contracts | 423 | 1.63 |
| Value | £494,470 | £1,901.81 |

Every single phone call was worth £27.73

# Tip #25: It is as easy to sell big as to sell small

## Part Four - Mastery

# CHAPTER 26
# Beware the 'Pubic' speaker
## The Full Formula

In August of 1996, I set up on my own. I called my venture Quest Education and Development. It was a play on QED, which in my Euclid's Geometry was always put at the end of a proven theorem and meant 'quod erat demonstrandum' (which was to be proved), but every schoolboy translated as 'Quite Enough Done'. My quest was to find business owners where the 'It wasn't that I couldn't. I'd never been shown how' principle could help. When you've always worked for someone else, doing it on your own is quite a step. The first critical question is, 'What are you selling?' Nic had always said, "What I love about instructing Neil's classes is everyone sticks. They know what they're there for, and they're motivated to stay the course." I was good at getting people to open up, share their deepest issues, and offer them a solution they could take away and make a difference. There wasn't the language for it in the mid-nineties, but I was coaching before the term hit the collective consciousness around 2001 and became the latest bandwagon ten years later. I started wearing out my well-polished shoe leather and talking to old clients. Instead of selling them courses, I sold myself as a one-to-one trainer and consultant. I had a one-page synopsis of all the areas I could cover with my smart, newly designed letterhead. I used this summary sheet for three years before someone pointed out one terrific faux pas. In the list of options I was offering was 'Presentations' and 'Pubic-speaking'. This woman said, "Ooh. I'll have some of that," and pointed to pubic-speaking.

One of my first clients was The Crown Agents (CA). The director I'd worked with before didn't notice the spelling mistake either, so I was coaching twelve of his senior and up-and-coming managers in 'The Art of Pubic Speaking'. I ended up consulting and coaching there for eight years. I even had my own pass. I remember Bryan saying to one of his colleagues, "Have you been Tusoned yet?" When you become a verb, you know you've broken through. Praise indeed.

One of the most effective techniques you can ever learn is that of mnemonics. This is where you let an object represent a concept. If you craft it well, with twenty-one objects you can talk or present for three hours without notes. Steve, one of the chaps at CA, was flying out to Kyrgyzstan. When he got off the plane, he was informed that he had to make a presentation the following morning to the trade minister. Because we'd been working together, Steve had what I called 'His-Back-Pocket-Talk' with him. By simply writing down the mnemonic anchors on one sheet of paper, he created the presentation in fifteen minutes flat. It took away all the stress and pressure. It also landed them a juicy contract.

What of that storm that was circling a couple of chapters back? It had ebbed. Then it had flowed. It waned, and then it waxed. There had been highs and lows, peaks and valleys. And then it was gone. Just like that. As my friend Geoffrey would say, "Piff-Paff-Puff." Gone. To be honest, my ego was shattered. It took a lot of antidoting and alcohol to regain my natural equilibrium. That equilibrium took another wobble when I took a phone call from my old St. Louis friend Phil one evening, "Neil. Sandy's dead. She shot herself!" What was incomprehensible was I'd only seen her three months before. She'd come over with a friend, and I'd spent a very pleasant three days with her. She'd been down to Portchester to stay with my parents. She was back to her vivacious, vibrant best. I guess the volatility was still there, just very, very well-hidden.

What of my son? I would have James every other weekend. As he grew and became more interested in things, we'd take trips into London. When he was five, he was utterly fascinated with dinosaurs and what better place to go than The Natural History Museum in Kensington? I'd been over to Blackheath to pick him up, and we were on the tube going through central London when James suddenly said, "Dad. I'm confused. I'm white. That man there is brown (pointing); he's yellow, he's black. But you're red." The black guy opposite fell off his tube seat he was laughing so much. I was mortified and, yes, very red.

Besides working and James, I threw myself into promoting the little book I'd written. One of Teresa's friends in Bristol had designed a better cover for it, which added some cost, but the margins were still excellent. Nic ran a packaging company and I had him design some point-of-sale boxes. I again wore out more shoe leather, going to every bookshop in London where I'd offer them the point-of-sale (POS) box with ten books for £20, which matched the publishing discounts of the time. I then started selling them into gift shops, the first one being Diva on Upper Street in Angel, Islington. The beauty of POS is they are little silent salespeople providing you can get the right location. Right next to the till is the absolute best spot. Orders started coming back.

The MEP we met earlier who wanted to be re-elected wasn't, but Blaire and Brown were, and the whole Brit Pop and Cool Britannia thing started with a giant fanfare of optimism, characterised by that great cheesy grin. Blair always reminded me of the Cheshire Cat, which, of course, is in Alice in Wonderland and an apt metaphor for what was to follow. Some of that optimism must have leaked out of Whitehall and oozed its way down to Tooting. I started writing again. The impetus was a frustration I had. The fashion at the time was for companies and organisations to publish their mission statements. Every time I saw one, I wanted to gag. Every time there was always one vital component missing, the executive or management consultants always came up with statements that lacked something.

I developed a model, 'The Vision Triangle', which ensured nothing would ever be missed again.

## The Vision Triangle™

The anchor for remembering it is Rudyard Kipling's great quote:

*I have six honest serving men:*
*They've taught me all I knew.*
*Their names are: What and Why and When.*
*How and Where and Who.*

And I put the words around the triangle, as shown above. Even today, there are still consultants pushing a 'Why, What, How' framework. As my good reverend friend so aptly said, "Neil. You can have the best reasons, the best plans, the best strategies, but if it's the wrong time, the wrong direction, and the wrong people, you're fucked!" It's funny but frustrating that I've been banging on about this for twenty-five years now.

# VISION

Probably the greatest visionary statement made in the last sixty years is Kennedy saying, "We're going to put a man on the moon by the end of the decade." When you analyse this headline, you can see it is composed of two key themes: When and Where: the moon by the end of the decade. Visions are always about the journey, this is where we are going, and this is when we aim to get there. It's like being the captain on the bridge of a ship. Outside of the safety of the ship, passengers, crew, and cargo, they only have one objective: Where's this ship going, and when will it get there? By their nature, visions are headline statements, short, sharp, and direct. There's generally no room for argument: "This is the way it's going to be."

Vision is the domain of imagination and flights of fancy. It's all about instinct and intuition (Green, Gut and Go).

# PURPOSE

The moment someone utters a visionary statement, the other two axes immediately come into play, slowing the whole thing down! People start saying, "Why are we doing this? Do they have any idea of what needs to happen and who we need to get engaged in this?"

So why did Kennedy want to put a man on the moon? The geopolitical landscape of the time was all about two superpowers: America and the Soviet Union (now known as Russia). Kennedy wanted to show the world that America was better than Russia and that 'Capitalism' was better than 'Communism'. He wanted to galvanise the American people behind a grand endeavour. When you give the people a powerful purpose, they will go through hell for you. If there's no purpose, there will be no glue to stick people to the task long after the initial enthusiasm has died and faded away. I always say to people, "No, Why: No Way!"

Purpose is the domain of intent and desire. It's all about meaning and people: the Who and Why (Red and Feel).

# MISSION

The other axis that comes into play is the logical realm. "What does this space cadet want us to do now? Do they have any idea of the complexity and difficulty involved in trying to accomplish this hair-brained, not-thought-through flight of fancy?"

Once Kennedy had floated the idea, the grand vision, and got the people behind him, then the really hard work began. Plans had to be drawn up; research had to be carried out; experiments had to be conducted; money had to be found; tens of thousands of people and projects had to be coordinated; manufacturers had to be identified; astronauts had to be trained etc. etc. etc. NASA, sitting in Mission Control in Houston, coordinated the planning and strategy required, for the success of the original vision. It's the thinking that makes things happen and brings about the successful accomplishment of any grand scheme. If you get your thinking wrong, you will end up with disastrous consequences.

The mission is the domain of planning and implementation. It's all about tactics and strategy: the What and How (Blue and Think).

My paper was well received by those I was working with. I was beginning to think, though, that I may well be a lone wolf howling on my own. This is a theme to explore a little later.

## Tip #26: The full formula is: What and Why and When, How and Where and Who

# CHAPTER 27
## Quietness and Simplicity
### *Forgiveness and Freedom*

"You're the calmest person I've ever met in my life," she said. We were sitting on a coach at the start of a client away day I'd arranged for the managing director, his leadership team, and (get this) all the employees. Vince, the MD, was well ahead of the curve in creating the right culture to improve team engagement. I thanked Adrienne for her compliment. Why I was so calm and perceived that way requires some background.

Following my tussle with the turning gear all those years ago, it had left me with some physical issues. I had some residual trauma locked into my forearms that prevented me from rotating my wrists. I couldn't turn them, so my palms were flat and horizontal to the ceiling. It made taking change for a pint rather comical. Once again, Teresa had sign-posted a way forward by bringing my attention to the work of FM Alexander. The American philosopher and educator John Dewey was very impressed with his work. Fritz Perls, who created Gestalt therapy, credited Alexander as an inspiration. I sought a teacher and found Karen Wentworth in Wandsworth Common. Karen herself had trained with Walter Carrington who had been Alexander's teaching assistant. Becoming conscious of one's own body movements, posture, breathing, pain, discomfort, and stress is quite disturbing at first. It takes a few lessons of being gently guided to sit, stand, and walk before you realise how inefficiently you've been doing it. It was on the fifth lesson with Karen that the magic happened, and this massive release of twenty years of held-in muscular trauma left, and I could again turn my palms over freely. It was also very emotional, and I do remember tears (rare for me) and a series of shudders through my whole body. I continued to have lessons with Karen for two years, during which time I found out she was a Quaker.

Now, my relationship with religion could be described as combative and agnostic at best. One of my favourite books at university had been Bertrand Russell's 'Why I am not a Christian'. I remember telling Debbie that if I'd believed, I'd have been ordained. She got pretty upset at that. The thing I ended up loving about the Quakers is their quietness and simplicity. I found that out when I went along to Wandsworth Meeting House for the first time. A meeting for worship is held in silence. There's no doctrine, no priest preaching from a pulpit, no sermon, no strictures, no confession, no guilt. There's simply a belief that the divine (and you can call it whatever you want) sits within and is available to everyone, anytime, anywhere, and needs no authority figure to translate for you. You just need to sit in silence and listen for the small, still voice. It's the sitting in silence that is the discipline, and it is akin to meditation. Years later, I would describe Quakerism as a Do-It-Yourself religion. The term 'Quaker' is also a great sign of their humility. In the beginning, back in the 1650s, it was a term of derision. A Judge had said of them, "You're nothing but a bunch of Quakers shaking with indignation." They adopted the insult as a badge of recognition themselves, which diffused the insult and left the judge shaking with indignation. They knew about reframing way before modern folk.

It was this combination of learning the Alexander technique and my ability to sit in silence for an hour that brought about an inner quietness that Adrienne complimented me on.

Am I always full of calmness, serenity, and quietude? No. As you will have seen, I'm not a perfect human being. I'm flawed but always, always seeking to improve. The big lesson for me was learning how to sit in silence, and I loved it when I came across a quote from Blaise Pascal. Pascal is a much-underestimated French genius of the 17th century most famous for 'Pascal's wager', a pragmatic argument for believing in the divine with a cost benefit analysis attached. The quote that resonated with me was, 'People's problems stem from one thing alone, and that's their inability to sit in a room on their own in silence'. If I'm ever coaching a highly energised and stressed extrovert, I will constantly challenge them to start sitting in silence on their own. Start with five minutes and then gradually build up. Naturally, they will always say, "I don't have time," but the funny thing is that once they get it, they always have more time.

The away day we were on was all about customer service, and I had Nic help me do it. You've already seen that Nic likes a stage, and we put him on one. With Queen's 'We Are the Champions' playing at full volume, the curtains open to Nic sitting on his customised Harley Davidson roadster. Leaping off it, he launches into his presentation on 'Why customer service is so important'. We then had Vince and Ted, his sales director, lead discussions on how, their company, 'Standard' could be even better at delivering customer excellence, the importance of improving customer relationships, and the crux issue that happy customers keep coming back. This theme is, of course, precisely the policy that Jeff Bezos would follow so many years later with Amazon— to be 100% customer-centric.

On the bus back, Adrienne said to me, "That Nic. I think he's the noisiest person I've ever met in my life."

The tragedy was that Vince unfortunately died young. He was caught by a rip tide whilst on holiday with his family in Australia—great company to work with and very fond memories.

When I started writing again, thanks to Blair's contagious optimism, I dusted off the notes I'd made when I had had my epiphany ten years earlier. If you remember, I'd had a sudden moment of understanding and a very weird vision where I saw a young boy sitting under a lush tree with the word 'FREEDOM' emblazoned in the canopy of branches and leaves. At the time, I'd drawn a picture as a seven-year-old child would and realised that 'Freedom' was a framework with F standing for 'Face Fear', and I'd used Cynthia's story to illustrate it. Over the years, I'd scoped out three cycles going from childhood to young adulthood to maturity, each with a fourteen-to-fifteen-year time scale. The freaky thing was I was forty-two, about to start writing the third cycle and looking for a story that would illustrate 'Forgiveness' when a letter drops on the doormat. I remember looking at the letter, turning it over and thinking, 'Vaguely familiar handwriting, but I don't know anybody in France'.

I opened it with a strange feeling of wonder and worry and read:

*Dear Neil,*

*Greetings from the south of France. I hope this finds you well. I've realised that I am no longer angry with you, and I would like to make my peace with you. I've always felt a strong connection between us, and I would now like to feel that it's a healthy one. I would hope that by now you've learned a fundamental truth that feeling good, happy, and secure can only come from within. I hope I'm preaching to the converted here, but I also trust that our friendship allows me a little preaching. You are OK; it was only your behaviour that to me was bad, and you can always choose to change that ... It's odd writing this not knowing if you'll receive it or what your response will be if you do, but I feel that you are meant to read it, and so you will. I don't know if our paths will cross again in this lifetime, but I will think fondly of you and hope for your happiness.*

*Love Sonia xx*

You don't know it, but this was the third piece of the puzzle falling into place when I'd cleared the decks in St. Louis all those years ago. I now had a tangible idea of how to illustrate the chapter on forgiveness, and the third cycle fell neatly into place. Within two months, I had the first manuscript of what would be my second book which was at the time was called, 'Fred and The Freedom Tree'.

# Tip #27: Learn to sit in silence

# CHAPTER 28
## Three buses come at once
### *The house on the hill*

When you work for yourself, you need a little piece of luck every once in a while. My once in a while seemed to be about every three years when the phone would go. Someone would say, "Neil, can you help us with …." Don't get me wrong, I wasn't like the supermodels of the day where Linda Evangelista, one of the top five, famously said, "We have this expression, Christy, and I. We don't wake up for less than $10,000 a day." I got out of bed every day looking for work. Still, getting that occasional phone call was nice when people came looking for you. One of my big breaks was when Ian Fraser, the CEO of Reliance Security, called me up. Ian was the chap who had nicknamed me 'Neil with the shiny shoes', and when I went to see him, I made sure they were extra shiny. He smiled as he came round the corner into reception and said, "There's those shiney shoes!" Ian introduced me to Grant, one of his up-and-coming salespeople and asked me to coach him using my 'Art of Selling' process that he knew worked so well. Grant was an absolute delight to work with. Intelligent, curious, open, and extremely direct and forthright, which would be of personal benefit some years later. Ian was negotiating a takeover of another company, Hi-Tech, at the time, and I happened to know the owners a father and son team, Andrew and Steve Webb. Once the deal was complete, Ian asked Grant to move to the new Reliance Hi-Tech offices in Chessington, and Andrew invited me to create an in-house coaching and training programme.

'It's not what you know but who you know'. This saying, much like 'Interesting Times', has an English double edge to it and can be used to complement someone on successfully breaking into a new field or profession or used in a snide way when someone passes you by. What's often overlooked is that someone may have invested shed loads of work in the background before the big break came through. Mohammad Ali once said, "It took me nineteen years to become an overnight success." I'm currently at thirty-seven and counting. One small break I did get was finding a mainstream publishing house for the A-Z. I'd sold about 5,000 at this point with my wearing-the-shoe-leather-out approach and clients buying them for their employees. The break occurred when I was quietly having a coffee after a meeting at Wandsworth Friend's House. My friend Richard taps me on the shoulder and says, "Isabel would like to meet you." Unbeknownst to me, she had seen a box of A-Zs on top of the piano and had raved to Richard about how good it was when Richard said, "Would you like to meet the author?" Isabel was astounded. She'd picked up a copy a year before in Diva up in Angel, Islington and loved it. Isabel was writing her first book, 'New Habits' and had a contract with Hodder & Stoughton. There and then, she announced, "I'm going to be your agent and get you a book deal." True to her word, she pitched me and the A-Z to Hodders and Simon & Shuster, and a month later, I had a publishing contract.

It's an old joke, a cliché, that you wait ages for a bus, then three come along at once. It is a mathematical inevitability due to 'Queuing Theory'. My second bus was 'The Freedom Tree'. I again self-published it in my samizdat way and posted a copy to Cynthia, who had inspired me all those years ago. She sent me a framed picture with this note attached.

> *Neil,*
> *Thank you for your book, 'The Freedom Tree'. Your acknowledgements are very kind and greatly appreciated.*
> *I loved reading it, and you touched my heart in a special way.*
> *You are very talented, Neil. Keep writing to share your blessing with others.*
> *Most sincerely,*
> *Cynthia Micinski*

Another ship was on a voyage, and it was already being well received.

The third bus? I was approached by a German fellow, Peter Gerlach, who worked for The Royal Mail. He announced that he'd like to do a German version of the A-Z. I said, "That's fine Peter, but you can't just translate it; you'll need to do the same research I did but with a German dictionary. You need to find out the percentages of positive and negative words." He agreed. It would be a year before I saw him again.

One of the clients that had bought copies of the A-Z for all their employees was Thomas Sanderson, the market leader in conservatory blinds. It was started and run by an old school friend, Rob Thomas. Rob was a man who, as a boy, had vision. As you know, I grew up in a village that became a small town. To the north is a prominent hill overlooking the Solent. When we were fourteen, Rob could see, from his bedroom, a new house being built on the top of the hill. He said to himself, "I'm going to own that house one day."

Straight out of school, Rob went into business, first running his own fish and chip shop and then working in sales for a well-known double-glazing company. He quickly became their top salesman and always had to win the Fortnum and Mason Christmas hamper. When the company failed to deliver the promised company car, Rob decided to go it alone and started his own business on Drayton High Street in Portsmouth. He spent twenty years building his business until it was worth £1 million. For the next six years, he worked on building value for the company. Rob was passionate about what they did and believed firmly in incentive and reward whilst having what he called "serious fun." He fought hard to maintain that culture and believed it played a big part in Thomas Sanderson's growth over the decades. The desire for growth was in the DNA of the company.

Rob eventually sold Thomas Sanderson in 2001 for £25 million to a company looking to scale. It was two years later than planned, as he'd originally said he would retire when he was 44.

£1 million in value was building income. £24 million was creating equity and wealth.

Rob got the house on the hill.

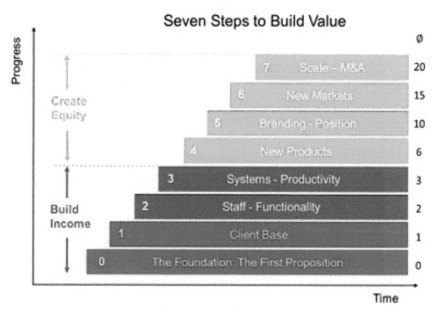

**Seven Steps to Build Value**

| | | |
|---|---|---|
| 7 Scale – M&A | 20 |
| 6 New Markets | 15 |
| 5 Branding - Position | 10 |
| 4 New Products | 6 |
| 3 Systems - Productivity | 3 |
| 2 Staff - Functionality | 2 |
| 1 Client Base | 1 |
| 0 The Foundation: The First Proposition | 0 |

Vision is really a question of how far you want to go. For Rob, £25 million was enough (he gave the staff £2.5m).

For others, they want to add another zero or two. Currently, there are only 51 organisations in the world with sales turnovers of hundreds of billions. There is not, as yet, one company that has hit a trillion in sales. Who will be the first?

# Add a Zero

## *How far do you want to go?*

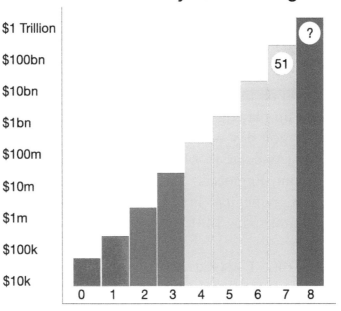

*Each Step Adds a Zero*

My vision has always been about creating a legacy. I wish to build a business that provides us with the lifestyle we want and takes us around the world. Going to university, living in the States, and running the Boston Marathon were just way stations on the journey. I have a few zeros to add yet.

## *Tip #28: Have a vision*

# CHAPTER 29
## Three Boxes
### *The Grand Old Duke of York*

If you're involved with business, you'll inevitably end up playing golf and/or watching rugby. My first ever golf day was with York in California. It was an ASHRAE (Association of Heating, Refrigeration and Air Conditioning Engineers) event. I remember it because 1. You always remember first events, and 2. I went round in exactly double par– 144!

The next time I played golf was when I was invited to the annual Bryden Johnson Golf Day at Hever. Hever is unique. Besides being right next to Hever Castle, the childhood home of Anne Boleyn, so lovingly beheaded by Henry the Eighth, it had this country's first par six-hole. This time, I completed the course in 122, knocking a mighty twenty-two shots off my handicap of seventy-two. Eventually, I took some lessons, bought my own clubs and steadily improved, relishing the birdies and pars along the way. My tip from Geoffrey Cotton was, "Don't lose any balls." On a Bryden Johnson day, I met John Gellett and his business partner Mark Zimmer, who had played rugby with the London Irish. They were about to sell their sales promotion company ZGC to a fast-growing Canadian group for a princely seven figure sum. They were both miles better at golf than me, especially Mark, but I had skills they both admired, and they would eventually seek me out.

Golf and rugby are not the top topics of conversation on a Quaker retreat. Woodbrooke, the former home of George Cadbury, is a study centre in leafy Bournville, Birmingham, offering short courses on personal spiritual growth alongside active training on peace-making. I'd enrolled on a three-week programme called 'Peace and Reconciliation'. These are marvellous skills to know about when you are a commercial coach and consultant working with corporate leadership teams. How do you bring warring factions to the table? How do you resolve the legacy of bitterness within a divided community alienated by utter hatred? How do you reconcile 'Them' and 'Us'? The Quakers were awarded the Nobel Peace Prize in 1947 for their continuous commitment and actions for peace, so they know a thing or two about all this. The context needed to start the process is always finding a point of commonality that both sides can agree upon and where each side sees the other as a human being and not othered (that is, outside, demonised, diminished, seen as less than). Once the sense of humanity is restored, the slow process of healing can begin. One of the highlights for me was learning more about non-violent resistance— the actions and challenges you can take against oppressors. Walter Wink was an American scholar who highlighted that turning the other cheek and walking the extra mile were acts of reclaiming your own power in the face of tyranny.

When the arrogant superior strikes their subordinate across the right cheek with a hefty backhand, asserting their superiority and power, turning the cheek is the subordinate's way of changing the power dynamic of reclaiming their own sense of power and control. The aloof superior can no longer slap them in the same way when the left cheek is turned. Turning the cheek is the powerless equivalent of giving them the finger. There is a similar and enlightening story for going the extra mile. I'll tell it to you if you ask me kindly. It seems counter-intuitive, and it certainly goes against the primaeval instinct of fight or flight that is still deeply ingrained in us all, but exercising the will in the face of that stimulus and using passive non-violence can bring an end to oppression. Part of me loves the idea. Part of me feels unsatisfied and wants divine retribution.

The other highlight of my time at Woodbrooke was meeting their artist-in-residence, Adam Boulter. Adam would help me bring 'The Freedom Tree' alive.

In May 1999, Hodders released 'The A-Z of Positive Thinking', and the Daily Mail made it 'Book of the Week' announcing that the book's overall effect was uplifting. I remember another editor saying, "This little book should achieve cult status." It's not happened yet, but I live in hope.

When you publish a book, you immediately look for two things:

1. Is it in your local bookshop?
2. Will you see someone reading it on the tube?

I'm pleased to say I experienced both.

Just after the release, Peter came back to me announcing, "I'm not happy, Neil. We are not as positive as you English!" Peter discovered that the English language is indeed more positive than German but also much more negative. German is emotionally flatter. English can be more expressive, both for the good and the bad, as shown in the table below.

## English is more Positive!

|  | Positive | Negative | Ratio -/+ |
|---|---|---|---|
| German | 3.6% | 7.7% | 2/1 |
| English | 5.4% | 18.7% | Over 3:1 |
| Ratio E/G | 50% more + | 240% more - | |

And why had it taken Peter so long? I'd used my schoolboy pocket English dictionary. Peter chose to use the 'Duden', a thumping great doorstop of a book. I congratulated him on his excellent work, and he set about finding a German publisher. There's a future PhD sitting there waiting for the right researcher who wishes to dig deep into the different languages and a culture's sense of optimism and positivity.

One of the ideas I started using in my work was something my son and a client I was doing a road show for taught me. I was interviewed about the concept, and the following is the dialogue:

*"The grand old Duke of York, he had ten thousand men, he marched them up to the top of the hill, and he marched them down again. And when they're up, they're up, and when they're down, they're down, and when they're only halfway up, they're neither up nor down!"*

"I had to smile as I watched and got a thousand bankers at a time to participate in the old nursery rhyme. They rose as one, they fell as one and they buzzed with energy and laughter as one. From Manchester to Birmingham to Brighton, it's the best fun I've ever had in a suit."

"But why?" she asked.

"Well, I'll tell you why shortly, but do you remember me telling you about James and how I got him to start managing his temper tantrums when he was about eleven?"

"Kind of," she replied.

*"We were getting a birthday card for his grandmother one Saturday. As we're walking to Fareham post office, he starts to go off on one in the middle of West Street. It was quite a scene, I can assure you. I let it go for a while, then took hold of his shoulders and started screaming back. He's so shocked he immediately stops and starts laughing, telling me what a crazy dad he has.*

*'Yes, I am, and I'm about to get crazier because I will teach you the biggest lesson of your life in the next five minutes. James, fundamentally there are three kinds of people in the world - Happy people - Neutral people – Unhappy people. Just see them all as being inside three different boxes. Which of the three boxes would you have been sitting in?'*

'Guess the unhappy box, Dad,' he responded with a curious expression.'

'Right. So, look around you as we walk down the street and tell me which of the boxes people sit in as we go.

'OK. That was fun,' he said as we arrived at the post office. 'What did you notice?' I asked him.

'Well, unhappy people just seem to radiate this zone of gloom around them which you don't want to get close to, and happy people just give off a wave of attraction, and I found myself drawn to them. The neutral people were just calm.'

'Good observation,' I replied. 'Now I need to draw this out for you to explain the lesson. I'll draw the boxes first from bottom left to top right, and I'll number them 3, 2, and 1 see.

# Three Boxes

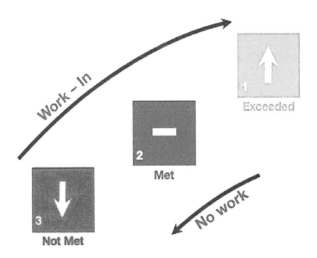

*Now, people's happiness can be likened to their energy levels. When they're happy, they're up; when they're unhappy, they're down. So, I'm going to represent that with three symbols.*

*An up arrow, a down arrow, and a neutral sign, which is just a dash. Now, do you remember the last time you saw your grandfather?'*

'Yes. He was a legend 'cos he gave me twenty pounds pocket money instead of ten.'

'How did that make you feel?'

'Very happy indeed. I suspect you will tell me that that is an up-arrow event.'

'Quick thinking, I am indeed. Now, the thing about energy is that it's always going to flow downwards over time. Hot things get cold. Rivers run downhill. Money gets spent. I'm going to put this up arrow in the top right-hand box 1. Now, do you remember how you felt the week before when your grandfather gave you your usual tenner?'

'Yeah. I just felt OK about it. I guess I'd gotten used to him always giving it to me as I left. I can see that that will be the neutral sign in box 2, and you don't have to ask me about box 3 because I can see that that's when he didn't give me anything.'

'Do you remember how you felt as we drove away?' I asked. 'I was really upset.' He replied.

'Do you remember why you were upset though?'

'Because I was meeting up with Dan, and I was expecting to get the money that evening so that we had something to go out with, and I had nothing, and it was *just so unfair, and I bet he didn't treat my cousins that way!' he started to shout.*

'OK, stop now. Here's where the lesson really comes together.

*Box 3 is all about that negative energy and emotion. Most negativity is caused by someone having an expectation that is not met or a promise not delivered, an expectation that is thwarted. The key thing to understand, though, and if you get this, you'll be light years ahead of all the other kids you know and most of the adults too, the key thing is that ninety-five per cent of all that down energy is self-generated because someone had a fantasy about their expectations, or they made an assumption about something, or they took something for granted. In other words, there was never any conversation, agreement, or clear rules and boundaries around things. Then, when it didn't happen, they got themselves upset.'*

'But dad,' he interrupted. 'If you don't get something, you're going to be upset. I don't understand.'

'No James, and neither do most of the human race. The big lesson is that you control your emotions and feelings. No one does it to you. You do it to you. It's your responsibility to control your own energy. When it does it to you, you are simply being a victim, and then you're at the effect of things, and you will live a box 3 life, which is a woeful and sorrowful thing.'

'OK, Dad, I think I get it, but what do I do to stay out of box 3?'

'Well, the sane place to live is in box 2. This is where you cause things to happen. You become the architect of your own future. This is where you have conversations with people about things. You draw up contracts and agreements. You get clear with people about how things are going to be. You share your thoughts and expectations with people. Then, if there's any disagreement, you get to make choices about what to do. Those choices may mean you negotiate a compromise, or it may mean you decide to walk away. The fact is that it's a cleaner way of conducting things, and it stabilises the energy.'

'Seems like a lot of hard work to me.'

'And that James is exactly why most people end up living a box 3 life. It requires work, and people want to go with the flow and have an easy life. The tragedy is it ends up not being an easy life. The easier life is the one in which someone takes responsibility and ends up making things happen for them. Now, I just need to check in with you to see how much of this you have understood. Here's the back of a paper bag and a pen. You teach me son.'

'Well, Dad, the way I see it, there are these three different squares. In this one is a house where the roof is blown off, all the windows are smashed, and the door is hanging off. There's also thunder, lightning, and sheets of rain. People are huddling together and look pretty miserable. In this square, the people have taken responsibility for looking after the house, and you can see them looking out the window, all warm and cosy *as the storm passes. And in square one, there's brilliant sunshine, flowers are blooming, there's a dog, and a couple looking very happy indeed having a picnic on the lawn.' 'That's brilliant, James, very good indeed. So, the next time you start like you did back in the street, I'm simply going to name the behaviour; I will call you 'Box-3-Boy' and ask you what you're going to do to change your attitude. OK?' 'Sure, pops. You certainly are one crazy guy.'"*

"Yep," she said as she smiled, "You certainly are; how many fathers have talks like that with their children? Now, I can see the correlation with the Grand Old Duke of York. Were you doing something with them about energy?"

"I was," I replied. "I was starting an exercise about getting them excited about something and wanted to show that we control our own energy levels and attitudes, but there was another reason, too."

"Do tell," she said.

"Well, the guy I was doing the tour with had bet me before the first show that I couldn't get one of the bankers up on stage to recite a nursery rhyme. I smiled as I took the bet and said to him, 'What's it worth if I get all of them to do it?'" "Brilliant," she said. "That's just so brilliant."

Golfer John sought me out first. He was now COO of the new group, and they were going for an extensive rebrand. John wanted me to help him prepare for the launch presentation using my 'Art of Presentations' paper. When I had set up on my own, I had quickly collected all my ideas on selling, public speaking, communications, assertiveness, presentations, motivation, and leadership into short papers. It enabled me to create some consistency and leave my clients with some tangible asset they could refer to. John loved my approach, but more importantly, his PA, Harriet, noticed the change and told her boyfriend about it. Little did I realise how momentous this work with John would prove to be as the millennium slowly came to a close.

I had a friend from Canada over recently (Bob from Newcastle). He wanted to go uptown and walk along the Thames. I stopped at one point by Cleopatra's Needle and said, "The morning after the millennium, I rode up here on my bike. That road there (The Embankment) all the way to Putney Bridge was a carpet of empty champagne bottles." I think the Millennium party was the biggest party I ever missed. I literally avoided it, but that's the character I am. I don't do hype. I don't do pumped-up emotion. With the clocks ticking over and the world not crashing down around our ears, what was the 21st century going to bring us?

## Tip #29: Sanity is living in box 2

# CHAPTER 30
## I invented coaching (or so I thought)
### The Internet age begins

The dot-com bubble burst, along with the dreams of many entrepreneurs and start-ups, pouring thousands of well-heeled executives into the employment market.

For some reason, they all wanted to become executive coaches. Talk about perfect timing. Jonathan Jay started The Coaching Academy in 1999, which was incorporated in February 2000, and the dot.com bubble burst in March. The Coaching Academy grew to become the largest life coaching course provider of its kind in the world, and Nic became Jonathan's top trainer. It would eventually be taken over by the lovely Bev James, of whom Joe Wicks recently had this to say, "Bev turned me from a young guy with enthusiasm and ideas into a businessman with a strategy and a clear vision for my future."

I often say I invented coaching, but the truth is I discovered something that already had a rich history of which I was unaware. Sir John Whitmore had gone to California's Esalen Institute in 1970, the birthplace of Humanistic Psychology, and met Tim Galway who had created a coaching process called 'The Inner Game'. Whitmore brought Galway's ideas back to Europe (with a license) and developed the theory into performance coaching. He co-created 'The GROW model' (Goals, Reality, Options and Obstacles, Ways forward) and was asked to apply his techniques with increasing numbers of businesses and business leaders. Hence, 'Business Coaching' began. When the time was right, culturally, in the UK, Sir John started to introduce the more transpersonal aspects of Roberto Assagioli and Carl Jung into his work (his wife Diana had founded The Psychosynthesis Trust in 1980). Thus, the softer, more people-centric, purpose-led side of coaching began to permeate the field, and the more 'Woo-woo' esoteric aspects that Sir John had first seen in California in 1970 became more acceptable to reserved Brits. The public hadn't been ready as yet for deep conversations about meaning and purpose.

"It wasn't that I couldn't. I'd never been shown how to." The fact is when people feel more confident about their abilities, they perform better. Today, life and business coaching is a multi-billion-dollar industry that has been embraced by the leaders of global corporations, including Steve Jobs and Mark Zuckerberg, movie stars and even a few presidents.

But what is coaching? The first use of the term 'coach' in connection with an instructor or trainer arose around 1830. It was Oxford University slang for a tutor who 'carried' a student through an exam. Therefore, the word 'coaching' identifies a process used to transport people from where they are to where they want to be. I always say, "It's the ability to create space for someone to see the answers that are right in front of their eyes." When people are constantly doing, ceaselessly striving, continually worrying, they can't see the wood for the trees. Allow someone to take a step back. Allow them to get to the bottom of what is really going on. Show them some possible ways to get out of the hole. Coach, instruct, teach, and train them how to use a new tool, framework, or perspective and let them run with it; voila, magic happens. All you are doing is supporting someone to achieve a specific goal with appropriate guidance. Coaches need superb communication skills and a range of tools in their toolbox to help clients shift their perspectives and discover different approaches to achieve their goals. The biggest skill they need is the ability to get their client to accept responsibility and flip their own 'Will' switch. As a coach, you know your work is done when you see them initiate that switch. Just as I learned at university, the context is you learn how to teach yourself. With coaching, the context is to show people how they can take responsibility for initiating their own changes and be independent in the complete sense of how that is defined. 'Flip-the-switch'.

The dot-com bubble may have burst, but it didn't slow down the inexorable rise of the internet. Tom Hanks was in a movie with Meg Ryan in 1998 'You've Got Mail'. I can remember the sudden need for everyone to get e-mail. My first account was set up with AOL and a dial-up modem. Appropriately enough, I had my first e-mail romance shortly afterwards. The ability to send letters, documents, and images instantly and get an immediate response was simply miraculous. Snail-mail to e-mail indeed. Add in websites, mobile phones, and text messages and a revolution in communication and how we do business rapidly unfolded.

The way we were communicating may have been undergoing a revolution. However, it didn't alter the fact that people still needed to be able to present their ideas in public forums to other people, and many were, and still are, terrified of doing it. By now, I had a proven package, 'The Art of Presentation', and I was consistently delivering it to businesspeople. Harriet, John's PA, called me up one day and told me she was passing my details on to her boyfriend. Kevin called me shortly afterwards. He explained that he needed some help with presentations, had heard from Harriet about my work with John, and asked if I could meet with him and his boss, Gary. Their firm Garban had recently merged with a company called Intercapital run by Michael Spencer, who would eventually become the Tory party treasurer and Lord Spencer of Alresford.

Kevin took to the programme like a duck to water. Gary was so impressed with the results (Kevin's position within the group and the product he was championing caught the executives' eyes) that he also asked me to work with him. Looking back on the words they used themselves to describe the process, you can clearly see a description of the coaching process described above:

> *"This has been the first time that I have taken a real step back to look at myself from the outside in. The process has been a roller-coaster ride of highs and*

*lows during an unforeseen difficult period. Through guidance and understanding, I have been able to look at things in a different light, and I have achieved clarity in many areas that I was unsure of. Going forward, I feel I have been given the cement to build the foundations of a strong base to create opportunities and solutions to reach my goals of a more flexible career. I've gained— 'Self-confidence, organisation, discipline, presentation skills at conferences, direction and vision'."*

*Kevin*

*"I was looking for self-confidence, presentation skills, motivation and influencing skills. I got that and much, much more, along with a substantial promotion. Thanks." Gary*

I've been asked many times over the years what coaching qualifications I have. I can remember one lady, a trained psychotherapist, spitting out her tea when she found out how much I charged and that I was not 'Qualified' to boot. I always say the same thing back: "I invented coaching. Why would I lower my standards?"

Perhaps I should start my own accreditation?

## Tip #30: Flip your own 'Will' switch

# CHAPTER 31
## Hunter's pace
### *Listening for the quiet visionaries*

My running partner during these years was Adam, the artist in residence from Woodbrooke. He was living on the edge of Battersea Park. We would often run past the Peace Pagoda and along the Thames. When we were training for the annual London Marathon, we'd start in Tooting, head for Wimbledon Common, cross the A3 into Richmond Park, and gradually work our way up to two loops. One halcyon day we realised that we had reached the fabled 'Hunter's Pace' where everything just fades into the background, and you can run forever. It's a lovely feeling, akin to being 'in the zone' and having a 'runner's high'.

I had often shared the outline of 'The Freedom Tree' with Adam, hoping he could create some illustrations. Having a coffee and breakfast after one of our epic runs, I broached the subject. I asked why he'd been unable to do anything and saw that the question had made him uncomfortable. He finally replied, "It's embarrassing, but I'm dyslexic and reading your book is just too difficult for me." I nodded, showing that I understood and quietly said, "Why don't I read it to you then?"

The Beautiful Run

And that's what we did. I spent an afternoon reading through all the stories and incidents that illustrated the principles of the first three cycles of growth from childhood to maturity. Within a week, Adam had come back with thirty-seven fantastic watercolours. 'The Freedom Tree' was alive with colour and on the path to publication.

Peter came back with a German publishing deal. He'd struck up a relationship with Vera Birkenbihl, a noted German management trainer who specialised in the topics of brain-friendly learning and teaching, as well as analytical and creative thinking. She had sold over two million books and loved the A-Z so much that she put her name to the German edition 'Positives Denken von A bis Z' and wrote a short preface. An international bestseller, you can't scoff at that. Sadly, Vera died, but the book continues to be sold to this day.

My biggest learning at this time was becoming aware of Robert Greenleaf and his Servant Leadership concept. Greenleaf felt a growing suspicion that the power-centred authoritarian leadership style so prominent in US institutions was not working. To an introvert, the idea of quiet leadership from within satisfied me in a way that the anathema of loud, full-of-themselves, look-at-me types never will. The people who will always be remembered are the visionaries. These key people acted as catalysts and galvanised large numbers of people into a cohesive and focused effort. Yes, some were loud, like Churchill and Kennedy, but many were quiet, like Gandhi and Mandela.

A core theme of Greenleaf is that similar historical figures are in our midst today, but we are not listening, or we are not yet ready to. This conundrum is compounded too by the fact that visionaries are often named as such after the fact and with the benefit of hindsight.

Steve Jobs said, "We designed our first computer because we couldn't afford to buy one, and then it snowballed. We didn't sit in a chair one day and think, 'My God, ten years from now, everyone is going to be using PCs.' No, it didn't happen that way; it was much more of a gradual process; we saw the potential of what was right in front of people's eyes, what had been staring at them for years."

It is afterwards, after all their persistence and hard work has borne fruit and resulted in success, that people are lauded as 'Visionary'. The fact is, they do not call themselves visionaries but come to be called visionaries.

Anita Roddick of the Body Shop was quoted as saying, "I just needed to make a living to support myself and my children; there was no grand design to build this massive international company; it just happened along the way as our vision grew." If you are a leader who desires, dreams and admires coercive power, command, and control, you'll probably throw this book across the room now.

Those still reading will recognise the wisdom of listening, learning, and looking for the prophets that are amidst us right now.

My parents had their 50th wedding anniversary. I enjoyed the three parties they threw, knowing full well that it was never going to be a party I'd be hosting myself. The first of the three was a garden party in the home I'd been born into all those years ago. It was full of neighbours, friends, and past colleagues, as they were both now retired. The second was held at the ram-shackled, slightly adrift Sallyport Hotel in Old Portsmouth, with the ghost of Buster Crabb, a real-life James Bond, haunting the corridors. This affair was somewhat more private with their very best and closest, plus me and Yvonne who I brought down from London. They weren't expecting me at the third, held up in Scotland (my mother was Scottish, after all), but I showed up anyway, much to their surprise. I had a habit of surprising my parents over the years. Some were good. Some were frowned upon. Some it's best not to speak of.

Shortly after this series of parties, I was invited to present at the Young Quakers' Yearly Gathering in Birchover, Derbyshire. Peter Tatchell, best known for his activism for gay rights, less so for human rights, had the slot before me, and one young joker said, "You've got a tough act to follow!" That wasn't a problem, and I wowed them with a two-hour workshop on 'Loving Yourself', which is as far removed from any of the corporate stuff I was doing as you can imagine. It brought about a combination of tears, cheers, and bursts of laughter. It's one of my all-time favourite workshops ever. In The Druid Inn with Adam afterwards, he suggested that I put my skills to work on a grander scale and help the Quakers themselves promote their message. Aren't seeds incredible when they take root? This one certainly did.

It doesn't matter what anyone did in 2001, does it? It'll only ever be remembered for one thing alone, and that is 9/11. Where were you when you first heard about it? Everyone has a story, don't they? I was in the gym. Fitness First – Balham, but it's really in Tooting. I was on one of the running machines watching a bank of TV screens, which suddenly all switched to this spectacle of the first plane going into the North Tower of the World Trade Centre in Manhattan. Everyone was flabbergasted, stopped what they were doing and just stared in disbelief. 'What a terrible accident' was my first thought. Then sixteen minutes later, another plane hits the South Tower, and I went, "That's the Palestinians fucked then," because, at that time, any act of terrorism like this would be laid squarely at their door. Few people had heard of Osama bin Laden and Al-Qaeda. No one could have envisaged the forthcoming twenty-plus-year war on terror. The attacks killed 2,977 people, excluding the hijackers themselves, injured thousands more and laid lower Manhattan to waste. When both towers collapsed within the next two hours, those magnificent York chillers I'd gone to see so many years before were well and truly buried.

## Tip #31: To Lead – Serve First

# CHAPTER 32
## *Burying demons*
### *£10, £100, or £1,000 per hour?*

I t was time to bury some of my own demons. Early in the new year, I flipped-that-switch and exercised my own sense of will by choosing not to drink. I quickly noticed that not drinking can threaten some people. When I was inevitably asked why, my stock answer was, "Because I was extremely good at it." I knew that I was just laying down new neural pathways and that what initially feels strange in the beginning will eventually just become a new habit. After all, I'd mapped out the model years before, so it must be true.

It is incredible how much more energy, time, and clarity one gets. I poured mine into two projects, Quaker Quest and E3, a training company. The former is still going twenty years later. The latter quietly fizzled away but became a stepping stone. Something I often use with clients is called 'The Respect Exercise'. Write down the initials (across the page) of three people you personally know and respect. Below each one, write down what it is you respect in them. Here is my own example.

# Respect Exercise

| RN | RT | NR |
|---|---|---|
| Energy | Drive | Energy |
| Chutzpah | Success | Makes Money |
| Commerciality | Vision | Risk Taker |
| Charm | Salesmanship | Talk to anyone |

Every time I do this exercise, I can guarantee that what someone sees in someone else is what they seek within themselves. You now have a window into my own soul. What am I looking for?

When I got the opportunity to work with Nic Rixon (NR above), I sensed that some of the attributes I was looking for would rub off. If you remember, Nic was the chap that, when I first met him, just wanted to be up the front instructing the class. In time, he became an excellent Dale Carnegie instructor, the top trainer for Jonathan Jay's coaching academy, and a sought-after motivational speaker while still running his own very successful packaging company in Mitcham, South London. Nic is an adventurer who is always seeking the next thing that will excite him. I'll never forget his fortieth birthday when his friends decorated the top of the cake with everything he had chased since his school days. It was hilarious with high-board diving, fast motorcycles and cars, scuba gear, Hi-Fi, palm trees, a plane, a motor home, a stage, a country mansion, fish-pond, and his wife, son, and daughter. Nic's latest quest was to create a training company, and he asked me to help. The impetus had been a phone call he made, "Neil. I've just been to see a possible client, and I screwed it up. I've told him I will send him someone who knows what they're doing. You. Can you also teach me how to sell?" I naturally said yes and, following Nic's introduction, got a great engineering client down in Kent. I started coaching Nic on 'The Art of Selling'. We set up E3 Training and had an excellent little book of clients by the summer, including one very large pharmaceutical company.

Coaching Richard, the managing director of the Kent engineering company, taught me as much as him. One day, he was struggling with time, which is often an entrepreneur's issue to which they never find a solution. The fact is we all have precisely the same amount of time, 8,760 hours a year. It's what we invest it in that is the great differentiator, and most people waste it on doing the wrong things. I had Richard do a 'Time-Log' capturing where he was spending his time and energy and finding out what he was doing on a daily and weekly basis. I then gave him three coloured highlighters: red, blue, and green. I explained that red was support-oriented tasks: estimating; finance; mail; administration; facilities etc. Blue was customer-oriented: sales; manufacturing; delivery; customer service etc. and green was strategic: planning; visionary; bigger-picture; wider-horizons. Richard then went through his list and highlighted in colour every item. I explained to Richard that each of the colours had a monetary equivalent: red work was worth £10 per hour; blue work was £100 per hour; and green work was £1,000 per hour. We stood back. He looked at his logs, and I could see a glimmer of understanding creeping into his expression.

Suddenly, he exclaimed, "So I'm wasting all my time doing £10 per hour work!" "Yep. Get your wallet out. Show me what you've got." He took his wallet out and pulled out £350 in cash. I said, "See, all this time you've been spending estimating seventeen to twenty hours per week? What would you pay an estimator?" "Twelve to fifteen pounds an hour." "Well, take that £350 and go hire one so you can spend your time doing what you should be doing to grow this company. You make two hundred grand a year, which is one hundred pounds an hour, so every hour you spend below stairs doing lower-grade work, you're doing yourself a disservice!" The penny dropped. The pound dropped when he realised what he could achieve if he started doing the work that would bring in £1,000 per hour, real high-level, high-value, equity-boosting stuff that really excited and motivated. When he left the coaching session that day, Richard had a spring in his step.

I summarised it all for him with the model below called 'The Story of Building a Business'.

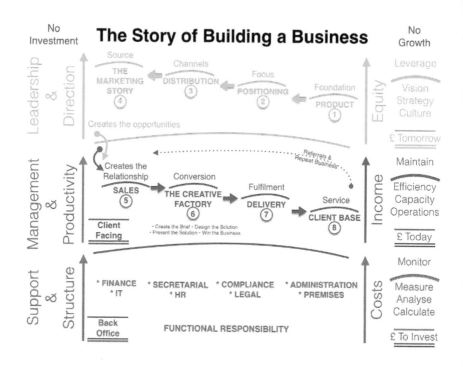

# Tip #32: Get clarity on where you invest your time

# CHAPTER 33
## The best-kept secret
### *Fighting the 'Blob'*

'You can't fight City Hall' is a great American saying that taking up the futile fight against petty or impersonal bureaucratic authority is a waste of time. The Child Support Agency (CSA) set up in 1993 certainly fit the bill of being that fortress of futility. Three years previously, I'd started to receive letters from them demanding that I pay them substantial amounts of money. The fact was Liz and I had a perfectly acceptable financial arrangement already in place, and they didn't need to be involved at all. But the 'Blob' wouldn't listen, the demands kept coming, and I kept ignoring them. Then, one day, I received a summons to appear at Wandsworth County Court. Fortunately for me, I took along a solicitor, and we were lucky to have, sitting that day, a Stipendiary Magistrate who knew something about Law. When the CSA stated that they had brought me in for non-payment of a now five-figure sum, my solicitor simply asked, "Where's your evidence that Mr. Tuson owes you this money?" The CSA chap spluttered and said, "It's in these printouts."

At this point, the Stipendiary Magistrate said, "I can see you have some printouts, but where's the evidence, the proof, that this man owes you the money?" At which point the CSA chap threw his hands up and withdrew. As far as I can see, they hadn't ever been challenged to prove that the sums they levied were actually real. We smiled as we left, but the 'Blob' wasn't done with me yet. They appealed, and the next stage was Crown Court, which rolled over, accepted their Barristers' arguments, and found against me, much to the chagrin of my solicitor. With a steely glint in her eye, she said, "We're going to appeal this in the High Court because what just happened is a travesty." True to her word, we lodged an appeal but didn't get our day in court. I received instead a letter of undertaking from the secretary of state that I would not be pursued any further. Some very clever bods in the 'Blob' had realised that our appeal had an excellent chance of winning, thus undermining the very fabric of the CSA and its process of pursuing perceived miscreants like me. It's a shame, really, because the maverick in me who loves to tilt lances at windmills wanted the fight. Quite rightly, the CSA came in for some shocking criticism, with Tony Blair himself saying it wasn't properly suited to its job and Sir Archy Kirkwood, the chairman of the Work and Pensions Committee, saying, "There is a systemic, chronic failure of management right across the totality of the agency." I was fortunate. Others who committed suicide due to the Kafkaesque machinations of 'City Hall' were not.

My other project, 'Quaker Quest' had begun the summer before. It's a play on the Carlsberg advert where I'd made a note that Quakers were probably the best-kept spiritual secret in the world today. When I returned from the Birchover gathering, I was introduced to some friends from the Hampstead meeting: Marie, Alec, Mike, Jean, and Geoffrey Durham. We joined forces, and together, we created the process of softly introducing people through a series of six informal open evenings. We held them every Monday evening at Friends House opposite Euston station, cycling through the sessions so that there was no beginning and end. The sessions focussed on equality, peace, faith, worship, the spirit, and silence. Geoffrey and I wrote the first pamphlet called 'Silence & Worship'. Others followed in due course. We got it off the ground remarkably quickly for a Quaker project, opening the doors to our first enquirers in February. It was, and is, a remarkable success, and the pattern has been replicated throughout the Quaker community here and overseas.

Geoffrey was still performing and touring. For those who don't know Geoffrey, he had been the 'Great Soprendo', an outrageous Spanish magician for many years, and he appeared on many children's TV shows, including Crackerjack. He was at the time married to Victoria Wood and appearing as a regular contributor on Countdown with Carol Vordeman. I asked him if he'd come to my 100th Movers and Shakers as a special guest. I was delighted when he accepted. Everyone was astounded when he performed his signature trick, 'The Newspaper Tear', which is #31 in The Magic Circle's '50 Greatest Magic Tricks' ever list. Geoffrey has publicly described his life with Quakers as "the single most inspiring, moving and rewarding thread running through the whole of my adult life."

Late in 2002, Nic casually commented about some Australians coming over to launch a business coaching concept. He'd been invited to meet them in January and said he'd check them out.

The best-kept secret was, by this time, on a roll and regularly attracted thirty to forty enquirers to Friend's House, Euston. I've always told people about public speaking that, "People accredit the person at the front of the room with much more intelligence than they actually have." The fact is when you are centre stage, people notice you. Now, that can have good and bad consequences, but like my Chinese story earlier, 'Good/ Bad – Who knows?' I caught the attention of Mary, who regularly helped us out and would eventually be a significant contributor. She had done some major work in Bosnia following the Balkan civil wars, specifically in helping communities to reconcile and peacefully co-exist after horrendous atrocities. We started a slow courtship with long country walks in Kent, trips to Suffolk, and a weekly backdrop of the TV show '24', starring Kiefer Sutherland, which many people were slowly becoming addicted to.

Nic checked the Australians out and immediately invited thirty people to an introduction in the West End. I have to admit I was intrigued. Nic was mesmerised. He flew to Australia to take part in one of their conferences and do a week of training on their methodology. Whilst he was out there, he asked me to put a room full of people together to pitch to upon his return. I chose the Aerodrome Hotel on the Purley Way, Croydon, which was the original London airport before Heathrow. It was an apt location because when Nic came back, we had a swift lift-off with a new company called Shirlaws. I liked their methodology because it was intuitive, simple, and instinctive. Unlike Action Coach, launched about the same time by Brad Sugars, and EOS, the Entrepreneurs Operating system, launched a few years later by Gino Wickman, it wasn't prescriptive, systematic, or process-oriented. All you needed was an open mind, the ability to create a conversation, some blank pieces of paper, and some coloured pens. Then, provided you could get yourself in front of a business owner, the magic could begin. Instinctive, in-the-moment coaching rather than 'Coaching by Numbers'. It was brilliant until the 'Silly Bollocks' began.

Nic threw himself into Shirlaws just as he threw himself off the highest diving board he could find when he was ten. He had said he wouldn't do it unless I wanted to, too, but trying to stop him would have been useless. The best thing to do was catch up and learn as much as I could as quickly as possible and use it by finding clients. The first client we signed up was Bryden Johnson, the accountancy firm I had first called on a decade previously. I couldn't make it to the first coaching session as I was off to Zagreb in Croatia to meet up with Mary. After a night in this magnificent Austro-Hungarian city, with a rich history dating back to Roman times, we took a train to Rijeka and a ferry to the lovely island of Cres. Here, looking at an Adriatic sunset, I found out that Mary was pregnant. It looked as though my immediate future would involve some decisions and decision-making. What better time than to learn how to do just that?

# Tip #33: Do you want to be noticed? Get on stage

# CHAPTER 34
## Arguments drain the energy

### '42' is the answer you're looking for

In life, the key lesson is to listen contextually. What do I mean by that? Whenever you hear someone talking, rather than listening to all the words and information, listen to find the theme, the crux issue, and the thing driving all those words out of them. The problem for most people is they habitually dig deep into all the details and thus get caught up in the story, absorbing and buying into all the juicy details. If you are a coach and you buy into the story, you're not doing your job; you need to be one step removed. That doesn't mean you're detached; it means you are serving your client by being one step ahead and allowing them to move out of their treacle. To listen for context means knowing what the prime contexts are, and in business there are only seventeen. Contexts are things that make sense of content. Let me illustrate:

The Mist and the Fog

An old proverb says, "If it's misty in the pulpit, it's going to be foggy in the pews!" How clear is your thinking and decision-making? It is certainly not a subject found in the school curriculum. This chapter will give you a decision-making tool you will use for the rest of your life. If you wish to move from confusion to clarity and be seen to be more powerful and decisive, then make sure you continue to read.

You come home from work one day and are all excited about an idea you have had for a fantastic holiday. Sat around the table after supper, you are about to share your excellent idea when your partner crisply announces, "I know where we should go for our holiday this year," and before you can even interject and say, "That's amazing. I've had a wonderful idea too." "South Africa. That's where we will go this year," and promptly leaves the room, failing to see the dismay on your face as you have been thinking and getting excited about Paris all day.

Sounds familiar? How long do you think that argument is going to go on for? Will you even manage to get your partner to sit down and listen? [Communication skills and awareness are obviously a factor here, along with assertiveness and interpersonal abilities]

I want to go to Paris; I want to go to South Africa – Impasse or Solution?

Let us look at this in more detail. There is what is called a contextual disparity going on here. Logically you have two people who have taken a position around 'Paris or South Africa'. Let us call that problem 'A or B'.

# A or B

Whenever anyone takes a position or stakes a claim, they immediately marshal all their arguments and gather all the evidence they have at their disposal for that cause.

I want to go to Paris because of 1, 2, 3 – X, Y, Z...
No. I want to go to South Africa because of A, B, C – 4, 5, 6 ...
Each time a position is stated, the argument becomes more firmly entrenched and embedded. The barriers are built. The fortifications become stronger. The barricades become higher. Taken to its logical conclusion, war, death, and famine will ensue.
What is happening is that the position and evidence are all about the detail—the Content—and what is missing is a context that can make sense of it all and show you a way out of the dilemma, the quagmire.
You will know when you are having an argument in content because the energy will be down, dark, and dismal. Context, however, provides clarity, energy, and a sense of lightness.

What is context, I hear you ask? – A quick illustration. We have a group of items. Let us say we have:

# Apples – Bananas – Pears – Oranges

What makes sense of them all? – The answer, of course, is fruit. Let us represent it this way – by providing a simple framework.

## Fruit

### Apples – Bananas – Pears – Oranges

Fruit is the contextual framework that makes sense of everything that sits below. You have stepped up one contextual level from the content to the context.

Context, then, is simply stepping up a level and making sense of all the content that sits below. The secret is to be just one step ahead of your audience. If you are too far removed, you will lose them totally and appear to be an out-of-touch space cadet. Let's say I start waxing lyrical about the need for shelter in sustaining indigenous life in the Arctic, and you are there to find out more about pork belly futures; there is not going to be an iota of understanding or comprehension between us.

Back to our fruit – let us say you had to choose between an apple, a banana, a pear, and an orange. Commercially, this could be any meeting that involved a choice between several competing ideas, pet projects, or proposals. Usually, if one were to make a choice, it would be done at a content level, and you would have a merry-go-round of an apple, a banana, a pear, or an orange. Everyone will be fighting their corner for their apple solution, or people making side trades – I'll back your pear idea this time as long as you back my orange solution next time. If, however, we set a context of, say, Vitamin C for making the decision:

# Vitamin C

## Apples – Bananas – Pears – Oranges

We would all immediately pick the orange.

If we become crystal clear at a contextual level first, the resolution and decision will also be instant and immediately evident. The secret to good, quick, clear decision-making is to work at the contextual level.

Back to our earlier couple and the impending war over a holiday. Rather than marshalling our forces for the details of where to go, let us look at why they would want to go on holiday in the first place. The reasons could be novelty, romance or adventure. If our couple were to choose romance, where would they go?

# Romance?

## Paris OR South Africa

Paris immediately becomes the answer.

## Adventure?

### Paris OR South Africa

South Africa.

Novelty? That would open up a whole new vista of opportunities:

### Novelty?

Greenland OR Madagascar OR Cape Verde OR Papua New Guinea

A context of 'Exotic' for the original fruits, what then?

## Exotic?

### Mangoes - Kiwis - Kumquats

The world of mangoes, kiwis, and kumquats is now on our culinary horizon.

What I have learnt is that the ultimate context is:

## Life – The Universe – And Everything

Anyone who has read 'The Hitchhikers Guide to the Galaxy' will know this to be true.

### Context & Content

### Life – The Universe – And Everything

### Food – Air – Water – Shelter – Heat

### Fruit – Vegetable – Grain – Fish – Meat

There is much more detail about this decision-making framework in Appendix 3.

## *Tip #34: If it's misty in the pulpit, it will be foggy in the pews*

# CHAPTER 35
## Rutting stags in the mist
### Connections and confrontation

I also realised that those contexts were precisely the same when applied to an individual, or, indeed, a personal relationship. This begs the question, "What are those seventeen contextual reference points?" Stick with me, and all will be revealed. (if you can't wait go to Appendix 5)

It became apparent when Shirlaws had their first conference in Sunningdale that Nic had introduced 75% of the coaches in the room. Most of those had come through his connections from The Coaching Academy. I'd met one of them, Steve Jones, a couple of years before when he came to one of our strategic presentation workshops in Windsor. We would always do a cheque raffle where we would let one of the participants pull a cheque out of the hat, and the person who wrote that cheque would get their money back. Steve pulled his own cheque out. Steve had been one of the driving forces in helping Fitness First grow from one gym in Bournemouth in 1993 to 360 internationally. He'd left with a nice little earner when the founder sold it to a private equity house for £404 million in 2003. Steve and I became fast friends.

Sadly, Mary and I were not. Following one spectacular, fiery, screaming match by the boathouses down on the Thames at Richmond, just along from Gaucho, we only saw each other one more time when Joe, our son, was a month old.

I was in Richmond for another conference. The next morning, I went for an early run in Richmond Park and came across one of the most spectacular sights I have ever seen. These two enormous stags were roaring and charging at each other in the early morning mist, locking antlers, butting heads, and pawing the ground like bulls. Their 'Rut' was producing clouds of steam evaporating from their exertions to prove who the Alpha with rights to the herd that year was.

These conferences were a bit of a 'Rut' themselves. There were three each year, designed to be educational, cultural, and motivational, but sometimes they became a bit of a mind-fuck. But not for me, Steve, and a chap called Jon. Edinburgh was the venue. You can tell, can't you, when a plenary session is not going to plan? I was certainly bored. The main man was losing it and suddenly said, "Do you want to be here?" I piped up, "No. I'd rather be running." To which he replied, "Off you go then. Does anyone else want to join him?" Steve and Jon did, and we went for an enjoyable run up around Arthur's Seat with fine panoramic views of Edinburgh, the Castle, Holyrood, Leith and the Forth. Jon was a very classy runner and came very close to breaking the world record for ten miles at his peak. From then on, our cards were marked as 'Trouble-makers', but frankly, we didn't care. We weren't bothered.

Edinburgh was a doozy for memorable events. With my friend Janet approaching me from across the room, let me tell it as it happened:

She said as he stormed off, "He didn't look too thrilled. What on earth did you say to him?"

I shrugged, smiled, and replied, "He came up to me and said, 'You're an enigma. I don't get you. I feel I know nothing about you'. And I simply said, 'Have you ever asked me a f'ing question?'"

"Ah. I see—your usual blunt and direct style. You do seem to have a way with people, don't you, Neil? Not a lot of feel there?"

"Nope. If you remember Janet, I'm the exact polar opposite of you. You're warm, flowing, and ebullient. Where I lead with intuition and instinct, you lag, and where you lead with feeling and empathy, I lag. This is why we work so well together. We perfectly complement each other. Sure, we drive each other crazy at times, but when we respect what each brings to the party, we perfectly compensate each other and come up with all the answers."

"What about Ian though? Where does he fit in?"

"I suspect he falls in between us and leads with his intellect and thinking. Clearly, he doesn't like direct and blunt responses, so a tad sensitive ..."

"Well, Neil, as a friend once told me, when you meet someone and you immediately take a dislike to them, you need to tell yourself, 'I think I need to get to know them better'. And just telling them to, 'Ask me a f'ing question' is not going to win you any friends, is it?"

"Well. It's not like I disliked him, but I get your point. Hey, look, let's find a way to bring Ian into a conversation later..."

I had begun to develop a communications framework that would eventually evolve into Perfect Teams. An important factor was the differences people have in their preferred style, and that can clearly be seen in the above conversation. I'm definitely gut and instinct; Janet is heart and feeling; Ian is head and thinking. There will be much more on this later in the story.

Returning from Edinburgh, I had a decision to make on where I was investing my own time and energy. For many years, I had invested much of it in the Quakers. Contextually, this would be the softer side of things. The truth is when you focus on soft outcomes; issues will eventually show up in the harder side of life and vice versa. For me, it was time to step back into the harder and more demanding commercial world and see where that would take me.

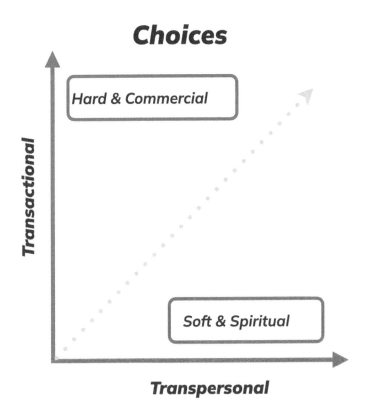

## Choices

The immediate result was earning a financial return, and I took James 'gliding'. If you haven't ever done it, do so. It's a magnificent experience with the acceleration, the soaring upwards, the exhilaration, the quietness, the effortless ease of following the thermals and over all too soon.

*Tip #35: Dislike them? Probably need to know them better*

# CHAPTER 36
## The 'Moose' in the room
### The Wonders of Yosemite

The conferences came and went. Bovey Castle in Devon was memorable for Steve falling flat on his face in a bog whilst the terrible trio were out running yet again.

It had taken a few years, but finally, Mark Zimmer sought me out. Steve and I were skiing in the French Alps when I took his call, and we agreed to meet when I returned. With all of his commercial experience, Mark wanted to learn how to be a coach. John had told him to hook up with me. It was a perfect partnership whilst it lasted. His initiation was at a conference in Cambridge, which was different this time because the Australians were absent for the first day. It was time for the English stags to 'Rut', and they failed abysmally. The request from the front for me to go running was easily ignored. The carnage unfolding before my eyes was much too esmerizing and just got better. Mark picked up that there was, in his terms, having worked for a Canadian group, 'A huge Moose in the room that everyone was tiptoeing around'. By the end of the day, everyone was ready for the evening activity, tenpin bowling.

As we're all trooping out for the transport to the venue, 'Tenpin', Jonesy shouts out so all can hear, "You wait all day for a decent coach, and one turns up in the evening!"

Behind us, thunder and lightning were boiling away among the wannabe stags. The following day, the Australian Alphas returned to save the conference and another set of games commenced. The aftermath was a major exodus of coaches, including my mate, Steve. Despite all these shenanigans, Mark stayed, and together, we created a major book of clients. I always say the same thing when people ask me what I gained from my association with Shirlaws. "I was considered an excellent coach beforehand. What I gained by learning to look at things contextually made my coaching an order of magnitude better." My life was stepping up, too. It appeared that four years of sobriety was paying dividends. I moved to a smarter, brighter, and roomier flat. I purchased a motorcycle, a large BMW 1100 tourer. James passed his exams and obtained a place at Portsmouth Grammar School. I banked the biggest cheque of my life To date. I also sketched out the complete framework for 'Perfect Teams' but put a lid on it for now. I ran my last London Marathon and raised around three thousand pounds for a friend's charity, 'Africat'.

Another thing I had to put a lid on was the affair that had started at a Wild West party with a bucking bronco, bumper cars, and a beauty. I'd never had 'an affair' before, so this was a new experience. Don't worry; the lid will be lifted in due course.

Nic put a lid on his past life for sure. He sold his packaging company, the equipment, and the land it was all on for a pretty penny. The 'Box Factory' was no more. He decided to build his dream house ten miles north of Madrid, but he also wanted to build a Spanish coaching business, which would prove challenging, even with his abundance of energy and drive.

My partnership with Mark was undoubtedly proving to be fruitful. With his contacts and my knowledge, we were practically at full capacity. I took a trip to San Francisco to attend a leadership conference. Mark Twain may have said, "The coldest winter I ever spent was a summer in San Francisco," but I thought it was glorious. What I also loved about it was that everyone walked, and because of that, the average size of San Franciscans must be ten sizes smaller than the general American population. My friend Charlie had, by this time, moved from Palm Springs. He was now living in Nevada City, an historic gold mining town founded during the gold rush of 1849. It is northeast of Sacramento and on the way to Reno, Nevada. I went to visit and felt I was in my very own cowboy movie with the Sierra Nevada mountains, Yuba City, Carson City, Lake Tahoe and the Donner Pass all close by. The Donner Pass is infamous for an incident that happened when a group of American pioneers migrating to California in a wagon train from the Midwest were delayed by a plethora of mishaps. They had to spend the winter of 1846-1847 snowbound in the Sierra Nevada Mountain range and resorted to cannibalism to survive.

Charlie took some time out from running his hospital, and we took a trip down to Yosemite. If you have never been to Yosemite, put it on your 'bucket list' it is spectacular. It is famed for its giant, ancient sequoia, the granite cliffs of 'El Capitan', the climbing communities' idea of heaven, rising 3,000 feet straight from the valley floor, and 'Half Dome'. The American photographer Ansel Adams immortalised its beauty with a renowned series of black-and-white landscapes in 1927. It is a wilderness in the truest sense. The second day there, Charlie and I decided to climb to the top of 'Half Dome'. What a blast. Seventeen miles and nine hours later, we get back to the campsite, drenched in sweat, and he says, "Let's go for a steak." We walk into this fancy-pants restaurant and get a table, and he says, "Do you fancy a glass of wine?" Did I ever? After seventeen hundred and thirteen days, I succumbed to a glass of Californian Pinot Noir. It was like the nectar of the Gods after we'd climbed the Half Dome stairway to heaven. There is actually a stairway at the top!

Late in September, I had a quick catch-up with Mark planned. He informed me that he'd accepted an offer from the British Olympics Association to be their sponsorship director for the 2008 Olympics in Beijing. Sadly, it ticked some corporate boxes that working with me would never bring. It proved to be a tremendous boost to Mark's subsequent success.

My success was getting 'The Freedom Tree' published on October 27th, 2006. It really is a beautiful book brought alive by Adam's vibrant watercolours. The fables, stories, and metaphors on life go through the first three cycles of life from childhood to young adulthood to maturity. Each cycle is about fourteen years, and when it was published, I was coming to the end of the next cycle, 'Mastery'. As I write this, I'm coming to the end of the fifth cycle 'Teacher'. It's no accident, then, that I'm now writing a book called 'Listening, Laughing and Learning – Wisdom Creeps Up on You'. My intention is that all these experiences and tips will teach you to look at something differently and allow you to create a shift for yourself and those close to you.

Those shifts will make more sense when you read the next chapter. Something had been bubbling away on the edges of my consciousness, just out of reach. I'd catch a glimpse of it, and then it'd be gone. It's very frustrating, and I'm sure you've had this feeling too. It took a Christmas party on Poland Street, Soho, thrown by Dan Bowyer, for it to reveal itself fully. Dan is now a very successful venture capitalist and was once in an early 90s boy band called Worlds Apart. At the time, he ran an IT support firm, 'The Engine Room'. He introduced me to Roman, who asked me what I did, and I replied, "The best way to describe what I do is to take these three forks."

I will get out of the way now and let the forks tell the story.

# Tip #36: Life comes in fourteen year cycles

# CHAPTER 37
## Take three forks
### *The pivotal factor?*

I walked up to the bar on Poland Street, Soho. It was two weeks before Christmas, ten years ago. I'm not one for networking and big social events, but Dan, my client, insisted I come along. He's very keen on these things, and there he was centre stage, being the exemplary host, which he would one day pivot into becoming a successful venture capitalist. It's the usual pre-Xmas vibe, with lots of excited, animated, loud people on the way to getting drunk and feeling the freedom the holiday season is bringing them. After several conversations of varying levels of interest, I find myself sitting quietly at a table towards the back of the bar with another introvert.

"Hi. I'm Neil."

"I'm Roman. What brings you here?"

"Well. I know Dan. We've done some work together, and you know Dan; he loves getting people together. How about you?"

"Yeah. I've done a few bits and pieces for Dan." "Like what?" I asked.

"I have a small tech start-up but have big plans for it. What did you do for Dan?"

"Let me see. The best way to describe what I do is to take these three forks.

They represent people and businesses in three different ways. This one on the left is 'Dependent'. The middle one is 'Independent'.

And this last one to the right is 'Interdependent'. Now I know the five things that people and businesses must do to move from a place of dependence to interdependence where things flourish, and people have a sense of accomplishment."
"That sounds very interesting. I'm intrigued. Can we meet up and talk about this some more?"
"Sure, Roman. Do you have a card? I'll give you a call tomorrow."

The following week, I walked up this tree-lined avenue in Finsbury Park, North London. Roman answered the door and ushered me into his kitchen. In true start-up mode, he was working from his kitchen table.

"I have to admit I've not been able to get those three forks out of my mind!"

"What do you remember about them," I asked.

"That they represent three different states. Dependence, independence, and interdependence, and that people need to do five things to shift from one to the other. I've been racking my brain as to what the five things are. I'm guessing vision is one; being good at something will help, and probably knowing people."

"That never hurts, does it? People and the ability to build relationships is one of the crucial factors. But you're missing the core crux issue, Roman. What do you think is the pivotal factor for someone to move from a state of dependence to one of independence where they create something bigger than themselves?"

"Feels like it's responsibility?"

"Bingo. You've got it. You see, two groups of people inhabit this dependent space. Some recognise that they need to take responsibility for themselves to advance, move on and up in the world. Some have not woken up yet or have abdicated their responsibility completely and are, therefore, doomed to stay in a dependent state for the rest of their lives. Those that make the choice to move forward, then seek out the ways and means of developing the other four factors."

"OK. I've got that. I've vision, relationships, and being good at something. What am I missing?"

"You're close, Roman. What do you mean by being good at something?"

"Well. I've earned my spurs, so to speak. I've been to Cambridge. I've worked in research. I've studied computer science. I've pulled them apart. I've built them. I've coded. I've developed bespoke software and solved the most intractable problems for people, and now I want to build a company that can do that for other people and businesses."

"What you've described there is that you've claimed a position for yourself. You've stood up and told the world this is what I can do. You haven't finessed or built a brand around it yet, but you've started the process. The missing piece for you is purpose. Why are you doing this? Why do you want to build a business? What does it all mean? Why do you get out of bed in the morning and continue developing yourself? Why do you invest in the future?"

"I see. That makes complete sense. And without these five factors in play, I guess people keep falling back down the rabbit hole to dependency?"

"Yep. That about sums it up. If you can't tick all five off, there's what I call 'Suck-Back'. This irresistible force that just keeps pulling you back until you completely sever it."

"Umm. I don't want that. How can you help me?"

"Good question. The way I usually work with businesses is to come in as a paid consultant. I'd spend a day with you, ask you a ton of questions, and get a complete brief from you. Based on that day of fact-finding, I'd put together a comprehensive discussion document that prioritises the three key things you'd need to concentrate on to flip you forward into that independent state. I must be honest with you, though, Roman; much as I'd love to work with you, you can't afford me!"

He looked at me and was silent for twenty seconds. "Let me be the judge of that. When can we start?"

**An Aside:**

*Roman invested twenty per cent of his annual turnover in the process. In the last ten years, the business has added two zeros.*

*It's gone from tens of thousands to hundreds of thousands to millions in turnover. It has grown from that kitchen table to an office for three, then fifteen, twenty-five, and now forty- seven. The plan is to add yet another zero. It has genuinely moved both himself and his business from a place of dependency to a powerhouse of interdependence.*

# Tip #37: You have to take responsibility

# CHAPTER 38
## The 'Nail'

### Are you crucifying yourself?

Hopefully, you're not saying, "Thank fork for that!" The truth is that the forks enabled the concept of three spaces to come alive, which has been such a breakthrough framework for me and my clients.

In November, I had my commercial breakthrough. Gary, who I had coached six years previously, called, saying he'd like to catch up. Garban-Intercapital was now ICAP plc, the world's largest inter-dealer broker. They had fine offices overlooking the Broadgate Circle near Liverpool Street. Gary was now the deputy CEO, and he credited his success to the coaching I'd given him. He now wanted my help with some key individuals in his team. I began with Jon, who ran the emerging markets desk and ended with Phil, who ran Euro SWOPS, and Carsten in Copenhagen. Over the next seven years, I was the principal executive coach within ICAP and worked and interacted with nearly 100 individuals in London, New York, Frankfurt, Copenhagen, and Bahrain. Their roles ranged from the main board level to the senior management team and Dep. CEO, Divisional MDs, ten desk heads, CIO, COO, Dep. CIO, HR and even the CIO's PA.

I worked with Front Office, Back Office, Credit, FX, Equity Derivatives, IT, Risk, and HR, coaching individuals (1:1), facilitating workshops, off-sites, 360-degree reviews, and being asked to do specific specialised projects. It was the gig of a lifetime, with fees approaching a cool million. Many of the people I worked with remain friends today. There were also some legendary characters whose stories and exploits can only be talked about at the back of a very dark, smoky bar far away from any PC police.

It wasn't all ICAP, though. I still had seven other clients, and I worked on my pet communication project whenever I lifted the lid. One of the tips I'd learned from Dale Carnegie all those years ago was, 'To live in day-tight compartments'. That is, live in the moment; just do what you can do right now, today. I had learnt to compartmentalise because I realised so many people didn't. One lesson I found useful just sprang into my mind one day. It was so vivid and intense that, for a while, I was pretty shocked. I could see myself being pulled apart, limb by limb. To my left, pulling my left arm straight out, stretching and straining all the ligaments and tendons, was the past with all my regrets, sorrows, and what-ifs of life. To my right, pulling my right arm so strongly that the joints were cracking and groaning, were all the promises and desires of tomorrow and the future. When I looked at myself in the mirror, what did I see? I saw someone crucifying himself, literally pulling himself apart between his past and future. As the sense of this painful image became real, it brought with it the knowledge that it was much more constructive and far less destructive to attend to living in the present moment.

Gradually, in the image, the arms released themselves and returned to a position of relaxation with the right palm over the left hand on my heart. Someone once told me that life will keep giving us wake-up calls until the day we take heed, pay attention, and wake up. At that moment, I woke up. What a f**king waste of time worry is. This image became a crucial component in my 'The Art of Dealing with Stress'.

My friend Joe was brilliant at doing stress. We were on a run one day around Wandsworth Common. He was moaning about this. He was moaning about that. Then it was them. Next, someone else. When he eventually took a breath and paused the moan tape, I started to tell him a story, still running, in a soft, slow, southern American drawl. "Hank's walking down the hot, dusty, deserted street when he sees his pal Earl sitting back in his old rocking chair on the front deck of his prairie-style house. Hank tips his hat and says, 'Hi Earl. How'll yawl doing?' 'Doing jus' dandy Hank. How'll's yarself?' At this point, the dog sitting next to Earl lets out a long howl. Hank looks at Earl, looks at the dog and says, 'All good, Earl. All good,' and the dog lets out another almighty howl. With the tumbleweed slowly blowing down the street, Hank and Earl continue their leisurely chinwag, intermittently interrupted by the dog's howls until Hank finally says, 'Earl? What's wi' yar dawg?' Earl looks at Hank, chews the end of his pipe, looks at the dawg, turns back to Hank and says, 'He'll be sittin' on a nail, Hank, sittin' on a nail.' Hank looks at the dawg and turns back to Earl, 'Why don't he move Earl?' 'Well, Hank. The nail jus' aint long enuff.'" Joe immediately stopped dead, looked at me, and said, "You cunt!" Then he smiled, and we continued running. Joe stopped moaning. By the end of the week, Joe got off the nail.

He quit the job he'd been moaning about so much and started his own business. He is now one of the most respected party-wall surveyors in South London.

The thing about stress and worry is it's never the stimulus, the event itself, that causes it; it's the continual ongoing excitation of the event after the fact. It's the mind whirling away, compounding the initiating issue until it becomes an all-consuming maelstrom of self-inflicted agony and angst. I'm an engineer, so I love it when I see something that can be applied in a totally unrelated arena. For instance, what could a bridge in Washington State possibly have to do with a worrywart in Worthing? In 1940, the Tacoma Narrows Bridge in Washington State was destroyed when the structure's natural frequency was matched by the gusts of wind blowing down the canyon. It went into resonance and collapsed. Resonance is the amplification of a frequency and ultimately leads to destruction.

Think about it this way. If I poked you in the arm once, you'd react, look at me askance and move away. What would happen if I continued to poke you in exactly the same place, at the same frequency, and you couldn't move away? The pain would gradually increase, and the anger would mount until a critical point at which you would explode. You would have metaphorically gone into resonance. I realised that this is precisely what people do to themselves. They let the negative event grow by continually exciting it. That first 'Eeeek' of the poke becomes a continuous stream of 'Eeeeks' where the negativity breeds more negativity. Focussing on the negative energy and constantly reinforcing it leads to 'resonance' and an eventual breakdown. The wisdom is realising that no one does <u>it</u> to you. You do <u>it</u> to yourself.

Don't be a victim. Remove yourself from being in a state of constant excitation.

## *Extra tips*

- Stop exciting the negative and focus on the positive.
- Even the darkest hour only has sixty minutes.
- What can you do in the next minute to change things?
- Relish the moment.
- Obsessing won't help.
- Michel de Montaigne said, "My life has been full of terrible misfortunes, most of which never occurred."
- Most of the things people worry about don't happen, but because they have focused on them so much, they become bigger and bigger and cloud judgment.

# *Tip #38: Get off the nail. Stop exciting the negatives*

# CHAPTER 39
# A trouble-maker and heretic?

## *Obama*

When 'The Freedom Tree' was properly published late in 2006, I sensed my life was coming together. I had learnt three years earlier that I must be able to create. I get incredibly frustrated if I'm denied the opportunity. When Nic and I joined the Australians, my first thoughts were, 'How will I be able to contribute?' As far as they were concerned, everything was sorted, and we just had to follow their lead. That became self-evident when I was called out at a national conference for 'tinkering' with their intellectual property. Obviously, I wasn't just a 'trouble-maker' but a 'heretic' too. Fine by me and an excellent badge to wear with pride. 2008 was a watershed year. I totally fell in love. James obtained ten GCSEs. Portsmouth won the FA Cup. I had spent my whole life hearing about the 'Glory Days' of Pompey being back-to-back Division 1 champions and holders of the FA Cup for six years running (they had won it in 1939). To see them beat Manchester United in the quarter-final, West Bromwich in the semi-final, and Cardiff in the final was deliciously delightful.

When James passed his exams to get into Portsmouth Grammar School, it had been a secret delight for me. I had missed out on a scholarship in primary school. What I missed out on saying earlier was that I took the general entrance exam the same year as the eleven plus. My parents told me I'd failed. Years later, I found out I had passed, but they couldn't afford the school fees. Ouch. Wheels within Wheels forty-five years later, James aced his exams, getting ten O-levels. Before his wheels fell off the following year (huge echoes of my inordinate desire to leave), he came up to town for some work experience. One of my Tooting friends, Gavin, ran a video production company in Soho, and James worked as a runner for him. I had a management seminar running one weekend and asked the MD if she minded if James sat in to get another layer of experience. They started treating James as one of the group members and involving him in the exercises. He was amazing. The MD's feedback was, "So much acumen, maturity, and confidence for a sixteen-year-old."

Friends introduced me to Cathy early in April, and I was utterly smitten. Lao Tzu says, "The flame that burns twice as bright burns half as long." This was ten times as bright, so it was over by September, and a gentle friendship remains to this day. Highlights are camping, Cornwall, motorcycle rides (she had a Harley), Leonard Cohen at the Albert Hall, and Neil Young in Hyde Park. The latter was a thank you because I'd introduced Carla, her daughter, to Gary at ICAP, and he'd offered her a job. Cathy also came to one of my 'Gift Days'. Based on the 'Freedom' framework with a workbook and everything, I'd first started these in the 90s with Teresa in Croydon. I can still see Lorna shouting out, "Of course. It's so f**king obvious. How could I have missed it?" as the realisation of what she needed to do hit home. I would run them at Friends House until 2010. Meanwhile, they are cocooned until the next cycle begins in 2025.

I was on a train once passing through London Bridge and onto Cannon Street. I had to laugh as this teenager said of Southwark Cathedral, "Cor. Look at that church. Why would they build it so close to the train tracks?" My running friend, the artist in residence and illustrator of our book, Adam, was being ordained there that summer. The idea of following that path had been a gentle and gradual calling over all the years we had run together. Following his ordination, he was appointed to St. Mary's in Battersea, one of the earliest church sites in England. William Blake, the stunning, mad Romantic artist and poet, was married there. His 'Ancient of Days' still stuns me today. Benedict Arnold, George Washington's trusted right-hand man until he turned his coat to the British, is buried in the Churchyard. Arnold is still abhorred as America's greatest traitor. It wasn't long before Adam got itchy feet to take him away from parish life. The last I heard, he was working for the Mission to Seamen in Toliara, Madagascar.

Nic's project in Spain was developing nicely. I flew out twice that year. The first time was for his inaugural conference in Madrid at the Westin Palace Hotel, half a mile from Puerta del Sol, the geographical centre of Spain. Following the conference, Nic couldn't wait to show me the plot of land he'd bought to build his dream house. Ciudalcampo is ten miles north of Madrid, with stunning views of Sierra de Guadarrama.

It is in these mountains that Philip II built the fabulous El Escorial royal monastery. From here, he planned the Spanish Armada invasion of Britain in 1588, which Sir Francis Drake so spectacularly thwarted. Not far from there is the infamous Valle de Cuelgamurous, Valley of the Fallen, built under the orders of the Dictator General Francisco Franco. He was buried there in 1975 but exhumed and moved elsewhere following a long, controversial legal battle between the left and right in Spain. The second time, we went up into those mountains, we stayed in a cute little boutique hotel in Robledo de Chavela, a mule ride from El Escorial. It was a coaching skills conference, and I did a good chunk of it in Spanish for the first and only time. Nic took me to see the progress on their dream house. It was emerging like a ship's superstructure from the hillside. Massive, magnificent, and quite magnetic. Still two years away from completion and hosting its first Christmas party and Linda's surprise 60th.

Did I have a sense of 'Mastery' while this phase of my life unfolded? Sometimes, I did, and sometimes, I didn't. One incident did affirm it. The three forks had developed into the 'Three Spaces' model.

Roman had explained it to Polly, and she'd asked to meet me. Polly was an exceptional woman. Unfortunately, she is no longer with us. A barrister by training, she'd given it all up to pursue her dream of getting the United Nations to agree to an international crime of 'Ecocide'. That is, any corporation that was found to be raping and pillaging Planet Earth would be prosecuted by an international commission for said crime. She explained it to me in her Islington flat. "When slavery was still commonplace in the nineteenth century, William Wilberforce

## *Three Spaces*

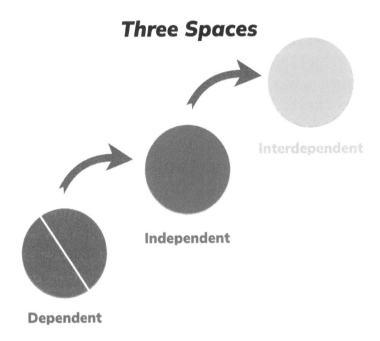

Interdependent

Independent

Dependent

and the Quakers who supported him continually came up against the same argument. 'It would be commercial suicide for the corporations that were vested in the practice to forego the use of their slaves'. At the time, only three hundred corporations were involved. People often say, "What can I do? I'm just one person." In 1746, one person decided to do something. His name was John Woolman, and he was an early abolitionist in colonial America. Woolman walked throughout the American frontier, going from one Quaker community to another, quietly advocating emancipation for slaves. In 1772, he travelled to England and convinced the Quakers here to support the abolition of slavery. John Woolman's quiet consistency and continual expression of his concern about slaveholding gradually won people over. People began to see the evils of slavery and started condemning the practice. By 1783, almost all North American Quakers had freed their slaves. When slavery in the UK was eventually abolished in 1833, the year of Wilberforce's death, and in the US in 1865, all those corporations pivoted into alternative means of furthering their economic success. Today there are only three hundred corporations raping and pillaging the earth!" Polly wanted to meet me to get my permission to use the 'Three-Spaces' model in a presentation she was making to President Obama. I, of course, said yes. Polly greatly influenced Gail Bradbrook, one of the co-founders of Extinction Rebellion. Polly, like Woolman, never doubted that one person can quietly and consistently create change.

## *Tip #39: One person can make the world change*

# CHAPTER 40
## *Eyeballs being etched by cut glass*
### *Made of rubber and magic*

My work with ICAP started to take me internationally. First to Frankfurt, then Copenhagen, and New York. Frankfurt was superb because my oldest friend Steve, of copper fame, was now living there in the really funky area of Old Sachsenhausen. Downstairs was the excellent Apfelwein Dax, and along the street Zum Eichkatzerl, where we would catch up with a flagon of Apfelwein and the most scrumptious Veal Schnitzel imaginable. Steve was by now the European marketing director for Ferrero Rocher, the Italian chocolate company famed for its 'Ambassador' adverts in the 90s. I began flying to Frankfurt for a week every month to work with Paul, Alex, Jürgen, and Olaf. On one trip, they took me to watch Eintracht Frankfurt play Borussia Dortmund, which was managed at the time by Jürgen Klopp. He was every bit as animated as the English would see when he moved to manage Liverpool in 2015.

The fascinating thing about going to that game was the infrastructure and logistics. We simply drove up and parked right under the stadium. It was sublime. At Christmas, Alex took me down to the Christmas Market centred around

Römerberg, the old town centre of Frankfurt. The Allied bombing towards the end of World War II entirely blitzed this whole area. Compared to how we rebuilt our cities, I prefer the German style. You'd never know it had happened. I've said before that many of the people I've worked with remain friends today. Alex went on to become a coach himself. Being German, he naturally chose to get qualified by taking a master's degree. Jürgen texts me occasionally when he's tucking into his schnitzel in his favourite Sachsenhausen haunt of Adolf Wagner on Schweizer Strasse, and Bayern Munich has won yet again.

In 2010, I went to New York twice. I had been asked to work with a very senior chap, let's call him Harry, by the Chief Operating Officer. Part of the process was to include a 360° review before and after. One of the most graphic comments came from the CEO of the NY office on my first visit in February. "When Harry's report lands on my desk, I feel like the insides of my eyeballs are being etched by cut glass." My remit was to help Harry communicate his cerebral insights to an audience that didn't want the New York telephone directory landing with a thump each month on their desks. Just because he saw the world through an intellectual microscope, they didn't. Over the next eight months, Harry and I worked very hard on his communication, relationship-building, and presentation skills. The aim was to change people's perceptions and enhance his personal position within the company. When I returned to New York at the end of November, the CEO had this to say, "His report is now slimmer, understandable, concise, and very readable. He gets to the point now and draws us in. A remarkable change in him and the perception amongst his peers— quite a sea change."

There had been a sea change in New York from the last time I'd been 'An Englishman in New York' and there to run the Marathon in 1989. The twin towers I'd loved going up were still just a hole in the ground. I had a lump in my throat as I walked around 'Ground Zero' before leaving for the airport.

The delight of delights Portsmouth made it to another FA Cup final by beating Tottenham, which the renegade Harry Redknapp had gone to manage. This sweet victory was alas quashed by Chelsea in the final, where my son and I watched it from the Wembley Club section with courtesy tickets from ICAP. James was by now nearly eighteen and had finally given up on school, as his father had. Unlike me, he had yet to find something to pour his energies into. I did applaud, though, when his headmaster said to him before he left, "Frankly, James, you're a rebel without a cause."

Did I have a cause? The truth is I was a little bit lost myself. All looked good on the outside, or so I convinced myself. I was attending James D's excellent wine tastings and buying cases of terrific wine. I had as much work as I needed. I dined at Chez Bruce, the successor to Marco Pierre White's Harvey's, on Bellevue Road, Wandsworth Common, and often voted top of the list of Londoner's favourite restaurants. If not there, I'd be closer to home in Numero

Uno most nights of the week, causing my bookkeeper to comment, "Your local restaurant? They must like you very much!" The shoebox they were presented with each quarter was full of blue Numero Uno receipts. The signs were all there, but I wasn't looking or listening.

I was invincible and ploughing on. Then I found out I wasn't made of rubber and magic. I needed a small growth removed from my right cheek, and they wouldn't do the operation when I went in for it because I had high blood pressure. Me? An elite Marathon runner? High blood pressure? Pfft! But facts are facts, and my doctor issued a crystal-clear warning, "Cut way back. Quit drinking completely. Your blood pressure is unsustainable, and you are in stroke territory." When I looked in the mirror and honestly acknowledged what I saw, it was indeed a puffy, blotchy, overweight, and unfit mockery of a man. What I saw was a travesty of my true self, and I didn't like it. It hadn't happened overnight. Slowly going from running seven miles a day to seven a week, from drinking three units a day to twenty, eventually takes a toll. I was forgetting and ignoring everything I'd ever learnt and more. I was creatively dead, too. Something had to change.

It's often attributed to Einstein, so that's good enough for me, "Insanity is doing the same thing repeatedly and expecting different results." The year before, I'd taken off on my motorbike around Europe. It had been more of a wine tour with me staying at one point with James D and his family in this magnificent French Chateau that he'd rented for the summer in Noailly, north of Roanne, on the right bank of the luscious Loire valley. This time, I headed for North Wales because I needed to do something different. I toured Anglesey (unfortunately, Iolo was overseas), Snowdon, Portmeirion, the Baroque folly tourist village and home to 'The Prisoner', and down the coast to Aberystwyth. I blew the cobwebs out, or they were washed away; it rained so much, I gained some perspective, and I went for long, windy, wet walks. I started writing the fourth cycle of 'The Freedom Tree' and recording the first three cycles with Wigg, a good friend of Roman, in his studio in Queen's Park.

Dinner with a client following a long series of coaching sessions got me back on track. We were in Portal, a fine Portuguese restaurant just up from Smithfield the London meat market. Over dinner, he gave me three cards. In the first, it said, "Never has meeting someone had such a profound effect on my life. Thank you." The second said, "Thank you very much for giving me a happier husband … he even smiles too." The third said, "Neil. Thank you for making our dad a happier dad!!" It was signed by both his daughters.

In my thirty-seven years of listening and learning, I've never felt as honoured and humbled as I was at that moment.

# Tip #40: Take a step backwards to get perspective

# CHAPTER 41
## *Why don't meetings work?*
### *Genius*

As Jack and Jez left the meeting, they looked at each other and raised their respective eyebrows. Jack was the first to break the silence, saying, "Well that was a right royal c\*\*k-up!" Jez smiled and replied, "Yep. They sure need Neil's help."

"They certainly do," responded Jack, "How many steps did they miss? How many cues did they fail to see that it was all going pear-shaped? And did you see Gary's face? It was a picture of thunder!"

"Well, they didn't get to the point. There was no context or purpose that I could see. They didn't check in with us, at all, on our understanding and what we wanted. It was like he just wanted to waffle on about his own magnificence. It was a complete and utter waste of our time. I can't wait to tell our coach!"

Jack, Jez, and Mark were probably three of my best candidates. They certainly took all the learnings on board, and when Jack introduced me to Mark, he said, "This is Neil. He's a genius," which is, to date, the grandest compliment I've ever been paid. Mark made meticulous notes of all our sessions. When I saw the booklet he'd produced at the end of our programme, it gave me the idea of professionally producing my own papers, which are all curated in the 'Perfect Teams Academy'. But I'm getting well ahead of myself. What I had done with all three of them was drill them on the need to run effective meetings and have a winning formula. Why?

Whatever your role in an organisation—CEO, Director, Manager, Supervisor, Salesperson, Consultant, Coach—having the ability to successfully facilitate meetings is absolutely crucial. It is the key ability to differentiate yourself as a leader and goes the furthest in creating a favourable opinion with all the people who come into that meeting room with you.

How much time have you wasted in worthless meetings? How many times have you left a meeting muttering to yourself, like Jack and Jez above, 'FFS, what a complete waste of time that was?' Knowing how to conduct a meeting with a tried and tested, winning formula behind you will make you more effective and more persuasive and improve your image, position, and reputation for being someone who 'Gets things done'. Consistently facilitating meetings and ensuring that all the correct points are ticked off will win people over, get you more business and save you hundreds of hours a year.

So, you don't have to go seeking the magic formula here it is. It has seven steps:

# 1. Agenda & Expectations:

*The first stage is to set the scene.*

*This is all about getting people's expectations out on the table. i.e., you will have your agenda/purpose but find out what others want to get from your time together.*

*The agenda-setting consists of two pieces: A global agenda and the specific agenda.*

*Global is the overarching theme or topic.*

*Specific is what do you want to accomplish TODAY.*

*Tip 1. Ask people to write down three things they specifically want to get out of the meeting. Glean these specifics by going around the group asking for one contribution at a time.*

*Tip 2. Never attempt to run a meeting if you do not have a prime purpose or overriding context and idea of what you are holding it for in the first place.*

*Tip 3. Always have in the front of your consciousness that when you are facilitating a meeting you are effectively creating a relationship between two parties – you and your audience.*

# 2. Understanding:

*The second stage is all about getting the people into the room/ meeting with you.*

*This is about aligning things and finding out what their relationship is like with you or your subject. You want to find out if this is going to be an easy meeting or a tough gig. Are they for you or against you?*

*The easiest question is to ask,*

> *"What's your understanding of ... Today's meeting, this subject, our company, me and what I do?"*

> *If everyone answers positively and encouragingly, then you know you are onto a winner.*

> *If negativity and ignorance show up, you have to reposition yourself and what you're there for really quickly.*

*Note:     An Aside...*

*The more time you spend on the first two stages, the more success you will generally have. Clear specific agendas, expectations, and understanding—clear buy-in from the beginning sets up the whole meeting.*

# 3. Questioning for Facts & Feelings:

*You now need to create a safe space to have a conversation or discussion.*

*Have a questioning framework available to delve into the issues/concerns/facts about your topic. You are in detective mode, looking for information.*

*Also, be aware of when the energy/mood/feeling changes. You're looking for the feelings that are either going to help you or hinder you from finding a resolution.*

*People buy things/make decisions for emotive reasons. You're looking for the levers that are going to help you move things forward when you get to present a possible solution based on all the information you are getting.*

*This is the classic 'Get-the-Brief' phase.*

*The more space you create, the better the connection you establish here, and the more likely you are to create the right stunning solution based on your audience's needs and desires.*

*No feeling – No motivation to do anything. They will then not buy into any concept you create.*

# 4. *The Solution & Presentation:*

*The fourth stage is to create a solution, based on stage 3, which the group feels motivated to commit to.*

*You generally want to present your solution in such a way that it is visually compelling and leaves a lasting legacy.*

*This is where creativity really comes to the fore.*

*If you are in a coaching scenario then this is where you present one of the coaching frameworks or tools that you have in your portfolio.*

*If you are in a selling situation then this is where your skill in listening for what your client really wants provides clarity. You produce the magic solution to all their problems right out of the proverbial 'Hat'.*

*If you are in a 'Leading' position, then this is where your skill in accurately summarizing the mood and sense of the group enables you to motivate them into action.*

*Whichever scenario you find yourself in, make sure you leave a graphic visual image in everyone's mind of what the solution can, will, and should look like. This is the phase that creates the 'Promised Land' as something to aim for, to strive for. This is where you leave an indelible anchor like Kennedy or Martin Luther King with their legacies of 'A Man on the Moon' and 'I Have a Dream'.*

## *Paint your picture boldly and brightly*

## 5. Silence & Engagement:

*When you present something. Stay silent.*

*Let your audience process what you have presented. You are waiting for them to come back with questions. If you have come up with a particularly creative and compelling solution your audience will be 'spellbound', and it will take what seems like an eternity to process what you have just presented. Whatever you do, do not break that spell by stepping into the silence. The silence can last anywhere up to forty minutes! Yes, forty minutes. Hold your nerve and let them completely engage with your solution and process it in their own time. Always remember that your focus is on your audience's needs not your own.*

*When they finally come, questions show that they have engaged with you. They are what's called 'Buying Signals'.*
*Questions show that your message has gone deep, and they are now looking for more information.*
*If all has gone well in the preceding steps, they are in the zone with you and your solution/conclusion.*
*Questions typically fall into three categories: Time, Cost and Resource required.*

*When you respond, do so confidently, briskly, and clearly. Your audience is looking for certainty that you can deliver the solution for them, that you can indeed take them to the 'Promised Land'.*

# 6. Reality & Summary:

*The sixth stage is to quickly recap the meeting. Go back over everything covered in a confident and assertive manner.*

*We came together today to ...*

*We agreed that what you wanted to get from today was A & B & C ...*

*We've looked at all the facts pertaining to ...*

*We've examined what may get in the way and what might stop us moving forward ...*

*We've created a solution that we agreed is appropriate. We've examined the costs, structure, and value ...*

*We've agreed that X needs to do V, and Y needs to do W.*

*What questions do you have before we continue?*

# 7. Next Steps & Looking for Commitment:

*The final stage is to create commitment and reach cast-iron agreements on who will do what, who is responsible for what, and what the next steps are.*

*This all needs to be clearly defined, minutes taken and communicated.*

*No actions – No meeting of minds occurred.*

*Have you ever been in a meeting and left thinking to yourself, 'Well that's good. They didn't really finish with a call to action, and I've got off Scot free!'*

*That's because there was not an assertive finale looking for action and people to take responsibility for doing something.*

*Whatever you do ensure that you always leave plenty of time for an effective finish. As they say in sales – 'There's no point having a million-dollar presentation with a ten-cent close!' Make sure that you have a million-dollar close and that it seals the deal on your new on-going relationship. This is the relationship that you have created through your ability to facilitate an effective and engaging meeting.*

*Whenever you are going to hold a meeting, make sure that you address the following points. If you have recently been in a meeting or are soon going to be in one – which will be in five minutes if you are living in corporate land – then use the following checklist to gauge how effective it was. We can guarantee that the good ones tick all the boxes, and the poor ones miss several of the steps.*

| | Step | √ - X |
|---|---|---|
| 1 | Agenda & Expectations | |
| 2 | Understanding | |
| 3 | Question for needs. Facts & Feelings | |
| 4 | Create a solution. Present it compellingly | |
| 5 | Create the space for engagement and questions | |
| 6 | Recap and summarise the meeting | |
| 7 | Gain commitment and develop the next steps | |
| **Total Points** | √ = 3 — = 1 X = 0 Nailed it So-So Missed it | Max = 21 |

The meeting Jack and Jez had come out of? The chap had scored about three out of twenty-one at best. What do your meetings score?

# Tip #41: Learn how to be a champion facilitator

# CHAPTER 42
## *You should turn it into a 'Philosophy'*
### *A conversation with Carl Jung*

" **I**'d pay £50,000 to know what Neil knows," and Gary had been true to his word with all the work he'd passed my way over the last twelve years. A change was afoot. It had been a long time coming. When the financial markets went into meltdown in 2008 following the collapse of Lehman Brothers, I heard someone on the dealing floor say, "My ears were bleeding. It was so frantic and tense." ICAP actually faired very well, and I went on to have my best years ever. Good friends see things that you don't, though. One of them, Peter Bell, said over dinner at the Paramount Club, "I love what you have developed, Neil. You should turn it into a philosophy."

The true turning point was March 19th, 2012. Do you remember Ian, the chap who had nicknamed me 'Neil with the shiny shoes'? He'd introduced me to Grant, one of his up-and-coming salespeople and asked me to coach him using my 'Art of Selling' process all those years ago. Grant had been an absolute delight to work with. I mentioned before that he was extremely direct, straightforward and forthright. Grant had had a stellar career. Two years after we worked together, he went to Adobe. Adobe, of course, is famous for its portable documentation software for creating content with graphics, photos, illustrations, animation, and print, and it sparked the desktop publishing revolution. Similar to many great stories, Adobe was started in John Warnock's garage, which inspired Grant and his friend Dave, who worked for The Royal Mail, when they hit on their great idea. They found a way to make PDFs interactive and took their idea to the Inland Revenue. If you want to moan about filing your taxes online, Grant and Dave are your boys. As you can imagine, their idea took off, and they were able to sell their company for a handsome return. Let's put it this way: when I saw Grant shortly afterwards, he was driving a brand-new Bentley Continental. It was at this time that the pupil became the teacher. Grant very directly said to me, "Neil. Why the fuck don't you do all this for yourself?" which, of course, was an excellent question.

And so, I did. I lifted the lid on my pet communications project and went to work. Grant had challenged me on the 19th, and on the 21st, Roman offered to help. On the 27th, I had the inspiration for a character that would enable me to create a narrative about the twelve diverse characters you will encounter in your workplace. More importantly, it would allow me to show you how you can create your own perfect teams and double team performance. On April 2nd, I started writing on my monthly flight to Frankfurt. By May 4th (Star Wars Day), I had my first draft, and Roman began to help with the graphics and the modelling.

If you remember, I developed something called the 'The Vision Triangle' many years before. I could clearly see that people had distinct preferences for one of the sides over the other two, and that was borne out by my conversation with Janet in Edinburgh earlier and my lack of one with Ian, who had run away. I had always had an aversion to personality tests and psychometrics, but I saw their usefulness in creating conversations between people in a team. They validated that people have different styles and ways of communicating and leading.

## The Vision Triangle™

When I went back and looked at the source of the psychometric tests, I realised, as an engineer, that there was a flaw in the source code. So, I carried out a 'Thought Experiment' in which I had an imaginary conversation with Dr. Carl Jung. I proposed to him that we use his components in a revolutionary new way.

*Dr. Jung, you recently published your new book 'Psychological Types'.*

*In it, you propose that there are four main functions of consciousness: two rational functions (Thinking and Feeling) and two irrational functions (Sensing and Intuition).*

*You have additionally explained that these conscious functions are modified by two main attitude types: extroversion and introversion.*

*If I were to take you forward a hundred years, you would see that your four and eight-factor model, modified by Myers-Briggs in the 1940s, to a sixteen-factor model, is used as the source of all the personality and psychometric testing in the world. That is quite a legacy, and as a result, it is seen as one of the world's most established and well-respected models for personality and behaviour. Sixteen personality types became de facto the accepted norm. Currently, it is heresy to challenge something so respected and vested in by the psychological community.*

*As your 1921 text is the source point for everything that has subsequently come, I'm going to challenge you to look at it differently and see if we can create together a new instrument that is indeed fit for the 21$^{st}$ century.*

*Let's leave the two main attitude types, extroversion and introversion, as is and make them the core.*

*Looking at your functions of consciousness, you have these two rational components (Thinking and Feeling), and I must agree they are vital.*

*Where I beg to differ is when you start talking about the two irrational functions of Sensing and Intuition. If you look closely at 'Sensing', it is just a smorgasbord of leftovers and debris from Thinking & Feeling, so you had something to juxtapose against Intuition. Instead of considering Intuition to be irrational, let's raise it and put it on equal footing with Thinking & Feeling.*

*This way, you will have a central triad (a triangle of functions) that says we all do Thinking and Feeling and Intuition rather than your current 'Or' framework.*

*When you now run the combinations between the two attitudes (I&E) with the three functions (T&F&G where G represents Intuition), you will see six possible behaviour styles.*

*IT, ET, IF, EF, IG, EG*

*Then, if these styles are, in turn, modified by another of the two remaining functions, you have twelve very distinct and integrated characters. Each will have a very particular and nuanced way of seeing the world. Each will have a different way of processing the information in their world. Each will make decisions to act in distinctly unique ways. Raising Intuition to a primary level and giving it equality with thinking and feeling changes everything from a two-dimensional 4/8/16 factor model into a simpler, more memorable 12-factor model. The beauty and simplicity of 12 is you can position the characters around a clockface and give them numbers.*

*The application allows you to instantly map groups and teams, giving organisations snapshots of different teams alongside their strengths and potential weaknesses.*

In this conversation, Carl Jung replies to me at the end, "I do declare, young man. That is sound thinking. It provides clarity and equality to the functions. I like the idea of 12 Character Types rather than 16 Personality Types, and I always thought that that Myers-Briggs thing was just a parlour game anyway."

Using the components in this new way gives us the following:

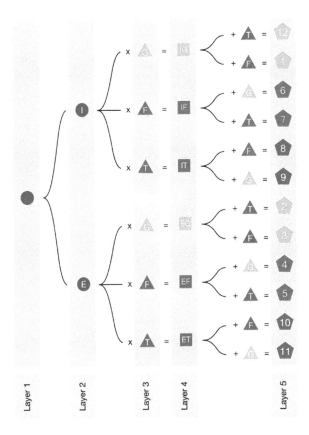

Twelve individual and distinct characters, and the beauty of twelve is that you can put them around a clock face. As you will see later, you can create instant, graphic, and clear team maps.

It took nearly a year, but early in January 2013, Roman and I started working on the coding for an online questionnaire that is at the heart of our business today.

# Tip #42: Do it for yourself

# CHAPTER 43
## 'I Have a Dream'
### Let's advance to an age of character

In my previous conversation with Carl Jung, I said, "Let's leave the two main attitude types, extroversion and introversion, as is and make them the core of this new model." Oddly enough, three weeks later, I had a graphic illustration of the differences between the two attitudes. Picture a group of people in a plush boardroom on Cavendish Square in the West End.

They rose out of their seats as one on one side of the boardroom table and collectively, with their arms folded, said, "What on earth are you talking about?"

On the other side of the table, their three colleagues were concentrating and writing away with no concerns whatsoever. What caused this dramatic schism, you are wondering? One minute beforehand, I had placed a single raisin in front of each of them and asked them to write down their answers to the question, "What is the raisin raising for you?" It's an exercise designed to illustrate the difference between 'Introversion' and 'Extroversion'. It's to test if someone can be quietly introspective. The three that dramatically stood up were archetypal extroverts; the three that were scribbling away and had no problems with the exercise at all were classic introverts.

I stood back from the group and held the silence. One by one, the three returned to their seats. The first one smiled and nodded. The second shuffled a little as if trying to escape from the room. The third scowled, muttered, and ground their teeth. After just three minutes, the three that had remained seated slowly finished the task set. I asked each of them to share what the raisin had raised. The three that had stood were flabbergasted at the responses. "That's just astonishing," said the first to sit back down.

"Where on earth does that come from?" said the second. The third remained silent.

The three scribes explained that they prefer to be given space and time whenever they are set a task or asked to do something. Being rushed to decide or being told to share their ideas doesn't work for them. As they started talking, the mood in the room lightened, and the understanding of the differences between the two sets became apparent. "I thought you'd completely lost it," the third stander said, "I was convinced you'd been smoking your socks! But I get it now. Glenn, Jo and I are so driven, so filled with impatience, so expressive, and wanting answers immediately that we've been missing the input these three can bring to the equation." The three scribes looked at each other and smiled. "Thank you, Sam," said one, "We've been struggling to find a way to explain the friction that always comes up in our board meetings, but this has just illustrated it completely. We're Introverts, and we love to create space and have time to ponder the issues. You are all natural extroverts. You love to fill the space and then rush off to the next thing. It's just a difference in style, isn't it?" she stated as she finished and looked back at me. "It certainly is. If you'd like to know more about the difference, I recommend you read a book called 'Quiet' by Susan Cain."

I smiled as I slowly walked to the flip-chart. I looked around the table. "Has anyone read it?" "Not yet," said one of the scribes, "but I've already Googled it, and I love the subtitle— 'The Power of Introverts in a World That Can't Stop Talking'.

Yes. I like that idea very much indeed."

"Susan Cain goes on to say that it would be practically impossible to get into Harvard Business School today unless you portrayed yourself as having a personality that you are extroverted, outgoing, powerful and confident. The big 'I AM'. She explains that this is a consequence of the 20th century's infatuation with 'The Extrovert Ideal' and the 'Myth of Charismatic leadership'. The 20th century became an 'Age of Personality' whereas previously, it was deemed that a person's character was more valued.

"Introversion and Extroversion are of themselves two critical factors in determining a person's preferred style. They have the biggest effect of all the factors involved."

The way I like to illustrate the differences is:

© Rob Arnold - Perfect Teams - 2023

Introverts like to create space. Extroverts like to fill the space.

How does this show up in your team?

## Character vs. Personality

A classic moment in Nelson Mandela's 'Long Walk to Freedom' is when an Authority figure confronts him and a friend. They dared to challenge his demand that they immediately run an errand for him. "Do you know who I am?" he shouts. Mandela's friend calmly replies, "No. I do not know who you are, but I know what you are!" as they proudly walk away ...

To me, this moment exemplifies the clear distinction between character and personality. What are you? Vs Who are you? Humility and diffidence vs. Ego.

Characters are forged in adversity, born of struggle and are a triumph of will. They are about substance over style. They are about a quiet inner power. Personality is deemed to be a gift, a confection.

The roadside is littered with the egos that have fallen and taken their companies with them. Big, loud personalities blindly leading prominent companies into oblivion (Skilling at Enron, Fuld at Lehman Bros, Diamond at Barclays, 'Fred the Shred' at RBS, Philip Greene at BHS).

Unfortunately, 'Big Extreme Extroverts' will never be able to listen. Quietness and the acknowledgement of it is pure anathema to them.

It's time to return to an 'Age of Character', a quieter, more introverted and thoughtful age where a person's character counts more than their 'personality'.

# What is the difference between character and personality?

Prior to WWII, the field of psychology was led by German-speaking countries and the term character was often used in place of personality. In fact, the school of psychology that was predominant in these countries during the late 19th century and early 20th century was known as 'Characterology'. When you investigate the words' etymology, you can see a clear distinction, too. Character comes from Greek roots and has an innate, intrinsic context of being engraved marked, and is about moral strength. Personality has Latin roots and has an extrinsic context of being made, adopted and worn as in a mask. Character is, therefore, something you work on over time. It goes deep and requires time to form. Personality is something more superficial. You can simply pick up the mask and adopt or act the character.

The pendulum fully swung from an age of character to one of personality, though, when the term personality, which was dominant in English use, came to be preferred after the end of WWII, particularly in American academia.

I choose to focus on character, not personality.

I started exploring the twelve characters you might find in and out of work. What strengths does each character bring to the equation? How can you best pick and mix the variations to create, build and sustain a perfect team?

To me, character trumps personality every time.

I'll leave it to Martin Luther King to have the last word, "I have a dream that my four little children will one day live in a nation where they will not be judged by the colour of their skin but by the content of their character."

# Tip #43: Character trumps personality

*Part Five - Teacher*

# CHAPTER 44
## A fiscal cliff looms
*The Big 'C' & 'D' world*

It looks like it's all coming together nicely, doesn't it? There were cracks in the fabric, though—a surprise VAT inspection and a request for a meeting with Human Resources (always a bad omen). Obama had talked about 'The Fiscal Cliff' at the end of 2012. Well, I reached mine when ICAP pulled the plug. Going from a good six-figures a year to zero overnight feels akin to falling off 'El Capitan'. 'So Long, And Thanks For All The Fish', except I didn't move to a parallel universe where everything was still OK. [If you don't know the writings of Douglas Adams, this comment may just have gone right over your head]. I hit the proverbial brick wall at the end of the road. Splat. Just like the 'Road Runner'.

I'd written a paper on precisely this scenario called 'Transitions' and how you manage your way through it, never expecting in a million years that I would have to experience it myself. This is what I wrote:

*The feelings that are generated when people hit a transition with no prior knowledge quite often is a world of hurt and frustration known as the 'D' world. The initial frustrations and stresses start to overwhelm. People begin to feel DISAPPOINTMENT, DISMAY, and DEPENDENT. They start to become DISILLUSIONED, DISEMPOWERED, DEPRESSED. They may initially DENY that anything is occurring by becoming DIASSOCIATED and DETACHED, but eventually, if the right steps are not taken, behaviours such as DRINK, DRUGS, and DEPRESSION will manifest, and these ultimately can lead to DEBT, DIVORCE, and DEATH.*

*It is a DARK, DISMAL, and DANGEROUS place full of DOOM!*

*This phase is where people just want to run away and give up. It is often accompanied by avoidance techniques.*

*The only way out of this pit of despair is to take action and do something. This cycle of negative feelings has to be broken, and that can only be done by getting into practical action and utilising logic and thinking.*

*This is the 'Melt-Down', the breakdown before the breakthrough. It can be seen as being the red phase.*

I pretty much had every one of these feelings. Despite all the gifts I'd received from Roman and Grant, the next four years of my life would be a challenge, to say the least. I was declared bankrupt by the Inland Revenue. The bailiffs took away my motorcycle. My mother died. I was sidelined in a business venture. Two good friends died of cancer. I found out I had cancer myself, and a kid shouted out from a car one day, "Hello, fat belly." In the immortal line of Kenneth Williams, 'Infamy... Infamy... they've all got it in for me!'

This wasn't a triple whammy but an 'Octuple Whammy'. And when that hits, there's only one thing to do— take a step back. I've said several times that you have to be one step removed to be a successful coach (and you can insert leader, manager, and supervisor there). You have to operate from a contextual layer, one removed from all the hubbub and stuff that is going on around you. I was just too involved and close to it all. I found myself getting caught up in a myriad of details and events. I had to get a proper perspective and remove myself for a while, step away and get an eagle's eye on what had transpired and find the arc that it all hangs from. And so, I started going on long walks first for an hour, then two, then three. Once a week, I would walk all day.

On one of my walks, I remembered coaching a friend who'd had a similar meltdown and had lost a couple of businesses as a consequence. I called him up, and he reminded me of the story I'd told him at the time. The young boy comes running up to the village elder, shouting, "The donkey's fallen down the well." The elder goes to look, and sure enough, there's the donkey at the bottom of the well, braying away but none-the-worse for its fall. The elder looks up and orders the villagers, who have gathered, "Go get your shovels." They and the young boy looked stunned. "Go on then. Quick. Quick." And off they scarper returning with their shovels. The elder looks down the well and tells the villagers to start shovelling the sand into the well. They are very reluctant but gradually begin doing as they're told. The elder calls a halt after five minutes, looks down the well and shouts, "Shake it off. Step up." The elder repeats this process until the donkey can step out of the well. John said, "When I was in that pit of despair, your story reminded me to look at what I still had, and that was enough to get me through. Sure, I had to readjust and do some research, but I wasn't as far down as I felt." I had to shake it off and step up.

What helped me step up was acknowledging what was still working in my life. I had a product I could sell. I had a new website and platform. I still had three clients. I had a book of intellectual property. I had a new bank account. I had friends. I found out I could claim my Navy pension. I had a supportive and loving wife. That's eight strokes of luck, but not as poetic as a whammy. By taking a step back, I broke the negative spiral of despair. I had forced myself into a logical and rational space where I could start to make sense and do something. In the transitions paper, this is the blue phase, and I had this to say:

> *When people or businesses end up in the red phase with all the associated feelings, it is generally because they did not take the time to invest in the next phase of development to shift them into the green growth phase. The writing may have been on the wall for months, if not years, beforehand. The solution, then, is to go into a phase of logic. Logic neutralises the negative energy of the 'D' world. This is where you start to rationalise, research, and find a different way forward. The blue thinking phase is a period of stabilisation and consolidation. This is where you begin to cast around for a way out of the mire of doom and gloom. This is where you just start to do things. It's all about action rather than paralysis. People develop the habit of doing things, trying out new solutions, looking for ways out of the pit of despair. Providing you find the right solution and implement it, you will shift yourself or your business into the next phase*

*of renewal and fresh growth. If it is not the right solution, providence will show you quickly, and the process will begin again – a process of research and logic. So, this is often a phase where people seek expert advice and start to retrain or learn new skills. For some businesses, it may require bringing in new talent that's up to par to take the company into its next growth stage.*

*A feeling of calmness characterises this phase as the chaos is stabilised and dissipated. People seek to consolidate by finding appropriate solutions.*

My breakdown lasted three years. Getting the all-clear from the fabulous Dr Kate Newbold, my oncologist, at the Royal Marsden on October 7th, 2016, and the second all-clear from my surgeon, Dr Kim, at St. George's on February 23rd, 2017, gave me the impetus to dust myself down and move forward. As the transition paper says, the third phase is characterised by confidence and the start of something new:

*Once decisions have been made about how and why things have to be done differently, it's all down to implementing the changes fast.*

Right choices – Right changes – Right Cure

*The green phase is all about renewal and transformation. It is about creating a whole new world. With the right solution implemented, confidence grows, and things start to take off again. This is the beginning of a whole new cycle of growth. How do you feel when you get through this transition? More often than not, it is accompanied by a feeling of pride in a job well done. The business owner draws breath and says TFFT!*

## The Three Stages of Transition

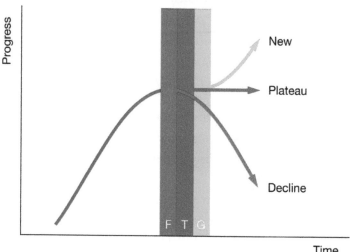

I've always said, "Live on the edge because that's where the energy is." It's also where the danger and turbulence lurks. Transitional states are boundaries between different energy levels where things change state, ice to water, water to steam. It's where the order of magnitude shifts. Businesses go from £100,000 turnovers to £1 million to £10 million to £100m to £1billion etc. And every one of those shifts comes with rewards and penalties—the secret is learning how to manage the transition without getting caught up in it. I became well and truly caught up. It, therefore, took considerably longer to get through. A world of renewal and fresh energy started when I finally shook it all off and stepped up.

*Tip #44: Shake it off and step up*

# CHAPTER 45
## Let me turn your world upside down
### *'He took her for a six-mile walk'*

I probably need to go back and fill in some of the open loops I've created by swiftly galloping through six years of my life.

Let's start with a 'loving and supportive wife'. I'd previously, as mentioned, put a lid on the Wild-West party affair. On the morning of April 27th, 2012, there was a flurry of text messages as I walked to an appointment in the West End. She finished with, "I don't want to hurt you," to which I responded, "Don't hurt me then. Love me." By the end of the day, the lid had disappeared and was never seen again. I made her wait a year before she could move in. Three years later, just after I'd been diagnosed with cancer, I proposed. Caroline and I were married on August 5th and have now been married for seven years. How she puts up with me, I'll never know. Shake it off and step up.

I had my 60th birthday in 2014 and decided to have a party, which is unlike me. Caroline is an ace organiser and helped me. I decided to have it at 'The Wheaty', which had undergone a massive refurbishment and on the night, we filled it with around one hundred and twenty guests. I had friends and family there from every period of my life, many of whom have already been mentioned. I had to do some detective work, but I'd even tracked down Winchester Vaughan, who came with Liz, his new wife-to-be. In planning for it, I pulled together my all-time favourite songs list, starting with Vera Lynn's 'My Son-My Son', the number one on the day I began, through to David Bowie's 2013 'Where Are We Now'. I gave the list, all 684 songs, to our DJ of the night— Big G. There was also a live band fronted by my old friend Paul. I didn't know it, but he'd written a song just for the occasion, set to the tune of Peter Sarstedt's 'Where Do You Go To (My Lovely)?' It had a recurring chorus of 'And you've never failed to amaze me, with the number of women you've met. But I think the compliments they gave you were going straight to your head … Yes, I do'. It went down a storm and raised a colossal cheer led by Jonesy, Nic, and my son James. Shake it off and step up.

It was great to catch up with Vaughan after so many years. A year later, he's inviting me to his 'Stag Night' in Bath. I'm not sure how we got onto the subject, but he reminded me that I should check out my pension from the Royal Fleet Auxiliary. Sure enough, I had one sitting there with a lump sum attached, too. Shake it off and step up.

One of the friends at the party was Julian from Mekon. They had been a client of mine for twenty years in one form or another. Jules flew acrobatics for Great Britain, and he had given me a card, "Let me turn your world upside down!" On March 5th, 2015, at White Waltham, he did just that and took me out for a 'Sortie' along the Thames Valley with a big loop-the-loop over Caversham Heights before returning. It was, as I put in my diary at the time, "Absolutely Fucking Awesome!!!" Shake it off and step up.

Another friend there that night, from Caversham, was Janet. She has been a constant in my life for many years. She is ever supportive, loving, giving, and honest with me, even when I'm being an idiot or shocking people with my directness. She was there that night with her best friend Jane and Glynn, with whom I was working on a joint venture. Shake it off and step up.

And then there was 'Three Forks' Roman. He'd helped me build the heart of a new platform and get the graphics and modelling right. We'd already secured some new work with two marketing groups and the London Stock Exchange with the new website. One of the marketing groups was run by the charismatic Peter Franks, who was there that evening with his charming wife, Giselle. Unfortunately, Peter was one of my friends who succumbed to cancer shortly before I was diagnosed myself. My other friend Peter Baker couldn't make it because he passed the week before at the Royal Marsden, a place I would become very familiar with, although I didn't know it then. Shake it off and step up.

It was walking that kept me sane through all this time. When Caroline moved in in 2013, we started a routine of walking together around Tooting Common. To be honest, she struggled to do even two miles but gradually got there. I can remember visiting my parents in Portchester. We went for a walk, and my mother told a neighbour, "He walked her six miles. He did. Six miles," as if I'd punished her, like an errant dog, by taking her for such a long walk. Month by month, we went further and further and just before my cancer was diagnosed, she said she'd like to do a marathon one day. After my treatment, I asked if she still wanted to do it, and she said yes. The thing about marathons, whether you're running them or walking, is to get your daily average up and slowly increase the length of your weekly long walk or run from eight to ten to twelve, etc., until you can comfortably do twenty. It will amaze you what you can do if you just take the time to slowly build up and have the discipline to stick with it. It's all about building muscle memory and putting the miles in the bank. We started training in November, and on March 25th, 2017, Caroline walked her first marathon—twenty-six point two miles. It's not bad for someone who struggled to walk two initially. Shake it off and step up.

The thing that stuck in my mind throughout this time was my determination that I wouldn't allow these setbacks to defeat me. I went to a client meeting two days after my initial surgery. My runaway friend Jon was now running a cracking business, Deltatre, in Wimbledon, for the founder Paul Bristow. He loved what I'd developed and wanted to do a team workshop with the board. Some issues were developing, and he knew I could help him flush them out into the open. We booked the workshop for June 1st, a week after my radiotherapy and chemo started. It was quite a moment when we persuaded the two directors who were clashing to admit it to the whole room openly. The workshop left such an impression that Paul, who went on to create the European Championships Games, invited me to Geneva in 2021 to work with his new team. I could have made all sorts of excuses, but that's not my style. Instead, I ascribe to the Finnish ethos of SISU that talks of stoic determination— the tenacity of purpose that will make you apply your willpower to persist and overcome all obstacles. It's about resilience, determination, grit, and staying power. I decided that with a strong purpose and the clarity of my aim, I would have even more determination to move past all these poxy challenges.

Talking of fortitude. At the beginning of this period, just after my 60th birthday, I went uptown to see the Poppies at the Tower. It was a powerful, potent and moving piece of art marking one hundred years since the first full day of Britain's involvement in the First World War. The artists Paul Cummins and Tom Piper had these ceramic poppies pouring out of the northeast bastion progressively filling the moat around the Tower between July and November. There were 888,246 of them representing every British military fatality—lumps in throats and gratitude for the fortitude of those who sacrificed everything. My problems paled into insignificance with the backdrop of those poppies.

# Tip #45: Be determined. Don't let setbacks defeat you

# CHAPTER 46

## You're an engineer? It'll probably work then!

### Duelling Banjos

O ne day I am walking down this street. It's a very familiar street. Familiar faces. Familiar things to do. Familiar distractions. There's a deep hole in the pavement. I fall in. I flounder around saying to myself, "I'm lost ... I'm so hopeless ... Who's done this to me? ... Who's fault is this? ... This isn't my fault." It takes forever for me to find a way out.

Later, I am walking down the self-same street. There is still a deep hole in the pavement. I pretend that I do not see it, but I fall in again. I say to myself, "I cannot believe this. I'm in the same place again. This is not my fault." But it still takes me a long time to get out.

Again, I am walking down this street. There is still the same deep hole in the pavement. I can see that it is there. I still fall in. I cannot help myself. It's a habit. I say to myself, "My eyes are open. I know where I am. This is my fault." I get out immediately.

*I am walking down this street. There is still the same deep hole in the pavement. I see it clearly. I walk around it.*

*The next day, I walk down a different street.*

As I read this the first time, I gasped. It was like a thunderbolt. A great big slap in the face. The metaphorical whack on the side of my great big head. It's called, 'An autobiography of life in five chapters'. I call it 'Habit Holes' and ask myself, which one have I fallen in today?

The final piece of the puzzle that enabled me to shake it off and step up was the fifth chapter above. Walk down a different street.

In 2017, my wife worked for a mid-size city accounting company called Wilson Wright, across from Hatton Garden. This exclusive London jewellery quarter was most recently famous for the underground safe deposit burglary that may have netted the thieves £200 million. Michael Caine and Ray Winston made slightly less playing the elderly criminals who masterminded the heist in the movie, 'King of Thieves'. Caroline introduced me to Katy their Head of HR. Katy wanted to use my profiling tool to help her with team development throughout the firm. At this time, the business was called 'Do-Zen', a play on the twelve characters you'll find in organisations. The logo represents this concept because you can create a sphere when you bring twelve pentagons together.

Thus, twelve characters represented by all the numbers from one to twelve coming together would create total unity with all the questions a team would ever have being answered. I trained Katy on the theory, application, and management of the platform, and she duly started profiling the partners and employees of Wilson Wright with the intention that I would do a workshop with the partners at their next retreat in 2018. Katy then asked who else I was working with, and I explained that I was looking for introductions. She duly introduced me to one of the partners, Warren, and he invited me to his networking group early in the new year.

My walk down a different street started on January 8th. I flipped my 'Will' switch, and as Brad Pitt would say, "I withdrew my drinking privileges." Over the holidays, I looked at ways to differentiate 'Do-Zen' from the thousands of other management tools available. I'd already developed a sound proposition to take on the world of psychometrics by positioning against them and saying Jung's source code was flawed, but I needed something else. On a walk, no less, the piece of paper and pencil I always carry came out, and the concept of 'Team Maps' was born. I simply drew a clock face and put a coloured button for each team member against their number. Simple. Instant. Graphically clear. I spent a few days reviewing my records and creating the first twenty company team maps.

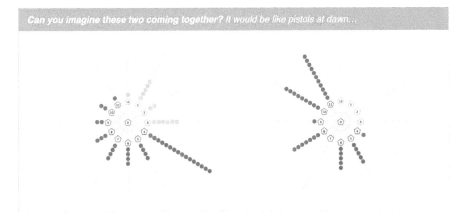

*Can you imagine these two coming together? It would be like pistols at dawn...*

These are two of the first ones I did. Can you imagine these two teams coming together?

I named this clash between two competing worldviews 'Duelling Banjos'. It would be like pistols at dawn or 'En Garde!'

Shortly after I had coffee with John and showed him the concept, he said, "Neil, that is a game-changer. No one else has got that. It's so simple and clear."

I also had a coffee early in February with a diversity consultant John introduced to me. I met Shelley at the Great Western, where I'd seen Robin Cook sneaking around all those years ago. At one point, Shelley asked, "Neil. Are you a psychologist?"

I said, "No, Shelley. I'm an engineer." She pauses for over thirty seconds before saying, "It'll probably work then," which has to be my favourite quote to date.

I finally managed to attend Warren's networking morning on February 20th. I freely admit that networking is not my preferred pastime, but if I am to build a new business, I must do it. It was a BNI meeting which had found a way of monetising networking back when I formed the Croydon Movers and Shakers in the early 90s. There comes a point in the proceedings where you have the floor for thirty seconds to tell everyone about you and what you do. I had been wrestling with the difficulty of succinctly explaining to people what Do-Zen was and could do. The jargon was I didn't have my 'Elevator-Pitch'. You're travelling in an elevator with a potential prospect and have thirty seconds to pitch your proposition. So, I'm sitting there, racking my brain on how to pitch 'Do-Zen'. Walking to the front, I say, "Hands up if you work in a team?" All the hands went up. "Keep them up if that team is perfect!" All the hands went down. "Perfect Teams. That's what I'm about." I smiled, walked back to my space and sat down. Immediately after the meeting finished, three people came dashing up to me, saying they wanted to talk further. One of them was Rob Boll, who became my first investor in what was now called 'Perfect Teams'.

Grant and Roman helped me with some of the early website build, and by April, we had the beginnings of a Perfect Teams proposition. It was enough to deliver a coherent message anyway, and James D, who I'd met at ICAP, and was now running the Humble Grape Group, booked our first workshop. James had grown his wine tastings into a chain of four bar restaurants in Battersea, Islington, Fleet Street, and Liverpool Street. He was about to crowdfund to expand that to ten within the year.

Rob had set up a company called Evoke Management, specialising in placing part-time, fractional finance, operations, and sales directors into companies. He was particularly interested in helping companies set up Employee Ownership Trusts (EOT). Naturally, any company going through a change like that, experiencing a growth spurt or needing to restructure, would require some help with team performance. Perfect Teams was the ideal plugin for him and his team to help their clients, so he trained to be a Perfect Teams licensee. This gave him access to all the intellectual property (IP) I had developed over the previous thirty years (published in three volumes) and the team profiling platform. That summer he asked me to extend it to his team. The night before the training day, he reiterated that he wanted to invest in Perfect Teams and help me grow it into a worldwide brand. The seed of the idea that Perfect Teams could be 'The Ritz, The Rolex, The Rolls Royce' of 'Team Development' was sown at The Ivy.

I was asked recently what my vision was. It is crystal clear:

- For 'Perfect Teams' to be the instrument of choice for the 21$^{st}$ Century.

- To be 'The Leaders in Team Development'.

- To help you, 'Create world-class teams that deliver outstanding results'.

How am I going to do that?

That's the $64,000 question, isn't it? Stay tuned.

# *Tip #46: Networking creates life-changing opportunities*

# CHAPTER 47
## Tectonic plates to windmills
### *PerfectTeams is launched*

Thomas Kuhn's outstanding contribution to the philosophy of science was his idea of paradigms and paradigm shifts. He described paradigms as the collective opinions of the time. A shift occurs when they are suddenly rendered obsolete and incompatible with new understanding. The great thing about human belief systems/constructs is they can change. The prevailing paradigm can shift. The Earth was once flat, and then it was round. Once upon a time, the Sun and the planets orbited the Earth, and then, one day, we all went around the Sun. Nothing had changed except the prevailing belief system. Thank goodness for Copernicus, Galileo, and the seafaring explorers. Fifty years ago, the Earth was stable; then, as my old running pal in St. Louis told me, tectonic plates were discovered. Suddenly, the paradigm shifted, and the world was turned upside down, or in this case, inside out. This was precisely what Polly was seeking to do with getting the UN to adopt an international law of 'Ecocide'. The same was true of John Woolman, who slowly walked from community to community, convincing slave owners to give up the practice.

They were both taking a 'tilt' at the constructs of a time and place. Hierarchies will always have a vested interest in keeping them going, as it creates an illusion of authority and control.

With Perfect Teams, I'm taking a 'tilt' too. Developing teams and doubling their performance doesn't have to be difficult or complicated. If you have the right tools, it can be surprisingly easy, and as an engineer, I like to make things easy. One client at the time said, "What I love about this, Neil, is you're not filling my head with your psychological credentials and mumbo jumbo. It's in plain English. It's simple, understandable, and I get it immediately."

Around this time, Richard and Nancy, from Long Beach days, came to visit. Richard, with his chutzpah, was now retired from OTIS. Appropriately enough, with Richard's nickname being 'Churchill', they stayed at the Hyatt Churchill on Portland Square before coming down to us and then venturing on to stay with my father.

Ronnie Scott's, in Soho, the Greenwich Maritime Museum, with its meridian and Harrison's Clocks, 'The clocks that changed the world' were some of the highlights. Harrison's clocks were revolutionary in allowing ships to determine their longitude at sea. Navigation from 1730 was revolutionised, and many lives were saved as a consequence. Dava Sobel retells the story in his fabulous book, 'Longitude – The True Story of a Lone Genius Who Solved the Greatest Scientific Problem of His Time'. Political shenanigans at play in the background, as always. A few weeks later, Wilson Wright had their 125th anniversary party at the Hyatt Churchill—a grand affair in the ballroom itself. Sitting at one of the tables, watching everyone have an increasingly drunken good time, an idea began to germinate or, because I wasn't drinking, brew.

Both take time, so I'll get back to this later.

When Richard and Nancy came down to us, I was no longer living in Tooting Bec. I can distinctly remember telling Lisa in California, "If I ever talk about moving to the suburbs – shoot me!" Caroline's best friend, Maja, lived in leafy, suburban Worcester Park with her husband, Rob A and their twins. We moved to a house just down the road. Rob became a fast friend, and I found out one day that he was an excellent cartoonist and illustrator, which proved to be very useful. He also liked fine Havana cigars, and we would occasionally put the world to rights puffing away on a Romeo y Juliette Churchill.

With the new rough and ready website and Rob B's support, business was starting to flourish. He introduced me to an engineering firm with offices in London and the provinces. Profiling over a hundred people, pulling together the fourteen different team maps, and organising each of the separate team workshops was very labour-intensive at this time. It was fruitful, though; the data and insights gained were invaluable to the directors and HR. For me, the highlight was presenting the concept to all the staff at King's College London just before Christmas. Getting a hundred and fifty people fully engaged and moving around the auditorium to show the mix of characters they had was a buzz. I'd forgotten how much I loved presenting and working a room.

The new year began with massive optimism. It would end the same way. Rob B made his investment, and shares were duly transferred. Finding an agency that could build what we required was a bit more challenging. After a couple of false starts, I was introduced to a developer by Shep, who runs a company called OptimaLife. He does exactly what it says on the tin. He helps you optimise your life. I took the train to Grantham, Margaret Thatcher's birthplace, to meet James and Clare of Envious Digital. I lifted the 'bonnet', so to speak, on Perfect Teams with a five-hour 'Show and Tell'. It was at times like this that I really missed Roman. The development process would have been simpler and faster if he'd still been involved. I met up with Clare a week later at Robin Cook's favourite hotel in Paddington. It looked to me that she and James had 'nailed' it. I shared the proposal with Rob B. and Roman, and they agreed. On March 27th, 2019, I gave Clare the green light. Twenty-eight years after returning to the UK with my tail between my legs, I received the first fruit. It popped into my inbox on April 25th—the new Perfect Teams logo, which we have subsequently trademarked and registered.

**PERFECT**®
T E A M S

It was amazing the effect it had. It was like a jack-in-the-box moment. Surprise! A friend has told me that it hits all the right psychological buttons, whatever that means.

If only the rest of the development had gone as quickly and smoothly. This 'Bear of Little Brain' regarding things to do with software and IT was on a rapid learning curve. Where art thou, Roman?

On practical matters, work was flowing in. I was coaching the CEO of the engineering firm. Workshops were being booked, and I was working on a major presentation for a soft launch of Perfect Teams at St. Martin's in the Field on Trafalgar Square. Rob B. had made another investment in International Leaders. This forum helps dynamic businesses grow, innovate, plan succession and exit. Rob intended to rejuvenate the London Leaders chapter with an array of engaging knowledge workshops that would have a powerful impact. These would be followed by ask-the-expert sessions designed to facilitate thought provoking discussions and provide invaluable insights to each member. Drinks, nibbles, and networking would tidy it all up. Rob had a videographer there, and we were able to capture it all for posterity.

If you've read this far and have a good memory, do you remember the tumble I took with Winchester Vaughan in the bright lights of Finsbury Park? We'd gone there to meet his brother Gary in a bar next to the Rainbow Theatre, a fabulous music venue in the day, now sadly a church. Before the tumble, it was a great night rubbing shoulders with Billy Idol of Generation X and Johnny Rotten. Gary was a magnetic force in a band called The Stukas, who were right on the cusp of breaking through. At the end of 2019, they were playing at the Hope & Anchor on Upper Street in Islington. This venue has been a sound destination for music lovers for fifty years now, and that night, they were headlining with The Wigs, fronted by Keith Brymer Jones, now more famous for 'The Great Pottery Throw Down' hosted by the delectable Melanie Sykes. Joy of joys, she was there in the basement watching it all alongside me and my mates Paul and Rob A. Unfortunately, Winchester Vaughan himself couldn't make it.

Boris had been elected PM two days before, ending three and a half years of constant parliamentary squabbling following the referendum. As we now know, the beautiful silence was very short lived. Nonetheless, I had an optimistic smile as the year turned.

## Tip #47: Challenge the 'Construct'

# CHAPTER 48
## Winnie-the-Pooh's pandemic

### *Emperors wear no clothes*

Someone once told me if you want to make God laugh, tell her your plans. She must have roared when she saw mine at the beginning of 2020, the year of perfect vision.

And what I saw was Perfect Teams in 12 cities and 12 countries by 2025. The last total eclipse of the Sun in the UK was in 1999. I can remember everyone heading to Cornwall to see it. I was coaching in the Crown Agents in Sutton at the time, and we took a break to go outside and experience it. The next total solar eclipse here isn't expected until September 23rd, 2090, but we had an unexpected total business eclipse on March 23rd with a complete lockdown due to the 'Chinese-Flu'. It's fair to say it completely f**ked my business.

The year had had a productive start. Rob A. dusted off his cartoonist skills, developing a set of twelve emojis, one for each character you might find in your team.

The Seer

The Challenger

The Go-Getter

The Connector

The Lover

The Guardian

The Discerner

The Planner

The Analyst

The Maker

The Director

The Judge

In February, Rob B. asked me to do another presentation for London Leaders, where I introduced my concept of the 'Quick & Dirty Business Plan' (QDP). The idea was to get everyone to have a business plan on one sheet of paper that they would have in their pocket. Again, being an engineer, I like to keep things simple. Most people have plans but don't have instant access to them. They always get stuffed away in a drawer or filed somewhere where they get quickly forgotten.

Here's mine from that very workshop:

## QDP - Where we are - January 2021

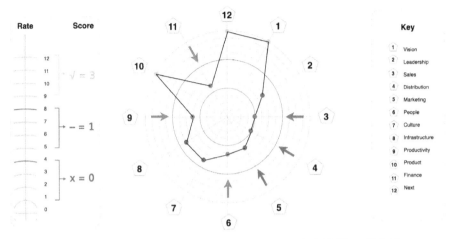

This business scored itself as 3 √, 7 -, 2 x for a total of 16/36 or 84/144

➤ Current projects underway   ➤ Next projects

As you can see, I needed to work on sales, distribution, and marketing within Perfect Teams. Until these three aspects of the business are fully resolved, it makes no sense to look at anything else. Having it in my pocket reminds me to stay focused on these three and nothing else. To be honest, as I look at it today, nothing has changed, except No. 6, the people part of the equation is beginning to nudge me, and No. 11 finance, because getting someone to invest in the business so that I can accelerate the plan after the pandemic, is of interest.

As you know, we had given our developers the green light for the new website and backend platform. The backend is where all the clever stuff is done with algorithms, report generation, and commercial payment systems. The frontend is a shop window where you entice people to take a look at your product, which, in our case, is Perfect Teams. We'd had a fabulous logo but here we are nearly a year later and no cigar. Fortunately, looking back now, I was able to meet Clare in Reading for a five hour complete download on February 27th and she resolved to get things moving. By now, we were receiving daily briefings on the impending pandemic with an epicentre in Lombardy and cruise ships being quarantined. With a global panic unfolding, a national lockdown was declared on March 23rd, 2020. The world would never be the same again. I mean, who had heard of Zoom, Teams, working from home (WFH), coronaviruses, or hybrid working apart from geeks, medical specialists, and some HR wonks thinking up the future of work?

Rob B., a man always ahead of the curve, hosted the first International Leaders meeting of the pandemic on March 25th on Zoom. I think I managed to sign up for an account that very morning. Full credit to Rob; he managed to keep and grow the network through the whole debacle.

I remember someone asking me the inevitable question, "How did I like working at home?" It became the de facto question, didn't it? Better than the weather one, in my opinion. I was used to it as it was what I did when I wasn't seeing clients. I remember quipping, "It's fine, but I'm no longer on my own!" Once my head understood all the new tech and applications, I found myself in a new groove. That's the beautiful thing about us humans: we have an incredible ability to adapt.

With all this free time on our hands mischief making became part of our new daily lives. Social media became rocket-powered, and cyberspace was awash with memes (who'd heard of those), short videos, and photoshopped jokes. WhatsApp was pinging left, right, and centre with new incoming messages. One of the memes that tickled me was one of Xi Jinping and Obama. I then heard that 'Winnie-the-Pooh' had been banned in China. Now, I'm not especially political, but I do believe that all Dictators, Despots, Autocrats and Theocrats should be mercilessly ridiculed, lampooned, and called to account. Dictators really are 'Dicks'. Sadly, too many people live under religions and regimes where that is not possible and risk death if they do. I, therefore, nicknamed the Chinese Emperor 'Jin-Ping-Pooh'. Within a week, I had this little ditty going around my brain like a word worm. I shared it with a friend, and by early April, we had a song and a little movie called 'The Jin Ping Pooh Song' which I posted on YouTube.

For the next year and a half, we were subjected to lockdowns, bans on social gatherings, no household mixing, tiering systems, local lockdowns, partial lockdowns, bubbles, rule of 3, keep your distance, constant queues. Christmas is cancelled, and then miraculously, with a vaccine slowly being introduced, things started to calm down, and normality returned. Unless you were travelling overseas or a politician. Because surprise-surprise, whilst they were dishing out all these edicts, mandates and rules, they were merrily breaking them themselves, with gusto, enthusiasm and a heavy emphasis on merry.

# The Jin Ping Pooh Song

Jin Ping Pooh who gave us all flu
Put us in a stew
Made us feel blue
With Jin Ping Flu Jin Ping Flu

Jin Ping Pooh gave us death too
What can we do?
When we're caged in a zoo
With Jin Ping Flu Jin Ping Flu

Jin Ping Pooh gave the world flu
No paper for the loo
Only allowed groups of two
With Jin Ping Flu Jin Ping Flu

Jin Ping Pooh hasn't got a clue
As his virus flew
We all went achoo
With Jin Ping Flu Jin Ping Flu

Jin Ping Pooh gave us something
new It wasn't for the few
We all feel the screw
With Jin Ping Flu Jin Ping Flu

Jin Ping Pooh will say it's untrue
That he gave us the flu
But we all know it's true
With Jin Ping Flu Jin Ping Flu

**Wouldn't it be ironic if it went viral?**

In the midst of all this mayhem, I had a little myself. It was sweet and sour. The sweet bit was my father's ninetieth birthday, held in the garden of the old family home in Portchester. Did we break the rules of the day? Possibly. It was good to get together with family and friends, and my father held court in his own inimitable way, happy to see so many people together. He'd hated the lockdown but had a magnificent beard as a result. The sour bit was he died less than two months later. The Chinese got him. Not the flu. The food. He broke a cardinal rule— never reheat seafood, especially leftover Chinese prawns. Food poisoning knocked him out for a week, and just as he told me on the phone, "I thought I was a goner there, son!" he passed the next day on August 19th. I dropped everything and spent the next two weeks in Portchester helping my brother Mark sort everything out—the things you find. We had to laugh as secrets tumbled out of closets.

The funeral was on September 11th, and I had this to say as a tribute:

> *It's traditional at times like this to say a few words.*
>
> *Ralph (or Rope as he was called in the Navy) was certainly a man of many words.*
>
> *His father was a man of few words; his sons are men of few words, but his grandsons? They again have the words.*
>
> *What were those words?*

*There were loving words and crosswords.*

<u>*Loving words?*</u> *They would often pour out as he sat in his favourite chair in what we called 'Rum Corner'. With a rum in one hand, a pencil in the other and tears in his eyes, he would raise a glass to his beloved Jean, whose photo stood amidst his many books, "She was the love of my life and the most beautiful woman!"*

<u>*Crosswords?*</u> *They were mainly for Mark, of course, him being the naughty son.*

*Well, there's the obvious lie in this tribute!*

No. *The crosswords were one of Ralph's many interests. To help him, he had his many dictionaries, thesauruses, lexicons, and encyclopaedias of fables, phrases, mythology, and history.*

*Other words?*

- *There were lettered words. With his beautiful and treasured calligraphy, which will live on in homes and offices around the world.*
- *There were Japanese words, again written in his perfect handwriting, with his penfriend of many years – Yumi. He was perpetually fascinated with Japan.*

- *There were words of humour with his legendary ability to tell a joke and spin a yarn with long, shaggy dog stories about his time in the Navy.*
- *There were lewd words/rude words. Two ladies down the 'Wicor' are still blushing after the last words he ever said to them just a few short weeks ago.*
- *There were musical words often accompanied by one of his many guitars, mandolins or, indeed, banjos.*
- *There were technical words associated with his skills in Technical Drawing, Archery and Ropework.*
- *Rope was certainly a man of many words and many interests. He'd only just bought a new banjo and was talking about having lessons, along with finishing off yet another bottle – of ropework as well as of Rum!*

*Words to sum up Ralph?*
*I'll let you choose your own favourite:*
*The Navy, Rum, Pirate, Barnacle Bill, Portsmouth, Portchester, Father, Grandfather, Scribe, Artisan, Joker, Linguist, Talented.*
*He was certainly a meticulous, devoted, and dogged man determined to succeed in all his interests and endeavours. Obsessive even.*
*Ralph wasn't a man to say fond words about religion. He'd have preferred a picture of the pyramids or the Sun to be up there on the wall in place of the cross. He did once say that he was a four-wheel Christian—a pram for the christening, a car for the marriage and a*

*hearse for the funeral.*

*So here we are today to pay tribute to a man who has taken his final four-wheel journey.*

*To finish let us share together the toast he learnt from his mother's sister - Aunt Juliette (one of the seven Abbott sisters)*

*"Here's to them that wish us well; all the rest can go to hell."*

# *Tip #48: Keep things simple*

# CHAPTER 49
## *Open for Business*
### *Constant and never-ending investment*

It's a funny thing to become the patriarch of the family. When this all began, I had parents, grandparents, and great grandparents stretching back to the 1870s when the US Civil War had only just finished, and the fight for the right to be free and not be enslaved began. And now, here I was, the elder of the family. Sobering thought I can tell you.

Finally, at the end of May, two months into lockdown, the new website was ready and launched. Four days later, we had our first workshop with a boutique insurance broker and our first online purchases. It felt good to be back, open for business, and see the initial investment paying off. The key word in that sentence is 'initial'. The truth is you will never stop needing to invest in your business. If the seed money is £10,000, you will need at least another £50,000 over the next three years, either from investors or reinvestment from income. 'The Story of Building a Business' introduced in chapter 32 has it writ large right at the top of the page 'No Investment = No Growth'.

One of the investments made earlier in the year was with a design agency. I met Adam and Laurence of Bunker Creative through International Leaders. Adam would help me start assembling my keynote presentations and blog posts so they reflected the brand more cohesively. Eventually, they would completely revamp the website that we had just launched. As I said, 'Constant and Never-ending Investment' (CANI). Many business development gurus will talk about the need for constant and never-ending improvements (based on Dave Brailsford's cycling achievements at the 2012 Olympics). Those never-ending improvements are merely the output of making an investment at source. Have access to a great designer that gets what you're doing. Keep investing.

Almost immediately after the new site was launched, I was approached by someone who wanted to take the concept to another country. Was I ready for this? Probably not, but 'in for a penny in for a pound' as my grandfather would say. I had to make some quick choices legally and structurally. The options are company-owned subsidiaries, in-country partners, franchisees, affiliates, associates, or licensees. The licensee route made the most sense at this stage, and I had our lawyer draw up the necessary contracts. There's that investment angle again. Make sure you have a good lawyer. We also created a website recruitment portal so potential licensees had a structured application process and knew the fees and commitment in advance. This is tied to our company values and published in our induction documents.

*Our Values – Simple, Clear & Light*

*Simple: The cornerstone product is simple to understand and explain. Because it is simple, people remember it and therefore use it. Underlying this core simplicity is depth, which strengthens the model. Always remember that there is beauty in simplicity.*

*Clear: We want and seek clarity in everything we do. This is especially true with our clients. That is why all the pricing is visible and transparent. We love cutting through moribund organisations and breathing life into them.*

*Light: Lightness of spirit is crucial to all our people. A light touch can have a more positive effect than a heavy hand. Our favourite quote is, 'There is not a shred of evidence that life is serious'. We strongly urge people who do not align with our values to look elsewhere.*

I also had to ensure that I could train someone and bring them up to speed quickly so they were getting an immediate return on their investment. Thus, 'The Perfect Teams Academy' was created. Unfortunately, the first licensee walked away after two months and even though we had a two-year contract, I let her go in good faith. It's funny how things happen, though. As she walked, someone else appeared. Erika seamlessly flowed through the whole process, and by Christmas, we had our first international licensee in South Africa fully trained and ready to go.

Things had been opening up through the summer, and I did a couple of in-person workshops in September. What a delight it was to be physically engaging with people once again. The first workshop was for John's Vistage group; the second was for the Officer's Association. At this time, people started talking about blended or hybrid working, and it became apparent that the world of training, coaching, and team development would have to adapt. Case in point: I did two virtual training workshops, one for Henley Business School, the same week.

The other additional investment made at this time was in marketing. As you will know from Chapter 19 my relationship with what I call the dark arts of marketing is mixed, to say the least. My experience has always been direct and hands-on viz-a-viz the direct mail approach I'd taken with Carnegie: The best way to generate leads then was to promote an event and invite as many prospective businesspeople as you could find. Create the event itself and make it two hours of 'Wow' wrapped around something interesting. All you have to do is find the potential candidates, and that is a painstaking process of canvassing, trawling through business directories, and talking to past and existing clients. Once you have the names, positions, and addresses you would begin writing the envelopes, add a name to the pre-printed invitation, insert, seal, and lick the stamp. Sixty an hour was about the maximum, so 2,000 invites would take a couple of hours a day for two weeks. Two thousand invites would get you forty people in the room. Then the magic would start, and the selling could begin.

The truth is everything up to the event is marketing, and I know I'm repeating myself but I will say it again, "I hate it—such a ridiculous waste of time for a salesperson." The outcome of all this effort is the event, and once you've wowed the audience, you have the right to call them to make an appointment. "Great to see you this morning. How does your diary look?" The simple statistics were that you'd get thirty-six appointments and twelve contracts/clients if forty showed up. The process worked exceptionally well.

What's changed? I still need to identify the target audience, but now I need emails. I no longer need to write thousands of envelopes and lick stamps, but I need an email database and a mailer to distribute my invites. But I'm not allowed to load the mailer up with speculative emails because that is considered spamming. It's black humour at its darkest. I know there are 44,000 businesses in the UK that employ over 50 people. Thirty-six thousand of them employ 50 -500 people. 5% of them will invest in team development and team leader coaching each year, and that's 1,800 opportunities for Perfect Teams in the UK alone annually.

I've invested in marketing, but it hasn't really helped me address the scenario above.

## Tip #49: Keep investing

# CHAPTER 50
## A life in numbers
*10,000 days left ...*

"What was that?" I said to myself as I heard this almighty thump from the floor above. I rushed upstairs to find Caroline, staggering around with blood pouring down her face. I quickly told her colleagues left hanging on the virtual conference call, closed the office door and attempted to find out what had happened without much success. All I heard was some incoherent mumbling. I put her to bed in the rescue position and told her colleagues, who were still in their virtual meeting. They said Caroline had complained about feeling dizzy and had asked for a breather, which was when she fell. I disconnected the call and returned downstairs, occasionally checking on her. When she finally came around, she was fatigued, confused, and disoriented but appeared to be physically fine. Three days later, it happened again at the top of the stairs, and fortunately, she didn't tumble down. This time, though, she started fitting, frothing at the mouth, talking gibberish, with her arms and legs spasmodically flailing around. It was very dramatic indeed.

I called 999, and she was taken to St. Georges in Tooting. On February 3rd, four days later, a doctor called. They can't say if it was viral meningitis or encephalitis. Either way, a severe inflammation of the brain and dicey, whatever the prognosis. It's still full lockdown for hospitals, so I'm not allowed to visit. Unknown to me at the time, until I started getting concerned phone calls from Paul and Neil (an old partner at her previous firm) she was in full-blown paranoia, experiencing hallucinations that I was dead and calling them. Essentially, Caroline's brain was under severe strain with impaired cognition, sporadic seizures and difficulty in speaking, being the most common symptoms. It was three weeks before things settled down, and she could return home. Little did we realise that this was just the beginning of a cycle of seizures, hospital stays, and periods of meltdown now spanning three years. Encephalitis is an extremely misunderstood and relatively unknown condition affecting the central nervous system. She survived, which gets a tick. Will she ever regain her full cognitive faculties? Hard to say. She's lost her career in the city but rediscovered her love of drama, so the Worcester Park Amateur Dramatic Society (WPADS) is richer for having an ardent collaborator and supporter whenever she is able.

I know I've nearly died twice myself. I've seen some good friends suddenly taken. There are increasingly frequent entries in my diaries for funerals. On February 23rd, on a walk, I had the graphic realisation that I only had 10,000 days left if I'm fortunate, based on current actuarial tables. This was my diary entry the next day:

*Yesterday (Tuesday – February 23rd 2021), I had the realisation that, if I'm fortunate, I only have 10,000 days left. Now, that is a very finite number indeed and quite a sobering thought. So, if I only have 10,000 days - I need to make sure that each and every one is well used and that requires clear instructions ...*

*Live, Laugh, Love & Learn (or Vivens, Riscens, Amans, Discens for the scholars) was a motto I composed 27 years (or 10,000 days) ago, and it's time to ensure that each and every day is comprised with those ingredients at its core. Sure, there are other things like making money and enjoying the moment, but those four aspects of living, laughing, loving, and learning pretty much sum it up for me.*

What do you think? Am I missing anything? Because with only 10,000 days left, I want to use them for the best of my ability and not miss anything.

I've been acutely aware of time ever since I did my 'Time Management' seminars, wowing potential clients for Carnegie. It's also part of my make-up, my DNA. The first question I always ask is, "When?" The key message in the seminar is that there are only 8,760 hours in a year, and it's what you do with them that makes the difference. I remember one seminar where someone in the audience shouted out, "No wonder you don't have a problem with time. You've got more than us." I'd put 9,760 up on the flip-chart by mistake. To save you time, I'm going to include a summary here of my seminar:

There are 8760 hours in a normal year. It is the great equaliser in life. It cannot be managed, but what we do ourselves and how we invest the available time is the real issue. This concept should more appropriately be called 'Self-Management'.

As Henry Ford once said, "Successful people become successful in the time that others waste." Mozart had fully 20,000 hours of musical tuition between the ages of three and ten! Is it any wonder that he became a musical genius?

## *Three Levels of Commitment*

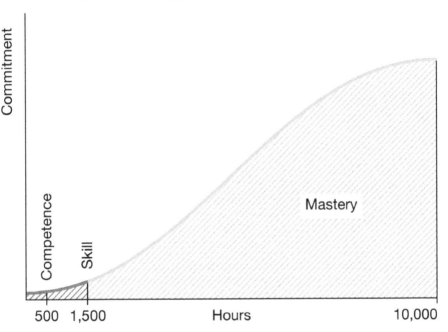

## *The Foundation of Mastery*

It takes 500 hours to become competent at something new, 1,000 hours to become proficient, 1,500 hours to become skilful, and 10,000 hours to master something. What areas do you want to invest your hours in?

In looking at 'Self-Management', there are some techniques that, if you were to adopt them, would help you better use the time available and become more efficient. There are seven techniques to adopt.

| 1 | Make Lists | Externalise the myriad of things calling for your attention. The conscious mind can only juggle and process 7±2 things at any one time. This is known as Miller's Magic No. 7. |
|---|---|---|
| 2 | Prioritise | Prioritise your lists in the order in which you are going to do things. |
| 3 | Quadrants | Be clear about the difference between 'Urgency' & 'Importance'. |

| 4 | 80/20 | Remember the 80/20 rule. Pareto was heard to say, "The important items on any given list are but a few of the trivial many". In modern parlance we refer to this as the 80/20 rule -that fully 80% of our productivity comes from 20% of the things we are called upon to do. What are your 80%ers? |
|---|---|---|
| 5 | Have Goals | If you don't know where you're going to you're unlikely to get there. Goals provide a focal point for your endeavours. Goals need to be short, medium and long term. Ask yourself, "Is what I'm about to do moving me closer to, or further away from, my goals?" |
| 6 | Beware Procrastination | Beware the dread disease known as 'Procrastination'. Mark Twain was fond of quoting, "If you're got to swallow a frog - do it quickly. If you've got to swallow two - then swallow the big one first!" Do the nasties first and free up your energy. |
| 7 | Keep a Time-Log | It is amazing how much time gets frittered away: by tiny inconsequential distractions. Be aware at all times where your time is being invested. |

# *Conclusion*

If you genuinely want to build your own value in your business, then learn how to manage yourself and your time. At the end of the day, the responsibility for being productive is yours alone, as there are only 8,760 hours in any given year. It is what we do with the hours— that will make the big difference. Mozart had eight hours of tuition and practice a day before he was ten. We will become competent if we do just an hour a day for a year to eighteen months. Three hours a day, and it becomes a skill.

Make your lists attend to the important rather than the urgent; do the things that have the maximum value. These are the things that count the most.

If I was to do the seminar today, I'd add another layer. A higher contextual layer, if you will.

How many days do you have left? My wake-up moment was realising it was only 10,000. That is 100 hundreds. In other words, 100 days is 1% of the time remaining for me, so I'd better make sure that each hundred days means something. A hundred days is a decent chunk of time. Make it count.

Bill Gates famously said, "People often overestimate what they can do in a year but underestimate what they can do in a decade."

# A life in numbers:

In a weird circularity, on November 20th, 2023, I'm coming to the end of the first 1,000 of my final 10,000. If I'm lucky, I'll get seven cycles of 14 years each for a total of 35,700 days. Everything becomes quite finite when you look at life in this way. It makes you appreciate the day you have and the moment you're experiencing.

As I write this, I can see my life in numbers:

2 – The number of times I nearly died; 2 sons; 2 wives; X girlfriends; 3 schools; 1 college; 5 universities; 10 ships;

19 addresses in 9 cities; 30 states; 44 countries; 23 jobs; 2 bankruptcies; 4 books; 25,185 days and counting.

Make every one of them count …

## *Tip #50: Do it today*

# CHAPTER 51
## Building a network
### Sceptical Horses

The days certainly counted in helping our 1ˢᵗ international licensee get up to speed. By spring, Erika was fully engaged and facilitating her own Perfect Teams workshops with her clients in South Africa. The first one she did was for thirty folks working for Rockwell. What was amazing to me was that someone I'd never physically met was using our IP in a foreign land. It was a beautiful realisation of our potential to help organisations anywhere, anytime, if we just build the network.

Life seemed to settle into a routine now of training, marketing, and delivering, which looked much slicker with the new keynote templates from Adam at Bunker. Every month, we would have a new article to post and use for promotion. We now have a library of thirty-five articles. They include Munch's Scream over Brexit, The Moon Landing, Identity and Diversity, Mission Statements, Teachers Not Leaders, and 11 Tips To Deal With Stress.

My favourite article, though, was the Sceptical Horse blog of July 20ᵗʰ, 2021, summarised below:

*What can you learn about creating, building, and sustaining your perfect team by comparing humans to horses? In this article, we are going to identify one of the key characteristics that separates humans from horses and highlight what that means for building a perfect team.*

*While preparing for a workshop with one of our clients, the company's CEO called to cancel the session. The company was a fast-growing, cutting-edge technology company, and around half of the team had PhDs. The team had the intellectual capacity to venture to the moon and back. When the CEO called us, he said he was getting a lot of pushbacks from the team, so much so that he did not want our facilitator to be subjected to their negativity and closed-mindedness.*

*I was on my early morning walk a week after the workshop was cancelled. It passes between two fields full of horses. Thinking back to the scepticism the CEO's team had shown towards the workshop, I was suddenly struck by a thought. A thought that literally stopped me dead in my tracks. I had never met a sceptical horse. Continuing with this train of thought, I realised that a horse operates purely in a sensory and instinctive way. Its brain does not have the ability to process information in an intellectual way as humans do.*

*Perfect teams are those in which different characters respect each other and do not judge. They balance the green (instinctive), red (emotional), and blue (intellectual) elements.*

*My client's team is heavily dominated by the blue (intellectual) element, whereas a horse is instinctive and sits in the green space— hence the comparison.*

*The team's reaction to the workshop told me that there is not much respect for other viewpoints within their team.*

*What might you notice in teams dominated by blue or green elements?*

1. **A team dominated by instinctive characters (the green element) over sceptical (intellectual, blue) characters:**

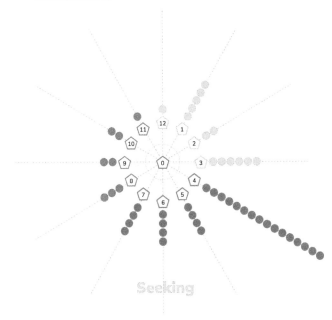

*As we can see, this first map shows a dominance of both red and green characters. This map is an example of a brokerage firm we worked with.*

*The organisation was dominated by ego and relationships, and the team members were focused on client acquisition and growth.*

*Most, if not all, of the time, though, that focus was not backed up by thoughts about processes and systems or the policies and procedures they needed to follow.*

*As a result, the team got into trouble with the regulators at the time, the FSA, a team that looked like this in our map below.*

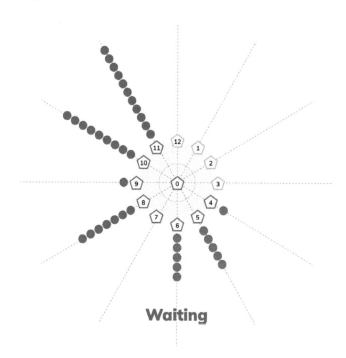

**Waiting**

*2. A team dominated by sceptical characters (the blue intellectual element) over instinctive characters (the green element).*

*Looking at this team map based on the compliance team at an International Clearing House, we can see that it is heavily dominated by blue characters - with few red and no green characters. It is a direct opposite of the previous map.*

*As you can imagine, with a compliance team, this group is focused on ensuring that rules, regulations, policies, and procedures are closely followed.*

*It is unsurprising that you would have had a total culture clash between the FSA and the brokerage firm.*

*From a business perspective, a team dominated by those blue characters will be heavily focused on the technical work of the business. It will usually lack any thirst for new relationships.*

*A world-class team?*

*Imagine, though, if you had a mix of the two teams. In this case, we recommended that the brokerage firm identify or recruit people dominated by the blue element to provide the structure and compliance element needed to balance out the current team.*

*Thinking back to the CEO's team earlier, by cancelling the workshop, the team will continue seeing the issues that come with being purely focused on the blue, process-driven world.*

*They need to identify the gaps that exist within their team and plug those with the appropriate people.*

*How balanced is your team? What gaps exist?*

But why was it my favourite? Because of the flack, it caused. One guy emailed me to say I was talking horse-shit. Another that I was off my rocker. If there's one thing I've learned in life, it's that how someone reacts to something (especially when they overreact) is indicative of how they react to everything. It's just their shit getting projected your way, and it never ceases to amuse me and make me laugh.

The emailer? He received the 'Knob-of-the-year' award.

We decided to step the marketing up a gear. We created a 'Coffee & Clues' morning geared towards helping businesses increase team engagement, which was deemed to be suffering due to the pandemic and WFH. I bought an email list from a broker of CEOs and Managing Directors in London and the home counties. Subscribing to an emailer was the next piece of the puzzle. I had the first two events in the summer of 2021. Two years later, we have now done fifteen. They get better each time and definitely bring in business. Sadly, they're not as joyous as those old early morning seminars we used to do with Carnegie. My next investment round will sort this conundrum out with an in-house database of those 44,000 businesses, with a well-oiled marketing team utilising it to its maximum benefit. I also want to see if direct mail and direct sales can work again.

The other area I started focussing on was using LinkedIn. At the beginning of 2021, I only had three hundred connections; today, we have nearly five thousand.

To say I was dismissive of the platform would be an understatement. I saw it as a complete waste of time. Social media was anathema to me. I bit my tongue and dipped my toes in the water. I followed the instructions: Be consistent; Be on message; Keep inviting; Keep interacting. I post daily. I write articles. I share things of interest, and some days it feels like something is happening, but mostly, to be honest, I feel like I'm farting in a thunderstorm! Ugh. I just felt it for the very first time since I started writing this book. A huge energy drain. It was like a 'Black-Hole' just appeared and sucked the living energy out of the universe. And that means that 'Marketing' and 'LinkedIn' are my 'Bêtes Noire. They need to be given to someone else because I detest them so much.

Listen to your energy and follow it.

On a more positive note, business was coming in. One of Rob B's team, Dave, is now a Perfect Teams champion. He is fully trained and accredited to facilitate workshops using the IP. The fabulous thing about Dave is that he gets higher Net Promoter Scores (NPS) than I do. You have to love it when the pupil outshines the maestro.

The highlights of the year?

- Getting the five-year cancer all-clear.

- A train trip to Geneva to work with Paul and his European Championship Management team.

- Getting to work with Dom and Simon of Selbey Andersen, who are building a dynamic marketing services group.

- This link will tell you what Dom thought of the process https://youtu.be/F6sh_ZENKLU

## *Tip #51: Follow your energy*

# CHAPTER 52
## *The magnificent Central Hall Westminster*
### *50 years later*

There's a fundamental difference between buying and selling. Nobody wakes up in the morning and says to themselves, "Today I'm going to buy insurance or a 'Perfect Teams' workshop." That was the core theme of that leaflet that guy in Grafton, North Dakota, had given me all those years ago, Albert Gray's essay, 'The Common Denominator of Success'. 'Successful people do the things that failures don't like to do', and most people don't like going out seeking people or prospects who don't want to buy. It's unnatural and goes against our natural inclination to want to be liked and accepted. Recognise that the percentage of people who are ready and willing to buy from you is infinitely smaller than the pool of people you can yet convince.

The fundamental dislike with selling is that we do not like to call on people who do not want to see us and talk to them about something they do not want to discuss. Successful people are influenced by the desire for pleasing results. Failures are influenced by the desire for pleasing methods. It is easier to sell to people who do not want what we have than it is to find people who do want it. Good salespeople prospect for needs regardless of wants and call on people who are able to buy but unwilling to listen, rather than willing to listen but unable to buy. Selling is, therefore, about uncovering a need someone didn't know they had in the first place. When you walk away, either you've sold or you've been sold. When you've sold, you've convinced them of the benefits and value of what you have to offer. When you've been sold, they've convinced you why they can't buy.

Early in 2022, I actually had a buyer. Now a buyer is someone who has done their research, knows what they want and is now seeking a solution. Jake had been on one of my webinars the year before and liked what he saw. He now wanted to talk to me about doing something for one of his clients and asked if we could talk. His client was a significant plc, and they were having their first conference for six hundred people in three years at Central Hall Westminster (CHW). Would I like to do a keynote presentation? The answer was an immediate yes! CHW is the most magnificent of venues, facing Westminster Abbey and across the square from the Houses of Parliament.

The Great Hall, where I was presenting, seats 2,200 and has the biggest organ I have ever seen. It hosted the first meeting of the United Nations in 1946, and the Jules Rimet world cup trophy, that England had just won, was stolen from there in 1966. As you can imagine, I was thrilled at the chance to present on such a stage, and yes, I got them to do 'The Grand Old Duke Of York'. You can see the results yourself by following this link: https://youtu. be/p-d6kHGeE-4 What was good about this was I wasn't just a 'One-Hit-Wonder' like Thunderclap Newman's 1969 'Something in the Air'; I had a second hit later in the year at another big event held at the Odeon, Leicester Square. Admittedly, they didn't have the 'Red Carpet' out for me, but I loved it, nonetheless.

2022 was a watershed year for me and Perfect Teams. We revamped the website yet again, Web 3.0, to reflect our more focussed approach, that Perfect Teams was about increasing team engagement and performance. Perhaps another buyer calling was an indication that things had matured. Tracey was now the operations director for an international car dealership, and she wanted me to do a workshop and coach a couple of the key people in the organisation. How could I refuse?

Earlier in the year, my publisher reminded me that it was the 25th anniversary of 'The A-Z of Positive Thinking' and that we should do a twenty-fifth edition to mark the occasion. I delivered the script to Chris late in March, and it was published on September 8th. It was not a good day to publish anything because something else happened that day. The Queen had died. Talk about a good day to bury a story, pun intended!

September was also memorable for me because we had our 50th cadet reunion in Southampton. There had been two before over the years. The 25th in 1997 at Townhill Park House, where all fifty-six of us had stayed for the first year, was just a dinner and drinks. The 40ᵗʰ at Droitwich Spa in 2012 was a short weekend. This was three days with a trip to the old house and a cruise on the steam ship S.S. Shieldhall out to the Solent and back. Caroline said the whole weekend was like being with seventeen 68-year-old teenagers, which I'll take as a massive compliment. It's amazing how the years just peel away, and you can still see the young lads in the old faces. In no particular order, it was great to see again the three Kevs, Iolo, Steve, Jimmy, Johnny, John, David, Andy, Guy, Carl, Jerry, Rod, Tom, and Glen, who had only just retired, being the youngest of our year. Missing were Simon, Chris F. and Dave G. Sadly missed was Big Sammy. One of the Kevs, Manx, sowed a seed that would come to fruition the following summer.

Caroline was getting fully engaged with WPADS. Am-Dram was evidently good for her. She certainly enjoyed helping out with 'Front-of-house' at all their performances. She'd even written a one-act play and recited it at the summer festival. With this in mind, I put her on the company payroll with the view that she'll continue to rehabilitate and grow into the role of our 'Events Manager'. We, therefore, polished off the year with our first-ever Perfect Teams Christmas party at Randall & Aubin's, a classic seafood bistro on Brewer Street in the heart of Soho. There'll be more there this year.

At the reunion, Kev planted the seed of an idea to do a mammoth walk on the Isle of Man, which, of course, is where 'Manx' is from. It's called the 'Parish Walk' because it goes past the eighteen parish churches on the island. The total walk is eighty-five miles, which has to be done within twenty-four hours, but there is a shorter one of just thirty-two and a half miles, which finishes in Peel where Kev lives. Kev has regularly done it in under seven and a half hours. I had some training to do.

I'm coming to the end of this story as it currently stands. With luck, there'll be another 9,000 days' worth to be told one day. The highlights so far this year have been:

- A new promotional video, https://youtu. be/0DUWaf6HdzM
- A new licensee in the education field.
- Erika in South Africa facilitating a Perfect Teams workshop with a multinational AI team in Costa Rica, Canada, USA, Kenya, Uganda, and South Africa simultaneously.
- The beginning of the Perfect Teams book 'What's Your Number?'
- Web 4.0 (there's that constant investment point being reinforced)
- Being told by a random stranger, "You've got lovely eyes!"
- This book itself.

Rob B. asked me to do a presentation at International Leaders on February 23rd. I'd been toying with the concept of Listening, Laughing and Learning since the beginning of the year, and this opportunity gave me a chance to test it on the road. It was exceptionally well received. Fortunately, Rob had his videographer record it, so you can watch it here: https://youtu. be/xyehO88mOXA

I started training for the Parish Walk in the new year. I had followed my formula of increasing the weekly long walks until I could comfortably do twenty miles. I then plotted a route to Box Hill and back, going up and over Epsom Downs. A glorious route that takes you along Stane Street, the old Roman road from Chichester to London, and past Lord Beaverbrook's grand old pad at Cherkley Court, south of Leatherhead, and now a Five Star Hotel. It's precisely a marathon, and I completed it twelve times between the beginning of February and the end of May. I also did two thirty-mile yomps by stretching the walk to Guilford along the North Downs. I knew I could do the distance, but what about the time? I figured we'd find out on the day.

Caroline and I flew to the Isle of Man on Mid-Summer's Day, three days before the race. Kev and Erika were brilliant hosts, and both mad about motorbikes with a garage full of them. The morning that we arrive, there's a tribute lap of the famous TT circuit in honour of a racer who died two weeks before competing in the races. I'm duly putting on borrowed leathers and riding pillion with Kev around the circuit on a Triumph Bonneville. What an introduction to the Isle of Man. It couldn't have been better. By the time I left I could visualise the TT circuit in my mind's eye. I was also determined to get myself another motorcycle.

The race itself was on Saturday, June 24th, starting at the National Sports Arena in Douglas. When it started, like any mass sports event, you're all bunched up, and it takes a while to get into your stride, but after half a lap of the running track, you can see the leading race walkers already heading out, never to be seen again. After a mile, I said to Kev, "How can this many people walk this fucking fast?" It was a revelation to me. I consider myself pretty fit and can walk three and a half miles an hour till the cows come home, but this lot were doing four, four-and-a-half, five miles an hour and a lot of them were not athletic of shape. I did pretty well for the first four hours, passing the halfway point at a steady four miles per hour, but I suddenly just ran out of gas. The next hour was hell. It was also a long, slow, relentless hill. Somehow, at the end of it, I regained my mojo and managed to get to Peel in eight hours and thirty-three minutes. Kev, bless him, had stayed with me despite my constant instructions to bugger off and go ahead, so we crossed the line together. Not too shabby for two old gits. My new goal? The whole thing. All eighty-five miles.

## Tip # 52: Keep making goals

## Part Six – Leader

# CHAPTER 53
## A quarter of a billion steps

### The first supper

I asked my friend Dan Bowyer how he had managed to add over 9,000 connections on LinkedIn in the last year. He said, "Find your community and engage with them in a 2-way conversation."

Perhaps that's my issue. I've been such a lone wolf (and proud of it) for so many years now that my insularity and independence mean I don't have a community or a tribe to communicate with.

As you can tell from reading this far, I like marathon running, endurance walking, solitude, self-reflection, reading, smoking Havana cigars, Scandi Noir, movies, and motorcycles. All prime activities of a lone wolf, right?

I am also, despite my contrary nature, driven to develop, grow, and promote Perfect Teams. I believe it will be the team development instrument of choice for the 21st Century.

I've always been active ever since I took my first baby steps back in Portchester. I took those first steps to the end of the driveway to wait for Steve to come home from kindergarten and tell me what a 'Copper' was. For many years, I kept running logs, so I know I was running an average of six to seven miles per day, let alone what I was walking. Some weeks, I would do over a hundred, so it's fair to assume that I have averaged at least 10,000 steps a day all my life. That roughly works out at 251,850,000 or a quarter of a billion steps. To get to where I am, I couldn't have missed one of them. I don't want to do my next steps alone.

I want to build Perfect Teams into the 'Rolex' of team development, for it to be the tool of choice whenever someone is looking to create a team, make it more productive, more engaged, more profitable.

It's challenging to summarise a lifetime's work as a proposition for potential 'Perfect Teams' investors. Below is my succinct summary:

- *Create a 'World-Class' team that delivers outstanding results.*

- *Perfect Teams shows businesses and organisations how to get it right quickly, efficiently and cost-effectively.*

- *Perfect Teams should be the first point of contact whenever anyone is:*

1. *Considering putting a team together or*
2. *Wishes to ascertain if they have the*
   a. *Right mix,*
   b. *Right dynamics,*
   c. *Right communication, and*
   d. *Right skill sets in place.*

*Perfect Teams will help you add value:*

1. *By getting it right the first time,*
2. *Provide you with a road map,*
3. *Show you how to do it,*
4. *Save you money, and more importantly,*
5. *Save you time exactly when you need it most –*
   a. *At the start of building your business,*
   b. *Restructuring it because it has functionally gone awry,*
   c. *Communication has broken down,*
   d. *Your team leaders have not been trained on how to lead a team.*

*Teams don't work unless you have the right people, good leadership, and brilliant communication, especially with regard to vision, purpose, and culture. For that to happen, I'm looking for smart, bright, intelligent, educated, instinctive, and clever people to walk with me. People with business, marketing, sales, advertising, promotion, logistics, planning, relationship, finance, leadership, social, and training skills.*

*Therefore, I am looking for twelve like-minded individuals with the desire and drive to help me build Perfect Teams into a global brand. Those who get involved will be my community, along with friends, associates, and clients, past, present, and future. My vision is to have a 'First Supper' at the Hyatt Churchill Library on Portman Square in November with myself and the first dozen advocates who are committed to helping me take Perfect Teams to the world.*

*If you are sports-minded, enthusiastic, entrepreneurial, ambitious, visionary, motivated, a maverick and desire to be a part of something revolutionary, get in touch. I'm looking forward to building a community and hosting our 'First Supper'.*

## Tip #53: Share your vision

# CHAPTER 54
## *What's next?*

### *The Great Con*

How do you finish a story that is still unfolding? Do I leave you hanging? Do I create an open loop? A what if? The beautiful thing about life is that it keeps growing, evolving, and unfolding from within. What's next? It will always be a surprise.

If someone tells you with certainty that they have the secret, that this is the solution to all your problems, it's a scam, a con. Solutions are never external fixes; they are always internal. Instant returns. Instant salvation. Instant wealth. Run a mile. We can save you, fix you, make you right. It's bullshit.

All you can do is listen, learn, and watch for the signposts that will help you find your own path.

If someone says, you should do this. Be very wary. Religions and cults just love to tell you what you should do. Religion could very well be the biggest lie ever told.

Become your own person. I'm in danger of overstating the obvious, but that will always be about you discovering your own sense of independence. Being around needy, dependent people will drain your energy.

I want to be surrounded by independent, strong, vigorous, forthright, exciting, energetic, enthralling, captivating, interesting, amusing, and galvanising people. People who can create and people who make things happen. People who seek and find solutions. You may desire this, too. For this to happen, you need to be independent yourself. I'm still working on it myself. I am not the finished article.

An aside: The Grand Art of the 'Con'

Once upon a time, I was involved with an organisation that started to feel a bit like a con. I was avidly ploughing through Terry Pratchett's works at the time, and in his book 'Going Postal' I read this:

'You get the punt – you get others so deeply involved that they don't dare fold. It's the dream, you see. They think that if they stay in, it'll all work out. They daren't think that it's all a dream. You use big words to tell them it's going to be jam tomorrow, and they 'hope'. But they'll never win. Part of them knows that, but the rest of them never listens to it. THE HOUSE ALWAYS WINS'.

I laughed as I read it, and the bubble of 'illusion' immediately popped. My eyes opened, and I saw that 'the emperor had no clothes'. For me, the con was over. Sadly, for others, it continued. Just like John said all those years ago, "People are always chasing and seeking the pot of gold at the end of the rainbow. No. It's never there. It's here now (and pointing). It's right there. You're sitting on it!"

Perhaps that's the last word. Be a maverick. Call it out. Challenge and dare to say to authority, "The Emperor has no clothes" or "He looks like Winnie-the-Pooh."

# QED

## *Bonus Tip #54: Call it out. Be brave*

# *Afterword*

Perhaps you have to get to the end of writing a book to know what it's truly about. The final editing process has required me to read through this book fourteen times so far. Chapter 34 talks about the difference between content and context.

I can categorically tell you content is energy draining especially when you have to go through it fourteen times! However, it is amazing how easy it is to discover what the context is. It jumped out and slapped me across the face like a wet fish. The context for this book is 'Self-Responsibility' and as I write this I can hear a whole gallery of giggling ghosts guffawing and holding their sides with glee saying, "Have you heard the latest? You won't believe it but Neil, yes Neil, has written a whole book about, wait for it, responsibility!". Ha-Ha-Ha. Ho-Ho-Ho.

In the 'Author's Statement' at the beginning I say, "… a life lived is continually unfolding … it's never going to be the perfect finished article … this book doesn't presume to be an idealised, utopian blueprint on how to live the perfect life …". But what if it was a step in the right direction? What if my 'Clarion Call' is 'To be a messenger for the virtues of 'Self-Responsibility'?'

There's no chance I'll ever be a 'Paragon' of self-responsibility, the ideal example, the perfect embodiment of the idea, the model of excellence (because I am not a saint) but I do know society needs people who aspire to be such.

My wish is that this book helps you to take that step yourself towards independence because that is where 'freedom' truly exists, and free people make things happen with joy, laughter, and love.

Let's all take that step together.

Neil Tuson - April 12th, 2024

# APPENDICES
## Appendix 1
### 45 beaches from Malibu - Newport

| | | | | | |
|----|----------------|----|----------------|----|------------------|
| 1  | Malibu         | 16 | Dockweiler     | 31 | Cherry           |
| 2  | Carbon         | 17 | Manhattan      | 32 | Long Beach       |
| 3  | Las Tunas      | 18 | Playa Hermosa  | 33 | Rosies Dog       |
| 4  | Topanga        | 19 | Hermosa        | 34 | Belmont Shore    |
| 5  | Castle Rock    | 20 | Redondo        | 35 | Bay Shore        |
| 6  | Will Rogers    | 21 | Topaz          | 36 | Seal Beach       |
| 7  | Ginger Rogers  | 22 | Torrance       | 37 | Surf Side        |
| 8  | Montana        | 23 | Terranea Cove  | 38 | Sunset           |
| 9  | Santa Monica   | 24 | Abalone Cove   | 39 | Bolsa Chica      |
| 10 | Venice         | 25 | Palos Verdes   | 40 | Huntington       |
| 11 | Muscle         | 26 | Royal Palms    | 41 | Huntington State |
| 12 | Driftwood      | 27 | White Point    | 42 | Santa Ana        |
| 13 | Marina Del Rey | 28 | Cabrillo       | 43 | 15th Street      |
| 14 | Charlie        | 29 | Alamitos       | 44 | Balboa           |
| 15 | Playa Del Rey  | 30 | Juniper        | 45 | Newport          |

# Appendix 2
## Cynthia's story (Chapter 15)

I had never been on a farm before. I'd spent all my life immersed in the dark, sharp, grey shapes of the city. So that first evening, just before the bright yellow sun started to dip towards the far distant horizon, I left the farmhouse and started to explore. Just to the left was a small winding lane gently descending to who knows where. 'And that's where I shall go,' I said to myself.

A little way down, around a couple of tight bends, I spotted a gap in the high hedgerows. Guarding the way into a huge field was a five-bar gate. I clambered over, and reaching the crest of a small hill, I stopped. At the bottom of the lush green valley, I saw a bright, clear pool of water. I started towards it. It was a beautiful evening. The sun was playing with the colours in the trees, bushes, and grass, so vivid, so fresh, so lucid. There were a lot of ducks at the pond, flying, paddling, feeding, and playing.

'How different the country is,' I thought. 'How fresh, how freeing, so clean, so full of wonder.' Suddenly, my thoughts were interrupted. I became aware that I was not alone. Something, somebody, was watching and coming towards me! I turned around and froze. There was something. It was huge. It was looking at me, and worse still, it was coming at *speed straight towards me. I didn't know what it was and, at that precise instant, didn't care either. I just turned tail and ran down the hill as fast as my little legs could take me. As I ran, I kept looking over my shoulder. It was still there and getting closer. I redoubled my efforts and, petrified, glanced back one more time. Suddenly, I tripped over my very own feet. Tumbling and falling to the ground, I cried to myself, 'Oh, no! I'm going to die. My very first day in the country, and I'm about to be killed.' (Suddenly, the big city looked so much safer, brighter, nicer). I lay there in a tiny heap, seeing my short but eventful seven-year-old life flash by, frame by frame. Nothing happened. I continued to wait for the now accepted inevitable, but still nothing. Still alive but shocked, I peeked out from under my arm. Through my curly, brown fringe, I could see with bright, blue eyes that it was still there. It was huge, and it was still looking at me with great, dark, black eyes. It was motionless, just quietly observing, waiting. 'But waiting for what?' I thought. Feeling a little braver and slightly less scared, I raised myself to my knees. Then, slowly to my feet. Whatever it was, it was now studiously ignoring me. Feeling much braver now (I was, after all, from the city), I decided to approach this thing and ever so slowly started to walk towards it. As I did so, the intimidating figure turned and started to walk away from me! I began to walk quicker now, feeling quite powerful, and it too started to walk quicker. It was about ten paces away, and I began to run, wanting to catch this huge thing. It was too quick, however and disappeared to the other side of the field, watching carefully lest I approach. I laughed with a combination of relief, courage, and joy. Walking down to the water's edge, I sat and pondered over what had happened. I gradually realized that there was a lesson for life here, that this big old cow (for that's all it was) had enabled me to begin to discover one of life's many unfolding secrets.*

*Years later, I realized that sometimes I went through periods of my life always looking over my shoulder, running away from things, issues, confrontations, problems, and events that were causing me pain and making me fearful. Sometimes, I ran away so hard, so fast, that my fears became fully realized, and I'd trip up and lay there all bloodied and bruised, paralyzed with fear, quaking, incapable of doing anything, doing nothing, just like my encounter with the cow of my childhood. 'Well, the next time I have one of these fears, one of these issues coming my way, I'm going to do what I did as a child,' I said to myself, 'I'm going to look it straight in the eye, stand up, look it straight on, see it for what it is, and run straight at it. I'm going to face up to my fears, accept them for what they are and then they will vanish just like my cow did.'*

# *Appendix 3*

**PERFECT
TEAMS**
A C A D E M Y

# Lead Your Business
Decision Making

PAPER 1:9

As soon as
questions of
will, decision,
reason or choice
of action arise,
human science
is at a loss."

Noam Chomsky

# Overview

"Should I stay or should I go?" This great song by The Clash sums it all up. The problem of decision-making revolves around that one little word – 'OR'.

To decide – comes from the Latin 'Decidere which means 'To Cut'. Deciding something, settling something, resolving something, therefore means making a cut between one thing or another. If you reflect back on the big decisions we all make in life you will see the same recurring pattern.

This great polarization is known philosophically as dualism. We all reach points in life, which in hindsight we call 'Crossroads', where we are faced with the decision of do we go 'Left or Right', 'Straight-on or Back'? The thing is, and what most people do not know, it is the OR that causes the problem; it becomes the issue and spawns the frustration, the indecisiveness and the procrastination, and creates arguments, anger and angst. If there was a better way, would that be worth looking at? Would it be worth considering?

Yes? Then read on OR stop now. The decision is yours...

| | | | With respect to |
|---|---|---|---|
| **Stay** | or | **Go** | Relationships – Jobs – Schools – Location |
| **This** | or | **That** | Things – Buying – Choosing |
| **Yes** | or | **No** | Health choices – Drink – Drugs – Diet – Marriage – Kids |
| **A** | or | **B** | Houses – Cars – Holidays |
| **Left** | or | **Right** | Directions – Forks-in-the-road – Forwards – Backwards |
| **For** | or | **Against** | Position – Politics – Ideas – Platforms |
| **Mind** | or | **Matter** | |
| **Me** | or | **You** | |
| **In** | or | **Out** | Commitment – Voting – Remain – Brexit |
| **Save** | or | **Spend** | Money – Resources – Rent – Buy |
| **Keep** | or | **Throw** | Possessions – Memories – Stuff – Letters – Photos |
| **Do** | or | **Do-Not** | Safety – Risk – Chances – Gambles |

# Decision Making

There's an old proverb that says, "If it's misty in the pulpit it's going to be foggy in the pews!" How clear is your thinking and decision-making? It is certainly not a subject found on the school curriculum. This paper will give you a decision-making tool you will use for the rest of your life. If you wish to move from confusion to clarity and be seen to be more powerful and decisive, then make sure you continue to read.

## AN IDEA

You come home from work one day and you are all excited about an idea you have had for a fantastic holiday. Sat around the table after supper you are about to share your wonderful idea, when your partner crisply announces, "I know where we should go for our holiday this year", and before you can even interject and say, "That's amazing. I've had a wonderful idea too...". "South Africa. That's where we will go this year", and promptly leaves the room failing to see the dismay in your face as you have been thinking, and getting excited, about Paris all day.

*The Mist and the Fog*

Sounds familiar? How long do you think that argument is going to go on for? Will you even manage to get your partner to sit down and listen?

[Communication skills and awareness are obviously a factor here too, along with assertiveness and interpersonal abilities!]

# A Framework

I want to go to Paris; I want to go to South Africa – Impasse or Solution?

Let us look at this in more detail. There is what is called a contextual disparity going on here. Logically you have two people who have taken a position around Paris or South Africa. Let us call that problem 'A or B'.

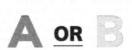

Whenever anyone takes a position or stakes a claim, they immediately marshal all their arguments and gather all their evidence for that cause.

I want to go to Paris because of 1, 2, 3 – X, Y, Z...

No. I want to go to South Africa because of X, Y, Z – 1, 2, 3...

Each time a position is stated the argument becomes more firmly entrenched and embedded. The barriers are built. The fortifications become stronger. The barricades become higher. Taken to its logical conclusion war, death and famine will ensue.

What is happening is that the position and evidence is all about the detail – The Content – and what is missing is a context that can make sense of it all and show you a way out of the quagmire.

What is context I hear you ask? – A quick illustration.

We have a group of items. Let us say we have:

---

**Apples** - Bananas - Pears - **Oranges**

---

What makes sense of them all? – The answer, of course, is fruit.
Let us represent it this way – by providing a simple framework.

---

**Fruit**

**Apples** - Bananas - Pears - **Oranges**

---

Fruit is the contextual framework that makes sense of everything that sits below.
What you have done is stepped up one contextual level from the content to the context.
However, is the new bundle of content that fruit now sits besides? That could be:

---

**Fruit** - Vegetable - Grain - **Fish** - **Meat**

---

And what makes sense of all that?

---

Food

**Fruit** - Vegetable - Grain - **Fish** - **Meat**

---

You can keep stepping up the contextual levels as shown. Food sits alongside:

---

Food - **Air** - **Water** - **Shelter** - **Heat**

---

And that is about:

---

**Life**

Food - **Air** - **Water** - **Shelter** - **Heat**

---

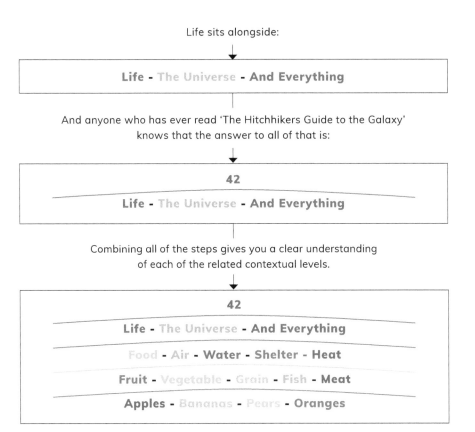

Life sits alongside:

**Life -** The Universe **- And Everything**

And anyone who has ever read 'The Hitchhikers Guide to the Galaxy' knows that the answer to all of that is:

**42**

**Life -** The Universe **- And Everything**

Combining all of the steps gives you a clear understanding of each of the related contextual levels.

**42**

**Life -** The Universe **- And Everything**

Food **- Air - Water - Shelter - Heat**

**Fruit -** Vegetable **-** Grain **- Fish - Meat**

**Apples -** Bananas **-** Pears **- Oranges**

Context, then, is simply stepping up a level and making sense of all the content that sits below. The secret is to be, just one step ahead of your audience. If you are too far removed you will lose them totally and appear to be an out-of-touch space cadet. If I should start waxing lyrical about the need for shelter in sustaining indigenous life in the Arctic and you are there to find out more about pork belly futures there is not going to be an iota of understanding or comprehension between us.

Back to our fruit – let us say you had to choose between an apple, a banana, a pear and an orange. Commercially this could be any meeting that involved a choice between a number of competing ideas, pet-projects or proposals. Usually if one was to make a choice it would be done at a content level and you would have a merry-go-round of an apple, or a banana, or a pear, or an orange. Everyone will be fighting their corner for the apple solution, or people making side trades – I'll back your pear idea this time as long as you back my orange solution next time. If, however, we set a context of say Vitamin C for making the decision:

---

**Vitamin C**

**Apples** - Bananas - Pears - **Oranges**

---

**We would all immediately pick the orange.**

**If we become clear at a contextual level first, the resolution and decision will also be instant and crystal clear. The secret to good, quick, clear decision making is to work at the contextual level.**

Back to our earlier couple and the impending war over a holiday, - rather than marshalling our forces for the details of where to go, let us look at why they would want to go on holiday in the first place. The reasons could be Novelty, Romance and / or Adventure. If our couple were to choose romance where would they go?

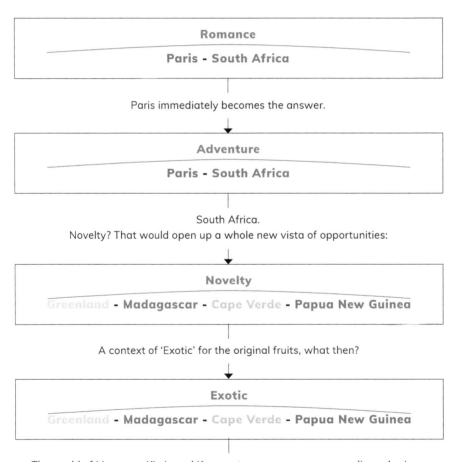

**Romance**

Paris - South Africa

Paris immediately becomes the answer.

**Adventure**

Paris - South Africa

South Africa.
Novelty? That would open up a whole new vista of opportunities:

**Novelty**

Greenland - **Madagascar** - Cape Verde - **Papua New Guinea**

A context of 'Exotic' for the original fruits, what then?

**Exotic**

Greenland - **Madagascar** - Cape Verde - **Papua New Guinea**

The world of Mangoes, Kiwis and Kumquats now appear on our culinary horizon.

# Application

The overall idea of the illustrated framework is to make sense amidst chaos. The tool is of most use when you cannot see the wood for the trees, or when you find yourself going round and round. Context gives you a helicopter view of the problem, issue or decision you are grappling with. [See Story 1 for an illustration of this concept]. Sometimes making a decision simply requires imagination as well as a process.

| | Process Rules |
|---|---|
| 1 | Always start by performing a complete mind-dump of all the issues and competing ideas onto large sheets of paper, or a large white-board. |
| 2 | Start to categorise and cluster the issues together. Look for the common themes that will emerge from the depths. |
| 3 | Chunk up by looking for the three sub-texts of what makes sense of everything. |
| 4 | Identify the single word that has the highest energy and leverage, - this is your emerging 'Context'. |
| 5 | Do not worry, and do not get too hung-up if you get the wrong word, or the wrong context. You will obtain feedback soon enough indicating whether you are on the right path. The feedback will point you in the right direction. [See Story 2 for a graphic illustration of this!] |
| 6 | If there is still an A or B question pending you are still in the divisive content. |
| 7 | Context takes you to an inclusive level where the conversation is about A and B. |
| 8 | Remember that content will always be energy draining. It is hard work. |
| 9 | Notice that context is energizing. |
| 10 | Test your decision. |
| 11 | Seek out feedback from people who like you but care about your feelings and attachments. Allow them to give you honest, robust criticism. Welcome it! |
| 12 | And last but by no means least – words of wisdom from a friend of mine – "Neil. You've thought of everything except for the possibility that you may be wrong!" Thank you Gary K. |

# Conclusion

As a leader, or a coach, you need to remain one contextual level away from the people you are leading or working with. If you do not you will end up being pulled into the mire. Transference will happen. You will end up 'going native', and find the tail wagging the dog. When this happens you will get feedback very quickly as you will notice your energy draining away.

The trick is to be just one contextual level above. That way you can provide leadership, clarity and guidance. Two contextual levels away and people will start to feel disconnected from you. Three contextual levels away and you will be seen to be aloof, arrogant and out-of-touch. People will say you do not have the 'common touch', you no longer have an interest in them, or that you have no idea of the 'real world'. You will be seen to be sitting in your 'Ivory Tower'.

**Leaders have clarity - the five C's**

Clarity

Context

**Content**

**Chaos & Confusion**

### AN ASIDE

*It is fast becoming a modern day truism that algorithms are often more accurate than human judgment. With the increasing advent of Artificial Intelligence [AI] watch this space.*

# Appendices

## STORY 1: THE HELICOPTER

"Do you remember that time we took James and his friends to Longleat for his birthday?"

"I most certainly do Mr. Cheat," she laughed.

"It wasn't cheating. It was helping," I laughed back.

"So what on earth has the maze at Longleat got to do with decision making?" she asked.

"Well they were just amazed at how easily we all got to the centre and back, weren't they?"

"They sure were."

"So buying the aerial postcard of the maze before we went in was quite a useful tool wouldn't you agree?"

"It was."

"Well in decision-making the most useful tool you can have is a helicopter view of the problem or issue, which means you have to have all the facts, all the facets laid out. One way of doing that is to externalize everything from your head onto one sheet of paper so that you can examine the complete landscape. What do you think happens as you do this?" I prompted.

"Well I can see that it's going to stop your mind going round and round in circles as you purge all the competing ideas."

"It does that and more. What else do you think will happen?"

"Well once I start to empty my mind it'll have room to breath again, and fresh ideas will start to come through."

"That's for sure. What also happens is that long forgotten and dormant nuances emerge from the sub-conscious, and this produces a much richer and creative process. Once you have mined your mind you can then examine what you've brought to the surface, but because you are above it and not grubbing around within it you can start to make sense of what is laid out in front of you."

"Well that makes complete sense," she responded.

"Good I'm glad you like it. To me this is the most critical component of decision-making. The technical term for it is 'Context-Content'. The helicopter view is representative of a definitive context. When you know what makes sense of everything that lies below you get incredibly energized. You are no longer lost in the maze or wallowing in the details and chasing your tail round and round."

*"The man who is denied the opportunity of taking decisions of importance begins to regard as important the decisions he is allowed to take."*

**C. Northcote Parkinson**

## STORY 2: THE FORK IN THE ROAD

I was talking with a colleague about decision-making. About the various critical points, the inevitable crossroads. He said, "I had a literal fork-in-the-road experience". "Tell me about it", I said.

"My wife and I had left Toronto to take a year out in Phoenix, Arizona. We were both somewhat jaded and disillusioned with our current careers. Having recharged our batteries and rekindled our relationship we decided to get back in the race. I had three firm opportunities. One was with an up and coming coffee concern in Seattle. Another was back in Toronto with a major marketing services agency. The third was in Norwalk, Connecticut at the brand new US headquarters of Labatt's brewery. Before leaving Phoenix I had already discounted the first option. This left Toronto or Norwalk? The second night on the road we treated ourselves to a night in the Union Station Hilton in St. Louis. We were downtown near the legendary Busch Stadium and had a fabulous view of the iconic Gateway Arch from our hotel room. Early the next morning we hit the road, still undecided on which destination we were heading for. Twenty miles and thirty minutes later, outside St. Louis and near a place called Troy, I came across my fork in the road! Straight on was route I-55, towards Chicago and Toronto – to the right and east was I-70 towards Pittsburgh and whole new unknown opportunities in New England. Decision time was getting closer. We looked at each other. We shrugged our shoulders, rolled our eyes and I swung the car right onto I-70 east. I had literally gone half a mile and my wife burst into floods of tears. As I now know, when it comes to decision-making, the universe gives you real quick feedback if you've made the right or wrong decision. Well, without a word, six miles and as many minutes later I took the off ramp and swung left and north on Highway 4 to rejoin I-55 and the road back to Toronto. Right/Wrong? Who knows? I do know that the HQ in New England moved back to Canada a few years later – that we've been married twenty-five years – and I've had a stunning career in marketing and advertising running major agencies around the globe".

# The Perfect Teams Academy

**CALL US TO FIND OUT MORE**

## ADDITIONAL RESOURCES

### THIS PAPER
· Additional copies £20.00 each
· Just let us know how many copies you require.

### OTHER PAPERS
· The Art of Facilitation – Paper 2:2
· Interpersonal Management Skills – Paper 2:11
· The Art of Managing Expectations – Paper 3:3

### RECOMMENDED
· 'The Empty Raincoat – Making Sense of the Future' by Charles Handy
· 'The Road Less Traveled' by Scott Peck

### BOOKS
· 'The A-Z of Positive Thinking' by N. James
· 'The Freedom Tree' by N. James
· Available from Do-Zen Ltd.

### THE VIDEO
· You Tube Video 'neilstabletalks' – Three Boxes

### LINK
· https://www.youtube.com/watch?v=l8eMlqotlPk

# Appendix 4

## *Get a message to Garcia:*

The phrase 'to carry a message to Garcia' was in common use for years to indicate taking the initiative when carrying out a difficult assignment. Tens of millions of copies of the essay were printed and passed on. It was written by Elbert Hubbard in 1899.

It expressed the value of individual initiative and conscientiousness in work. The essay's primary example is a dramatized version of a daring escapade performed by an American soldier, First Lieutenant Andrew S. Rowan, just before the Spanish-American War.

The essay describes Rowan 'carrying a message' from President William McKinley, 'to Gen. Calixto García, a leader of the Cuban insurgents somewhere in the mountain fastnesses of Cuba—no one knew where'. The essay contrasts Rowan's self-driven effort against 'the imbecility of the average man— the inability or unwillingness of people to concentrate on a thing and do it'. The point was this: McKinley gave Rowan a letter to be delivered to Garcia; Rowan took the letter and did not ask, "Where is he at?" He just got on with it.

The strong sub-text was that it's not book-learning young people need, but a stiffening of the vertebrae which will cause them to be loyal to a trust, to act promptly, concentrate their energies, and do the thing—'Carry a message to Garcia!' It's an early definition of the Finnish concept of 'SISU' as described earlier. Don't equivocate. Don't ask for detailed instructions. Don't hire a consultant or assemble a task force. Just take the letter and deliver it to Garcia.

When people learn to 'get the job done' like Rowan, extraordinary opportunities will come your way. Using difficult and challenging assignments to hone your natural talents mastering a discipline in a way that brings you great joy and serves the needs of others, and you'll be well on your way to discovering a 'calling' in life and embarking on a Hero's Journey.

# *Appendix 5*

## Seventeen contexts for life and business

| | |
|---|---|
| **• FOUNDATION** | What is your core product or proposition? What can you give to the world? What do you offer?<br>Your originating proposition and product are the foundation of your business. Product extensions help a company to leverage the client base that has already been created and, in turn, develop new distribution channels. |
| **• RELATIONSHIP** | What's your relationship like with yourself? Your family? Your team?<br>How skilled are you at building, developing, and sustaining enduring relationships?<br>What and where are your channels to market?<br>If you have a product proposition then finding and developing channels to market will be your prime focus.<br>If you have a distribution model, you already have access to a market and will wish to leverage your network by finding additional products. |
| **• FOCUS** | What is your value proposition?<br>Positioning gives a business a clear focus on what they're providing, who their market is, and their delivery style.<br>It feeds into how you take your product to market.<br>Do you choose a premium, medium, or low position?<br>Are you competing on price or service?<br>James Caan said, "Marketing is essential. You can have the best product/service in the world, but if nobody knows about it, what is the point!" |
| **• PERSUASION** | Marketing creates 'pre-sold' opportunities<br>Those opportunities now have to be converted.<br>Sales is essential. If your marketing is good, then this is about converting the opportunities. The hard way is to go out, knock on doors, and keep pitching your proposition.<br>A friend said years ago, "If you knock on enough doors with an alligator, you'll eventually sell it!" |
| **• FACILITATION** | The single most crucial step in selling is the ability to listen to clients and find out precisely what it is they want.<br>Getting the 'Brief' will take you further than all the sales training on the planet. Active, engaged questioning and listening and the ability to elicit emotional needs is the source of sales success. |

| | |
|---|---|
| • PURPOSE | What's your culture and your intent?<br>Studies have shown that people leave companies predominantly because of other people. Investing in a culture where everyone feels engaged, valued and respected pays dividends and increases the value of the business.<br>No why – No way! |
| • EXPECTATION | Expectations are all about energy. When exceeded, good energy is generated. When dashed, for some people, the world ends. Meeting expectations requires effort and energy, which is the world that proactive, responsible people inhabit.<br>See 'Three Boxes'. |
| • RESPONSIBILITY | Having people in a business that accept and take responsibility is the key to effective functionality.<br>Having a process that helps a business define those roles and responsibilities is seen as a "Godsend".<br>See 'Three Spaces'. |
| • EFFICIENCY | What's your financial efficiency?<br>Capacity is the ability to generate revenue for a business with its existing resources. Most companies do not have a formula for working out exactly what the maximum possible revenue is, and therefore, they fly blind, oblivious to an underlying inefficiency. |
| • STAGE | Where does your business sit in the recurring and relentless lifecycle they all go through? Knowing where you are and what's next helps you make clear decisions. |
| • VISION | "Without vision, the people will perish!" Vision is the imagination and inspiration that ends up compelling others to follow your dream.<br>How far do you want to go? How many zeros do you want to add? What value and legacy do you wish to bequeath? Conrad Hilton's dream was for a Hilton on the Moon!<br>See the 'Vision Triangle'. |
| • CHOICES | What sort of business are you looking to create? Is it an income/lifestyle business or a longer-term equity play?<br>The choice a business owner makes will dictate the kinds of investments they will or will not make.<br>Are you a 'Spender', a 'Saver', or an 'Investor'? |

| | |
|---|---|
| • LOYALTY | How many times do clients return to do business with you? Once? Twice? Thrice? Or do you have the magic fourth touch? Statistically, if someone buys from you four times, you have a loyal customer, which is yours for the losing. Ensure your interviewing process is designed around a minimum of four touchpoints. |
| • UNITY | The first thing that ever goes in a relationship is the humour. Humour only occurs when people are communicating. What's your culture like? Create a 'World-Class' team that delivers outstanding results. To achieve this, you have to know yourself first. Superb communication skills are crucial to developing an engaged, productive, and united company. |
| • FRAMEWORK | Do you have a consistent framework for making decisions? We can't see the wood for the trees! The right-hand doesn't know what the left is doing! Clarity comes from context, and that makes decision-making crystal clear. Context is energizing. Conflicts happen when arguments happen in content, and people can't find a common point of interest. You serve by not buying into the story. |
| • COMMITMENT | Hire for attitude. Train for skill. Businesses are all about people. One owner likened his business to working in a human laboratory. What skills are you committed to investing in for yourself and your employees? As a business grows, so do expectations and standards. What was adequate in the early days may no longer be fit for purpose. New skills and staff may need to be drafted in, and some staff may need to be encouraged to move on. |
| • ALIGNMENT | If you don't respect and appreciate structure, consider how you would get along without your own skeleton. The best structures are invisible and non-intrusive. In business, three key components must be openly addressed to minimize future disagreements and maximize alignment: Income, Equity, and Control. Create a dialogue around these before they blow up in your face. |

# *Acknowledgements:*

How do you acknowledge a lifetime of events, experiences, and experiments? Oh, that it was an experiment to be repeated, replicated, and ever so slightly adjusted. Do I detect a whiff of regret in that statement? Not at all. Just a constant curiosity and desire to play with things and life. It's just the way my mind, infuriatingly to some, works. I'm always looking for the mischief, the edge, the energy and humour in the conversation or event. Perhaps you've noticed that as you have travelled with me through the pages of this book. But who to thank?

Well, my parents naturally. They enabled all of this to come to pass. And then there's Caroline, my wife whose love and support aided me through the darkest of times.

The thanks that now follow are a random free association. Do not attach any importance or significance to their position. Some names have been changed to respect their privacy.

**There are those who helped:** Paul, Vaughan, Charlie, John G., Roman, Grant, Rob A., Rob B., Steve O., Steve J., Joe, Walter, Nic, DC Jr., Michael C., and Adam B.

**There have been my muses:** Debbie, Lisa, Beth, Sonia, Jane, Sandy, Liz, Teresa, Orit, Ali, Cathy, and Mary.

I'm sure a psychiatrist would have something insightful, profound, and unhelpful to say about the gender split there!

**There have been my clients and friends:** Peter and Conny, Janet, Peter F., Gary, Jack, Jez, James D., Phil, Jules, Lisa, Annette, Rich, Rob T., Bob W., Bob M., Iolo, Kev, Richard and Nancy, Adam R., Dave, John, Alex, Juergen, Ian, Adrian, Bryan, Aubrey, Carsten, Clare, James W., Geoffrey, Gordon, Neil, Hervé, Isabel, Jon, Jake, Lisa, Julia, Linda, Michael, David, Paul B., DC Snr., Tomas, and Ned.

I have to thank Paul for his thorough, diligent, and tireless editing. I own all remaining discrepancies.

Finally, there is my publisher, Chris Day and my charming, chatty, and charismatic son, James, who never ceases to amuse, educate, and challenge me.

To all of you, I say thank you from the bottom of my heart. The funny thing is there are only 75 of you, and I feel there should be twice that number so I could neatly match Robin Dunbar's magic 150! The only conclusion I can draw is that It's been a life half-lived or

I'm only halfway through. In which case, I look forward to meeting the friends I have yet to make.

# QED

# OTHER BOOKS BY NEIL:

The A-Z of POSITIVE THINKING

NEIL JAMES TUSON

25th Anniversary Edition

THE **A-Z** OF

**POSITIVE THINKING**

A NEW VOCABULARY TO CHANGE YOUR LIFE

NEIL JAMES TUSON

OVER 50,000 SOLD GLOBALLY

This brilliant, bewitching, bold, brave, bouncing, ballsy book of wise, worthy, and witty words will increase your vocabulary of positive language and help you to succeed in life, improve your mood and enrich your relationships.

It's fun: try playing with positive words when writing to friends and colleagues; enhance your CV with words which jump off the page and inspire confidence; above all, stimulate good energy in your life by the very words you choose to use.

"Shows you how to think positively and banish negative feelings. Putting the positive words together will make you giggle. The overall effect of the book is uplifting."
Daily Mail – Book of the Week

**The Press**

"The A-Z of Positive Thinking is definitely a good idea… It tells us that there are three times as many negative words as positive ones. The important ones – the positives – are listed and are called 'antidotes to negativity'. This book is a good introduction to positive thinking."
Women's Health Magazine

"Examples of how to think positively and banish negative feelings. Putting the positive words together will make you giggle. The overall effect of the book is uplifting."
Daily Mail – Book of the Week

"A call to accentuate the positive… Excuses and negative thinking are diseases that can blight your life. According to this book, positive words are the antidote. Positive words are the essential medicine, the cure, to give you the power of positive thought."
Farmers Weekly – Editor's Choice

## Readers Quotes

"Very clever and well written."
Jean McCulloch

"I stopped in the middle of writing a speech. I was frustrated, anxious, lost for ideas – until I dipped into your book. It got me back on track. It's Excellent, Accomplished, Fulfilling, Happy, Invaluable, Invigorating, Masterful, Powerful, Profound and Therapeutic. Thanks – Carpe Diem."
Ian MD, Reliance Group

"It is a truth that personal fulfilment is linked to the degree of control people feel they have over their own lives. This book helps people gain that control."
Nic MD, Serial Entrepreneur

"It made me laugh."
Linda MD, Packaging Team

"It's intriguing. I couldn't put it down. I had to read it to the end." Stefan – Owner, Eurostat Group

"It made me want to pick it up and reread it. I'm going to do just that tonight."
Ashley – MD, LA Design

"It made me smile. It made me laugh. I couldn't put it down."
Conny

"This book has helped me write that letter make that phone call."
Adrian

"I find your book so exciting and so wonderfully helpful. I have read it again and again, and each time, find deeper wisdom, a pearl of great price, or a light shining out of a particular sentence or phrase."
Marie

"There is no doubt your book is food for thought for the hungry – fulfilling a great need.'
Constance

'Enlightened people lead us back into truth… I believe you are such… you truly must go on with your work. You are a lighthouse in a storm-tossed sea."
Megan

"I thank you for your book. It enabled me to give a push to a boulder on my own road. Now, I can go a little further along the path."
Annie

"I thought it a pity some of the best passages were right at the end – hidden away. But where else could they be? A true student/seeker will go right to the end and find them."
Maja

"I know you will rejoice in the transformation your book brought about in the daughter of a friend of mine. "She was 40. Her marriage was on the rocks. Her children were neglected. She had a wretched job. She was overweight, ungroomed and uncouth. She popped in to see me last Friday. I would not have recognised her if her son had not been with her. She was full of light, beautiful, well-groomed, and happy. She has a

wonderful new job and is considered the best. She is interested in and caring for her children. She has lost loads of weight. She told me, "Two years ago, you gave me a small yellow book. I read it three times and decided I would do what it said, and I have done so faithfully ever since. Every morning, when I get out of bed, I go to my bathroom mirror and tell myself, 'I am loving, beautiful and successful'. The results have been quite dramatic." A wonderful transformation, Neil ..."
Constance

"I began to read your 'A-Z' in the bath and did not realise until I got to the end that my bath was cold, the bubbles had dissolved, and I looked like a prune! I was so captivated and empowered by this. What an incredible gift!"
Sarah

"I found your book very inspiring. It will help me a lot in the future as I start my career as a hospital doctor. Thank you."
Jan

"After reading your book, I have done three things. 1. Written an article based on Living, Laughing, Loving and Learning. 2. Helped lift my girlfriend out of a deep gloom. 3. Cheered up my grandma after her recent bereavement. Your book has a good effect on people."
Will

"I love the 'A-Z'. It was amazing how answers can appear from nowhere just by opening it on a random

page. The happy, healthy, horny and holy combination is definitely a reframe on life!! – I am full of admiration."
Liz

"Your 'A-Z' was a joy to read. It is a perfect gift and a complete insight."
Claire

"Thank you for writing your valuable, happy book. Smiling is important to me, and your positive antidotes make me smile. Let's smile some more and make the world a happier place."
Louise

"This book is easy to read, flows well and has excellent, strong, relevant content."
Piera

"I like this book very much and always have it by my side for regular reading."
David

"This book is absolutely marvellous, and I refer to it often. Thank you for sharing your experiences."
Gerry

"This is a very fine book. It gave me great pleasure, and I was very impressed. It helps restore the old 'Joie de vivre'. I believe this book will be a great success."
Dave

"Good book – Sensible stuff."
Denise

**Amazon – Readers Feedback: 4.7 / 5 STARS**

"Wonderful insight – this book changed my thoughts."
Marc – 4 STARS

"As human nature has it, we tend to tell ourselves what we cannot achieve instead of what we can. Neil's short but concise book turns around the negative thought process. Brilliant inspiration into life's wonders and what we make of them, all in words and how we use them. Recommended for those who want to be reborn."

"I bought this book for myself a long time ago, and it has brought so much to my life, even though it is only a small book. It is pure positive thinking in its very essence. You can have books that dilute it and waffle on, but why? Here is the very book you need. I am now here to buy this book for my teenage daughter, as mine, as so many of my best books have been borrowed – never to be returned."
Bojo – 5 STARS

"I have bought a number of these little books for different people and like it very much."
Molly – 5 STARS

"If you are interested in the effects of your thoughts on your life, this is a fab book to carry around in your pocket so that you can refer to it when you slip into negative thinking

mode. If you change your vocabulary, you are, in effect, changing your mind. A good, zippy, to-the-point book."
Shine – 5 STARS

"Love this book – One of the best."
Sam 5 – STARS

"Positive words – I positively know it will help!"
Bas 4 – STARS

"Your book encapsulates your attitude to life. It has changed my life. I love it!"
Caroline – 5 STARS

The Freedom Tree

Neil James
illustrated by Adam Boulter

This book contains allegorical fables, stories, and metaphors about life. Beautifully illustrated by Adam Boulter, it has been treasured by those seeking personal freedom.

It charts the first three phases of life, from childhood through maturity, and sets you up for the next stage of mastery. It is full of wisdom and tips to help you on your journey and will never cease to surprise you. It is simply full of joy.

"I've read a good number of personal development books, but yours is certainly the most beautifully written and inspiring book I've ever read. Congratulations."
Howard

*"Just finished your book. Loved it"*
Nic

*"I love this book. It is so beautiful, too."*
Jenny

*"I have finished reading your book and enjoyed it immensely – in fact, I have put it on my son's bed for him to read to support him in a relationship dilemma he is experiencing now."*
Ros

*"This book is amazing... I have to say it's the best book I've ever read."*
James

*"I want to say that having read it; it is so inspirational, honest, real, touches the heart and is unput-downable."*
Karen


*"I can only remember once before in my life when a book has had such an immediate impact on me. I cannot wait to share its message with many people who mean everything to me.*
*The book speaks to me of seasons. I felt as if I was travelling in time, past, present, and future while reading it. It made me remember so many things. It made me aware of incidents I have long forgotten or chosen to hide. It allowed me to bring everything I needed to see up close in a friendly, caring, compassionate and trusting way. I thank you for that. Somehow, what you wrote spoke to me on such a deep level. Your stories made sense to me; your quotes and poetry moved me. I read the poem you wrote over and over again, and it gave a name to something I had been unable to define.*
*I will treasure this book, Neil, and it will stay with me and move with me wherever I go. I find such peace in quietly picking it up and reading bits of it repeatedly.*
*Thank you for writing such an extraordinary book. I am so moved and touched by your words."*
Suki

## Coming next – Spring of 2025

Perfect Teams has fast become the 'Go-To' tool for team development in the 21st century. It provides a simple and memorable way for team leaders, HR Directors,and board directors to make sense of the people equation in their organisations.

Why don't teams work? Why do they suffer from dysfunction, absenteeism, and a lack of engagement? The three main reasons are:

1. The wrong mix of people
2. Mediocre team leadership
3. Poor communication.

Perfect Teams can help you solve all these issues.

Finally, the founder of Perfect Teams has been coaxed into sharing his insights in this easily accessible book.

As one client memorably said:
"You're an engineer? It'll probably work then!"

9 781915 465467